The Age of Em

CW00684226

The King. (N. W. Palace, Nimroud).

From W. S. W. Vaux, *Nineveh and Persepolis: an historical sketch of ancient Assyria and Persia*, London, 1850.

The Age of Empires

Mesopotamia in the first millennium BC

Francis Joannès
Translated by Antonia Nevill

Edinburgh University Press

© Armand Colin/HER, 2000
English translation © Antonia Nevill, 2004

Edinburgh University Press Ltd
22 George Square, Edinburgh

Typeset in Plantin and Gill Sans
by Servis Filmsetting Ltd, and
printed and bound in Great Britain by the Cromwell Press,
Trowbridge, Wilts.

A CIP record for this book is available from the British Library

ISBN 0 7486 1755 8 (hardback)
ISBN 0 7486 1756 6 (paperback)

The right of Francis Joannès
to be identified as author of this work
has been asserted in accordance with
the Copyright, Designs and Patents Act 1988.

The publishers thank the French Ministry of Culture – National Book
Centre – for kindly granting a translation subvention.

Published with the support of the Edinburgh University Scholarly
Publishing Initiatives Fund.

CONTENTS

The Age of Empires

Introduction

At the beginning of the first millennium BC, the Near East was emerging from two centuries of crisis, marked by vast movements of populations and the disappearance or dormancy of the majority of the great political powers. A system of sharing areas of influence among the Near Eastern kingdoms, marked by conflict but also by intensive diplomatic or trading relations, was followed, after the invasions by the Peoples of the Sea and then the expansion of the Aramaeans, by a long period of reunification. The first millennium BC in the Near East may therefore be described as the 'age of empires'. Indeed, the ninth to the first centuries saw the establishment of five great political constructions including Mesopotamia and the west of the Near East (western Syria, Phoenicia, Palestine): the neo-Assyrian, neo-Babylonian, Achaemenid, Hellenistic and Seleucid Persian, then the Arsacid Parthian empires. Their political centre of gravity, initially situated in Mesopotamia, later shifted now towards Iran, now towards the Mediterranean coast. Although they were characterised by the fairly marked dominance of one people over the imperial entity that was their own, they cannot be reduced to a standardised model.

In any case, to avoid the too general image of an East that was 'barbarian', then Hellenised and lastly Romanised, the unifying element we are concerned with here is the evolution of Mesopotamia, heir to a civilisation going back millennia, with its continuities and interruptions. Archaeological and, above all, textual sources are especially plentiful for this period of Mesopotamian history, and document the political, socio-economic and cultural aspects of its development. They enable us to evaluate the contribution of traditional heritage, formed originally by the constraints of the natural environment, but also of the uninterrupted transmission of structures of civilisation which were established in the second, even the third, millennium. But we must equally take note of new developments, produced by Mesopotamian civilisation itself, or introduced by its lasting opening-up to neighbouring regions, chiefly following the Persian conquest by Cyrus in the sixth century BC, then Alexander's in the fourth.

The history of Mesopotamia in the first millennium traditionally follows the political chronology of the empires; first, that of the Assyrians, up to 610, then of the kings of Babylon from 610 to 539, next of Alexander and his Seleucid successors, and finally that of the Parthians, starting from 141. The internal division into three phases of the history of Assyro-Babylonian civilisation in the second and first millennia, adopted by Assyriologists on the model of other ancient civilisations such as the Egyptian 'empire' or the three 'ages' of Greek history, resulted in two ternary sequences for Assyria (palaeo-, middle- and neo-Assyrian), and Babylonia (palaeo- or Old, middle- and neo-Babylonian). But this division, implicitly resting on the sequence birth–maturity–decline, is all the more conventional because it takes no account of the specific nature of the state constructions of the first millennium or that each of these periods covered at the same time, in Mesopotamia, political events (the 'neo-Assyrian' then 'neo-Babylonian' empires, for example) and also a state of language and writing; thus the description 'neo-Babylonian' is given to the textual documentation produced in Babylonia between the ninth and sixth centuries, according to the form of the signs of cuneiform writing and the special grammatical features of the Babylonian language it depicts. Similarly, when speaking of 'neo-Babylonian' society, religion or literature, one is referring to phases of Mesopotamian civilisation whose duration is longer than that of the political period

(610–539) from which the name is derived. The case is equally clear cut in Assyria, where the neo-Assyrian phase strictly speaking lasted only from 747 to 610, whereas the 'neo-Assyrian period' begins one and a half centuries earlier.

Lastly, how can the period of history stretching from 539 to the Christian era be characterised for Mesopotamia? From the cultural or socio-economic viewpoint, it is sometimes classed as 'late Babylonian'; but on many points it is a direct extension of the neo-Babylonian period, and the date at which it passes from one to the other remains problematic. The underlying problem is that of the end of Mesopotamian civilisation in itself. For a long time historiography considered that this end corresponded with the moment when Babylonia lost its political independence, in 539 BC, when Cyrus attached the neo-Babylonian empire to the nascent Achaemenid empire. But socio-economic and cultural data offer no evidence of any substantial alteration in Mesopotamia before the beginning of the fifth century. Similarly, people have used as a deadline the time of Alexander the Great's conquest of Babylon in 331, followed by the phenomenon of the 'Hellenisation of the East'. But this process has its chief significance in the Greek setting of ancient history; seen from the Mesopotamian viewpoint, it introduced no definitive upheaval. True, the Seleucid period of Mesopotamian history has its own particular features but, from many aspects, it is a part of the direct prolongation of the periods that preceded it. Consequently, in view of the close connection between the type of writing used in Mesopotamia and many characteristic elements of Mesopotamian civilisation, it is possible to suggest a long periodisation, based on written sources. The late date assigned to the last datable cuneiform tablet (an astronomical text of AD 75), like the resurgence in Adiabene (i.e. the Assyria of the Parthian and Roman era) of the worship of the god Assor (Aššur, Ashur), as local inscriptions attest, are further items which prove the durable quality of Mesopotamian civilisation in its region of origin.

The presentation adopted in this book, therefore, seeks to take account of the broad duration of this Mesopotamian civilisation over the whole of the first millennium, in its socio-economic, religious and cultural aspects. At the same time, this lengthy period is marked by sequences of political history which follow a quicker rhythm, present features in common but also include specific elements. For each of these great eras, defined as (neo-)-Assyrian, (neo-)-Babylonian, Achaemenid and Graeco-Parthian, I have also tried to study the interaction with the local social, economic and cultural substrata, highlighting the aspects of continuity and the most significant breaks.

NOTES ON THE SYSTEM OF TRANSCRIPTION

As well as personal names and the geographical names known from Biblical tradition or the historical works of classical antiquity (Nineveh, Sennacherib, Babylon, Nebuchadnezzar), Mesopotamian names have been rendered in the accepted Anglicised form, but the table given below will help with the pronunciation of other names: the vowel *u* is always pronounced as the *oo* in 'boot', the vowel *e* as the first *e* in 'whether'.

For consonants, the equivalents are as follows:

Category	Form	Pronunciation
Weak guttural	'	Not pronounced
Strong guttural	h	As in Scottish 'loch'
Emphatic sibilant	ṣ	'ts(e)'
Lisped sibilant	š	'sh(e)'
Emphatic dental	ṭ	Like a French 't'

Chapter 1
The world of the peoples of Mesopotamia

PLACES AND PEOPLES

The geographical aspect

Although the name 'Mesopotamia' itself, the country 'between two rivers', is a Greek designation, the inhabitants of this entire area actually defined their land in relation to the two major routes formed by the Tigris and Euphrates, making two vast regions: Assyria in the north, and Babylonia in the south. At the same time, an abstract vision of a single territory with Babylon at its centre was superimposed on this division into two separate entities.

Lower Mesopotamia

The virtually unrelieved alluvial plain which stretches from Sippar, in the north, as far as the Persian Gulf, and historically forms Babylonia, benefits from the vast amount of water contributed by the two rivers. Their use (in fact, chiefly that of the Euphrates) allowed the irrigated cultivation of cereals and date-palms on a huge scale. In the first millennium, the basically longitudinal network of the great irrigation canals, several of which made use of secondary beds of the Euphrates, was connected by a transverse network. The establishment of the overall system took place over a very long period, accompanying the gradual westward shift of the Euphrates' major bed, and at the same time aiming to link it with the Tigris. This complex network required constant

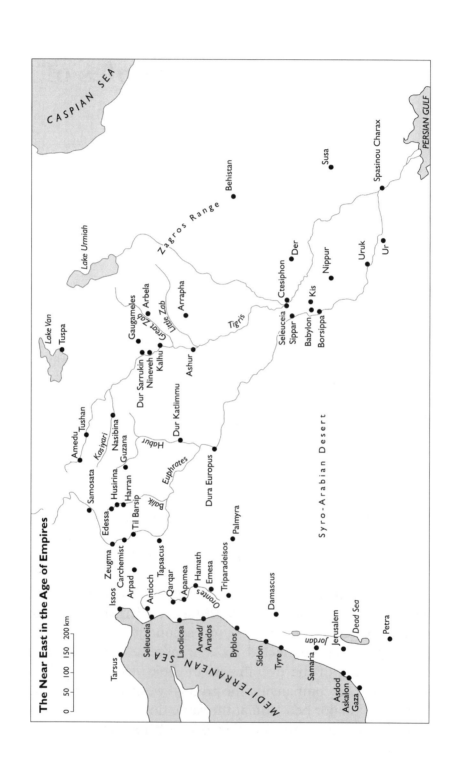

The Near East in the Age of Empires

0 50 100 150 200 km

CASPIAN SEA

PERSIAN GULF

MEDITERRANEAN SEA

Lake Van

Lake Urmiah

Zagros Range

Syro-Arabian Desert

Dead Sea

Tarsus

Issos
Zeugma
Carchemist
Arpad
Antioch
Tapsacus
Qarqar
Apamea
Hamath
Emesa
Triparadeisos
Palmyra

Seleuceia
Laodicea
Arwad/
Arados
Byblos
Sidon
Tyre
Samaria
Asdod
Askalon
Gaza
Jerusalem

Damascus

Petra

Jordan

Orontes

Til Barsip
Edessa
Samosata
Husirina
Harran
Balik
Nasibina
Guzana
Kasiyari
Amedu
Tushan

Dur Sarrukin
Nineveh
Kalhu
Ashur
Dur Katlimmu

Habur

Euphrates

Dura Europus

Gaugameles
Arbela
Great Zab
Little Zab
Arrapha

Tigris

Tuspa

Behistan

Susa

Spasinou Charax

Ctesiphon
Der
Seleuceia
Sippar
Babylon
Borsippa
Kis
Nippur
Uruk
Ur

maintenance and was very costly in labour. Most of the large towns in Babylonia were settled along or in immediate proximity to the Euphrates; the roots of their history lay in a distant past, and they served as religious, administrative and economic centres for the areas of irrigated crops which were developed on their periphery along the main irrigation canals. Three major groups of towns can thus be picked out during this period: a northern group, comprising Sippar, Kuta, Kish, Babylon, Borsippa and Dilbat; a second, in the centre of the country, around Nippur and Isin; and a third, to the south, with the towns of Uruk, Larsa and Ur. Within the network formed by these urban groups lived a population who mainly went in for livestock breeding, were more or less settled, and whose relations with the people who were dependent on the towns were not always peaceful. They were increased by inflows from the wider areas of the Syro-Arabian steppes and deserts, who sometimes arrived in massive numbers resulting in encroachments and settlements on the territory of the irrigated plain, before being gradually integrated with the population already there. The start of the first millennium had witnessed the peak of the Aramaean influx; around the beginning of the Christian era, Arab populations appeared in ever-increasing numbers.

Upper Mesopotamia

The wide space in the north which separates the Euphrates from the Tigris and forms the plain of Upper Mesopotamia, or Jezireh, covers the topmost part of the Fertile Crescent. To the east of this area, on the banks of the Tigris and in the region of the hills stretching from the river to the Zagros range separating Mesopotamia from the Iranian plateau, Assyria was formed, and was sufficiently watered to allow non-irrigated cultivation. In the Jezireh properly speaking, cultivable zones – along the wadis of the foothills of the Tur Abdin and the two tributaries of the Euphrates, Habur and Balih – alternated with almost barren steppes. Populations of transhumant livestock-breeders had similarly established their hold there. The start of the first millennium saw the constitution of Aramaean principalities; from the fifth century BC, groups of populations from the southern desert settled there, forming a new Arabia which was destined to last for several centuries. This region of Upper Mesopotamia had only a few large towns, which for the most part had been established along the Tigris and, in the middle of the second millennium, had been united to form the Assyrian state. However, in its geopolitical conception, this covered the whole area of Upper Mesopotamia, as far as the western bend of the Euphrates, but it had borne the full brunt of Aramaean expansion and, at the beginning of the first millennium, had been reduced to the original 'Assyrian triangle' between the towns of Nineveh, Arbela and Ashur.

The world of the Mesopotamians

For the people of Babylonia, who had conceived it, the view of the world was simple: from the Upper Sea (the Mediterranean) to the Lower Sea (the Persian Gulf) stretched a territory whose focal point was the city of Babylon. Around a central zone combining Assyria and Babylonia were the 'four regions of the world', divided according to the cardinal points. To the north, the land of Subartu, which had originally designated Assyria, covered the mountainous area beyond its northern frontier; to the west, the land of Amurru comprised the areas near the Mediterranean coast; to the east was the country of Elam, by reference to the kingdom formed in the south-west of Iran but which, in this division of the world, covered the greater part of the Zagros chain and the western edges of the Iranian plateau; to the south, the vast barren expanse of present-day Nefud and Nejed was not regarded as a truly defined entity, but extended in indeterminate fashion to the heart of the Arabian peninsula. The central role allocated to the town of Babylon was a historical heritage and did not actually match the true geographical reality. When Mesopotamia was incorporated into the political ensembles covering the entire Near and Middle East, it was at the veritable crossroads of the great communication routes, at the place where the Tigris and Euphrates are closest and where, through the Diyala valley, one of the rare routes of passage opens up between the Mesopotamian plain and the Iranian plateau, that the new capitals of the region were established: Seleuceia on Tigris, Ctesiphon, Vologesias and lastly Baghdad.

Reconstructing history

As they liked to arrange all the aspects of the world that surrounded them into ordered series, Assyrians and Babylonians of the first millennium sought to apply this method to the events of the past, and reconstructed a version of the history of humankind which, starting from antediluvian times, proceeded in a direct line up to their own period.

Lists of kings and dynasties

The Assyrian King List therefore rests on the principle of a single dynasty, harking back to 'kings who lived in tents', which extended in linear fashion as far as the neo-Assyrian sovereigns, erasing as far as possible accidental elements such as usurpations or a royal power vacuum. The Babylonians had resumed the cyclical concept, which saw dynasties connected with towns or major centres in the region take turns to receive the role of supremacy. Starting from the twelfth century BC, a second dynasty of Isin was recorded, then a second dynasty of the Country of the Sea, a dynasty of Bazi, an Elamite dynasty (comprising one king only), and a dynasty called 'of E'. But from the ninth century, this system was out of step with the theoretical view of Babylon as the one and only political capital of the country, and adherence to successive local references faded in favour of a continuous list, like the one current in Assyria. In this way rulers of foreign origin were incorporated, first Assyrians then, from 539 BC, even non-Mesopotamians.

Reconstructed history

This centralising view enabled contemporary events to be set into the flow of a sequence of development which harked back to a mythical past but remained perfectly coherent. In any case, they had no qualms about reconstructing certain episodes of that past by composing inscriptions or chronicles relating to the most celebrated of the earliest kings, such as the kings of Agade (2334–2193) or Ur III (2112–2004). These documents were intended to promote the importance of Babylon or the obligation on rulers to respect the traditional religious order. Such reworkings of the past may well have been much earlier: for instance, in the archives of the temple of the god Shamash at Sippar, Ebabbar, we may note the presence of several neo-Babylonian copies of a document probably of the Old Babylonian era but attributed to the king of Agade, Man-ištušu (2269–2255), who at the time of his reign had granted major privileges to the Ebabbar sanctuary.

Mythical ancestors

What applied to the sovereigns was also valid for certain of their subjects. Beginning in the neo-Babylonian era, the well-read were to be found inventing prestigious ancestors for themselves, frequently harking back to the Kassite period (eighteenth to fifteenth centuries BC). In addition to these educated people of the second millennium, attempts were made to trace ancestry back to the antediluvian Sages, the *apkallu*, creatures that were half-human, half-fish, who had received directly from the god Ea the knowledge on which the Mesopotamian civilisation was founded; and to their successors, the *ummânu*, experts who possessed technical, magical and scientific secrets. At the time when their canonical list was established in the first millennium, an aetiological myth of the *apkallu* was thus fixed, and to their definition as initiators of techniques was added the image of the *apkallu* as Sage, often linked with a famous king or kingdom, giving rise to a tradition that was prolific throughout the Near East.

THE REDISCOVERY OF THE 'ASSYRIANS'

External tradition

Biblical elements

For a long time the Bible was the only Near Eastern source to document the history of the neo-Assyrian, neo-Babylonian empires and their Persian and Seleucid successors, citing the names of kings (Sennacherib, Esarhaddon, Nebuchadnezzar), but mostly mentioning their history only in so far as it interfered directly with that of the kingdoms of Israel and Judah. A certain number of prophetic books, however, made reference to Nineveh and Babylon as considerable and dominant powers. The exile of the deportees from Jerusalem to the banks of the Kebar canal (*nâr Kabiru*, attested several times by cuneiform texts) constituted a major moment in the history of the Jewish people, and various episodes in the Book of Daniel took place partly in the royal palace of Babylon, the fall of the city to the Persians being the occasion of a famous episode. At all events, Mesopotamia appeared several times in the Bible, mentioned as a real place of origin, from the Garden of Eden to the Tower of Babel, by way of Ur, a Chaldaean town, the homeland of Abraham's family, and Harran in Upper Mesopotamia, where he stayed. In the main, however, Biblical predictions had come true: the power of the great capitals of Assyria and Babylonia had been shattered; these towns, and above all knowledge of their history, had disappeared under piles of bricks and earth. The data provided by the Talmud about Babylon and by the history of the Jewish community in Babylonia over the centuries were not much more explicit.

Writers of antiquity

Another collection of sources was available, however: the one supplied by the historical literature of classical antiquity, with descriptions regarded as direct, such as those of Herodotus or Xenophon, or based on fairly accurate knowledge, like Ctesias' *Persica* or Arrian's *History of Alexander*. It was therefore possible to reconstruct an initial plot of events specific to the history of the Near East, as is shown by the works of Diodorus Siculus at the start of the Christian era, of Justin in the second century, summarising the *Philippic History* of Pompeius Trogus, or of Eusebius of Caesarea in the fourth. But a precise determination of the periods or locality of events remained extremely blurred. The most detailed data on the formative elements of Babylonian culture and religion, provided by Berossus in the third century BC or to be found in certain writers of late antiquity, had not been incorporated into the corpus of the great Graeco-Roman historical tradition and were accessible only indirectly by summaries in the Byzantine period. Symbolically, it was the town of Harran/Carrhae, in Upper Mesopotamia, one of the major places in both neo-Assyrian and neo-Babylonian history, which gave refuge to the last representatives of paganism – the Neoplatonic philosophers whom Christianity had expelled from Athens in the late fifth century AD.

Travellers and scholars

The very places which had witnessed the unfolding of Mesopotamian history were regularly visited, however, and from ancient times; but access to the geographical whole represented by the former Assyrian and Babylonian territories was difficult in those days; it was situated at the point of contact between the Roman and Iranian empires, and for the most part was skirted by the big trading routes. The first travellers to the site of Babylon were fulfilling kinds of intellectual and religious pilgrimages: the rabbi Benjamin of

Tudela, around 1165; the Bavarian knight Schiltberger, around 1400, or the Italian Pietro della Valle, between 1614 and 1626.

Description of the ruins of Nineveh in 1644 and of Persepolis in 1655, by J.-B. Tavernier[1]

'Nineveh, which was built on the left bank of the Tigris on the Assyrian side, is now no more than a muddle of old hovels stretching about a league along the river. There are quite a few inhabited vaults or caverns, though it is hard to judge whether these vaults served as a dwelling for the inhabitants or whether there had been something higher above them, most of the villages in Turkey being as if sunk into the ground or barely reaching a first storey.

For in the end they are merely old columns, some standing, others lying on the ground, and a few very badly made figures, with little square dark rooms; all this together easily persuades those who, like me, have seen the principal pagodas of the Indies, which I thought well of, that Tchelminar [Persepolis] was formerly no more than a temple of false gods.'

From the eighteenth century onward, interest in oriental sources developed from the travels of scholars in the Near East, seeking to identify major sites, who noted down their findings and recopied inscriptions; for instance, the Frenchman Chardin between 1665 and 1677, the Dane C. Niehbur from 1761 to 1767, or the Frenchman A. Michaux in 1786. The frequency of journeys, publication of accounts of travels and initial appraisals accelerated in the early nineteenth century; they were predominantly British (C. Rich, J. Buckingham, R. Ker Porter), but also French (F.-R. Chesney on the Euphrates in 1836, E. Coste and E. Flandin at Persepolis in 1840–1).

---

[1] Sources of the extracts of texts are given at the end of the book, pp. 281–3.

Nineteenth-century excavations

Uncovering Assyrian palaces

The first palace to be discovered was that of Sargon II at Dûr-Šarrukîn, the site of Khorsabad, explored by the French consul P.-E. Botta in 1843 and 1844. The antiquities unearthed were exhibited at the Louvre in 1847. This first excavation was followed by that of the ruins of the palaces of Kalhu by the Englishman Layard in 1845, then of Nineveh, commencing in 1849, by a French mission (V. Place) and a British mission (H. Rawlinson). Relations with the local populace were not always easy, however, and the disturbed state of the country ended in a disaster in 1855, when the rafts transporting the antiquities brought back by V. Place from Nineveh were attacked and sank in the Tigris, 211 out of 235 cases being swallowed up. In 1872, on a dig at Nineveh, H. Rassam brought to light the cuneiform tablets from what was called Ashurbanipal's library. From 1903 until the outbreak of World War I, the German W. Andrae installed himself at Ashur; archaeology had entered a new, more scientific, phase and his excavations remain a model of their kind.

Babylon and Babylonia

An initial phase was devoted to the recognition and identification of the principal sites of Babylonia: Uruk at Warka, and Larsa at Senkereh, by W. Loftus; Ur at Muqqayar and Eridu at Abu-Shahrein, by J. Taylor, and Sippar at Abu-Habbah, by H. Rassam. Babylon and Borsippa had been the subject of a first attempt by F. Fresnel, J. Oppert and F. Thomas, between 1851 and 1854, but it ended in failure. When R. Koldewey took charge of lengthy and large-scale excavations, from 1899 to 1914, this enabled the town to be rediscovered in all the splendour of its neo-Babylonian era. The majority of the other large sites (Borsippa, Nippur, Sippar, Ur and Uruk) similarly yielded vast archaeological and textual documentation, some of which dated from the first millennium, while clandestine excavations, which were particularly active on the sites of Babylon and Uruk, fed a veritable international market in cuneiform tablets between 1870 and 1900. The stores of European and American museums were thus filled with tens of thousands of documents, many of which are still unpublished. The years since the mid-twentieth century have witnessed new archaeological enterprises which have often proved very useful in complementing the knowledge of major sites of the first millennium, such as Kalhu in Assyria, or Sippar and Babylon in Babylonia.

Texts and archives

Deciphering cuneiform

Somewhat paradoxically, the first venture in deciphering a cuneiform writing had been carried out as early as 1802, by G. Grotefend, well before the first archaeological undertakings, and concerned inscriptions in Old Persian from the Achaemenid sites of Iran, fairly faithful copies of which had already reached western Europe. The advantage of the Achaemenid inscriptions was that they provided a certain number of trilingual ones in Old Persian, Babylonian and Elamite cuneiform. The progress achieved in the decipherment of the Old Persian by H. Rawlinson between 1840 and 1850 thus enabled Babylonian cuneiform writing to be tackled. Once it was realised that it transcribed a Semitic language, subsequently called Akkadian, the language of the Babylonians and Assyrians (Akkad was north Babylonia in the third millennium BC), and that these signs could have a phonetic value (a sign = a syllable) or an ideographic value (a sign = a word), the basic principles were laid down. Later, it was possible to establish that the ideograms were not Akkadian, but a far more ancient language – Sumerian. From 1850 onward, the discoveries made in Assyria furnished a large quantity of Assyro-Babylonian texts, which stimulated the progress of decipherment. Assyriology's date of birth can therefore be fixed in the year 1857, when four learned scholars (H. F. Talbot, J. Oppert, E. Hincks and H. Rawlinson), working separately, managed to come up with identical translations of the same royal Assyrian inscription.

Types of text

Despite some unevenness of distribution in time and place in the first millennium, Assyro-Babylonian cuneiform documentation represents a considerable body of texts, touching on nearly every field: historical, socio-economic, religious and cultural. It is customarily divided into scholarly and practical texts. The first category contains historical, scientific, religious and literary documents; the second is a collection of texts from administrative and private archives. For the first millennium the first group is particularly rich, since it can avail itself of the two major historical sources, the annals of the kings of Assyria and a certain number of Babylonian chronicles. In addition, there are many royal inscriptions and lists of rulers or eponyms. But the abundance of this historical literature is not in itself a guarantee of objectivity: the purpose was to glorify royal deeds or write up events within the conventional interpretation of Mesopotamian history. The scientific literature, for its part, often adopted the form of a list, revealing a desire to catalogue their environment in its most material as well as its most abstract aspects, which was typical of the people of Mesopotamia. At the same time, it defined the scientific fields which strictly pertained to it: law, medicine, pharmacopoeia and mathematics rub shoulders with divination, astrology and magical conjuration. Indeed, understanding of the world according to rational principles was always supported by reference to the world of the gods, who were the sole possessors of true knowledge. Scientific literature was therefore closely linked with religious literature, which set down in writing the rituals and different types of prayers. The written form aimed not only at fixing a norm that would guarantee the result of addresses to the gods, but equally at using an instrument of intellectual mastery of reality that was supplied to humankind by divine agents. Despite their relatively small number in the corpus of learned literature, the Mesopotamian 'belles-lettres' of the first millennium are similarly of capital importance and include major works of Assyro-Babylonian thinking.

Archive problems

The practical texts, which for this period can be numbered in tens of thousands, are connected with the idea of archives: administrative archives of the sanctuaries, administrative and diplomatic archives of the palaces and private archives of the inhabitants of the large towns. Understanding this system of archives nevertheless presents a whole range of problems: very many texts were discovered by clandestine excavators, and therefore lack an exact archaeological context; moreover, some of these archives related to current affairs at the time when they had been deposited, whereas others had ceased to be used. The clay tablets on which the texts were inscribed might even have been re-used as building materials; so a distinction must be made between 'living' and 'dead' archives when interpreting the data they provide. Lastly, their dispersal in time and area shows that we do not have a homogeneous documentation at our disposal; at any given time, this or that site is either overabundantly represented by texts or missing from the documentation, and a general interpretation must therefore combine available data with hypotheses. The latter are based on the similarity of local situations in a given period, or rely on the permanence of certain facts over several centuries, or even from one millennium to the next.

Vanished documentation

Violent destruction, like that suffered by the large Assyrian capitals between 614 and 610, has often engulfed certain sites just as they stood, with their architectural and textual elements. Dûr-Šarrukîn is a special case, in that it concerns a palace which had been little used and functioned only partly up to the end of the neo-Assyrian era, before being totally abandoned. But where groups of buildings were regularly inhabited, as at Babylon or Uruk, a process of natural elimination levelled off most earlier constructions in the last stage of occupation and wiped out a good number of archives that had become useless. The most spectacular example is without doubt the great ziggurat of Babylon, which was used as a reserve of bricks for building and the enrichment of farming land for several centuries, and at present takes the form of a depression on the spot where a 90-metre-high edifice had formerly risen.

The rediscovery by clandestine excavators of several private archives of Babylon, datable to the sixth century but rarely going beyond the reign of Darius I (522–486), apart from being effected outside any known archaeological context, poses the still unresolved problem of the circumstances which marked their halt early in the fifth century. Similarly, it is difficult to know why the great administrative archives of the temples of Sippar and Uruk do not carry on beyond the same period. Another phenomenon which must be taken into account is the growing Aramaicisation of the Babylonian population, in both language and writing practice; it implies that there was an increasingly systematic resort to writing materials (papyrus or leather) which were unable to stand up to prolonged burial. Alongside the mass of documentation available to us, there is therefore an even greater mass which has disappeared, and may correspond to aspects of the history of this region that have now become inaccessible. The continuous use of the royal palace of Babylon between Nabopolassar (626–605) and Alexander the Great (330–323) thus resulted in eliminating the older cuneiform palace documentation on clay, then producing archives on perishable materials. When all is said and done, we have virtually no state archives from the capital of Babylonia.

THE EVOLUTION OF MESOPOTAMIAN HISTORIOGRAPHY

Babel und Bibel

The world of the Bible

The rediscovery of the Assyrians and then the great neo-Babylonian sites documented aspects of Mesopotamian civilisation which had a direct echo in the Biblical books. The historical aspects were the first to be recognised, but interest was redoubled when it was discovered that the literary texts of the Nineveh library corresponded with Biblical mentions. Prominence was given to the existence of a 'Babylonian' Noah and Job. Budding Assyriology thus served to establish the historicity of certain episodes in the Bible, and then to include the latter in a larger Near Eastern tradition, although it remained the major point of reference, sometimes to the detriment of aspects specific to the Mesopotamia of the first millennium, whose data were used to illustrate 'the world of the Bible'. Since the end of the nineteenth century and the chronological ordering of Mesopotamian civilisation, this view has largely disappeared, and the study of Mesopotamia is now considered in its own right.

Did history begin at Babylon?

There is no certainty that our view of Mesopotamia has become entirely objective. The way in which this civilisation is presented still frequently obeys the centralising schema of a point of origin which radiated its civilisation out to more or less barbarian peripheral areas. Must we therefore look upon Babylon as the single centre of a Mesopotamian civilisation spreading its influence over the rest of the Near East? True, the Babylonians themselves contributed to the elaboration of this notion, making their capital the quasi-cosmological centre of the world and, according to their own norms, unifying the diverse cultural traditions they had inherited. This phenomenon is registered by giving the name *Standard Babylonian* to the Akkadian language used in Mesopotamia for the learned works of the first millennium, or when it was found that the annals of the kings of Assyria were composed in Babylonian and not Assyrian, or that the Nineveh library was made up of works mostly originating from Babylonia. But a powerful intellectual unity in no way signifies uniformity; cultural or learned traditions specific to certain regions existed, and Babylonia itself did not form a unified bloc. The resurgence in the second half of the first millennium is a manifestation that deserves attention.

Oriental barbarians

The Bible and the majority of the writers of classical antiquity made the Babylon of the first millennium the paragon of the multi-ethnic eastern metropolis, devoted to worldly pleasures and lucrative activities, simultaneously splendid and terrifying. The fascination which the Orient exerted on the Greeks, by its wealth and power, was matched by an undoubted hostility in the face of the potential threat from its armies. But their knowledge of eastern reality prior to the Achaemenid era was poor, often indirect, the result of contacts with the Mediterranean coast of the Near East, and their reflections were often ideological or mythical. Even after the Hellenisation of the East, the interest of Greek (or Roman) thought in Mesopotamian culture remained very mild; Berossus' *Babyloniaca* reached only a limited readership, and Babylon remained first and foremost an exotic place, at the limits of imagination, as is shown by the success of the novel *Theogenus and Chariclaea* by Iamblichus in the second century AD.

The historical model of the Near Eastern empire

'Oriental despotism'

'Asiatic mode of production', 'hydraulic royalty', 'immobile civilisation': many modern interpretations of the political and socio-economic state of Mesopotamia have advanced aspects that are frequently ideological, primarily concerned with the neo-Assyrian and neo-Babylonian empires; but proclamations of an absolute royal power, as found in Mesopotamian official texts, are not necessarily an accurate reflection of reality. It has also been pointed out that the involvement of the authorities in the use of irrigation did not mean an absolute and centralised government control over the organisation of the country's agricultural activity; particularly in Babylonia, its management seems to have been largely dependent on local situations. The most organised attempts to exploit new land date chiefly to the Achaemenid period, and it was only under the Sassanids that the network of irrigation canals was completely hierarchised and interconnected. We must also bear in mind the existence of cycles of development which lasted a long time, showing that after a period of heavy decline covering the greater part of the second millennium BC and the beginning of the first, farming of land and urban population experienced a boom which began around the seventh century and continued for almost a thousand years. A certain demographic fragility in Upper Mesopotamia resulted in political vagaries that often had spectacular consequences for the population and prosperity of the region: after the glorious period of the Assyrian empire, its fall seems to have transformed the country into a human desert, but that also had to do with the way the territory was occupied, oscillating between nomadic practices and established settlements.

Great urban organisations and notables

Historical analysis quite rightly lays equal emphasis on the predominant position occupied by the crown and sanctuaries in Mesopotamia's economic life, with nuances that vary depending on the writer. While recognising their role, we must nevertheless not overvalue it: as L. Oppenheim shows, in particular, the vision of a virtually state-controlled economy must be strongly qualified in the first millennium.

The forces of economic life in Mesopotamia

'In Babylonia, the gradual salinisation of the soil, the blocking of canals (used for transport and irrigation), the weakening of the dykes, called for constant surveillance. The temple and palace, which could afford to invest the capital necessary to ensure that such work was carried out, saw their size and importance increase. From the latter half of the second millennium, the regular decline in the influence of the temple, and the corresponding rise in landed properties – kinds of feudal tenures granted by royal charter – must have caused fundamental economic upheavals. During the second half of the first millennium, it would seem that the growing role played by capital in the hands of 'private individuals' (with all the limits that the term covers as regards the Near East) certainly had the same consequences. The 'bank' of Murashu investing in new lands is perhaps an example of 'private' capital assuming responsibilities which, in the course of Mesopotamian history, had been exercised in turn by village communities, then the temples and then the palaces.'

The striking fact in Babylonia, not so much for its economic importance as for its social significance, was the existence of a category of urban notables who, while doing their utmost to build upon an often fairly restricted patrimony, took part in the economic activities of the temples and probably of the royal palace (though in the latter instance the sources are incomplete), deriving both prestige and revenue from doing so. This specifically urban feature meant that the occurrence was less developed in Assyria, where large townships were rare and a client system seems to have prevailed around the houses of the great Assyrian nobility, who were themselves dependent on royal favour from the eighth century onward. Viewed overall, however, the reality (as far as it can be grasped) of power-sharing in the Mesopotamia of the first millennium BC appears much more diffuse than one would think at first sight, and explains the enduring quality of a socio-economic organisation which persisted, through major political changes, until the beginning of the Christian era.

The notion of universal empire

The history of Mesopotamia in the first millennium BC cannot be understood without the background formed by the two preceding millennia, and many aspects of its civilisation were remarkably maintained during a very long period. The search for a historical logic, however, has led to the political history of this region being placed in a linear perspective: starting from the formation of the first kinds of political organisation during the third millennium, with the constitution of the Sumerian city-states, we emerge by a sort of natural evolution at the building of the great empires of the first millennium, with an increasingly affirmed multi-ethnic and universal purpose. It is not certain that the neo-Assyrian and then neo-Babylonian empires should be regarded as the logical culmination of an evolution that began in the great towns of Sumer (south Babylonia in the third millenium BC), or that the Achaemenid, Seleucid and Arsacid empires were a simple development of those that had preceded them. A certain accidental value of History must be taken into account: the development of the neo-Assyrian empire seems to have resulted chiefly from the country's militarisation in response to the Aramaean incursions early in the first millennium and the spectacular growth of the royal ideology that accompanied it. Not until the last part of the neo-Assyrian period was an imperial structure put in place, and the political set-up sought to acquire an organisation to match the overall scheme. Some writers even think that the Assyrian empire did not actually start until the reign of Tiglath-pileser III (744–727), with a phase of conquest under his reign and that of Sargon II (721–705), and then of maturity in the reigns of Sennacherib, Esarhaddon and Ashurbanipal (from 704 to 627).

Similarly, the neo-Babylonian empire resulted from a temporary expansion and did not lead to a truly unified whole. The kings of Babylon were first and foremost Mesopotamian rulers, centred on their capital. The Assyrian or Babylonian model of government was not conceived to be exported, and worked only within the geographical setting of Mesopotamia. Faced with the burning ideological obligation to outstrip their predecessors and eliminate possible external sources of rebellion, most of these sovereigns at first expanded their empire as circumstances dictated; but only gradually did they become aware that the geographical expansion they had achieved called for responses other than those models provided for them by Mesopotamian tradition. Conversely, from the official discourse of its rulers and their enterprises, it clearly appears that the Achaemenid empire was conceived as a universal empire, under the domination of 'Persian man', whose ruler had the duty of introducing an order that was as unified as possible. It is therefore only with great difficulty that a line of continuity can be traced between the first forms of political organisation of Mesopotamia in the third millennium and the empires of the first: they are above all the outcome of a series of circumstances.

Chapter 2
Political history of the Assyrian empire (934–610 BC)

Between 934 and 827, Assyria embarked on the conquest of the territories which had belonged to it in the second millennium but which from then on had been occupied by the Aramaeans. The result was impressive: in the reigns of Ashurnasirpal II and his son Shalmaneser III a vast kingdom was formed, connected with the Mediterranean once the stranglehold of the Aramaean states on the Syrian bend of the Euphrates had been broken.

An eighty-three-year long crisis marked a hiatus, after this over-rapid expansion, and brought to light deep social antagonisms in Assyria, while the powerful state of Urartu, in eastern Anatolia, was at the same time a constant threat on its northern frontiers. The reign of Tiglath-pileser III put an end to this period of internal and external stagnation, and led to a generalised venture of conquest of the western part of the Near East.

A kingdom of the traditional kind was succeeded by an empire centred on the royal personage, who was glorified by the clergy and was the sole possessor of authority. From 722, a new dynasty took over the destiny of the Assyrian empire and gave it its definitive dimensions under Sargon II, Sennacherib, Esarhaddon and Ashurbanipal. A certain number of structural weaknesses, however, provoked crises that shook the Assyrian empire and resulted in catastrophe in 614; in a matter of four years, the empire crumbled under the assaults of the Medes and Babylonians, and its capitals (Ashur, Nineveh and Harran) were captured and destroyed.

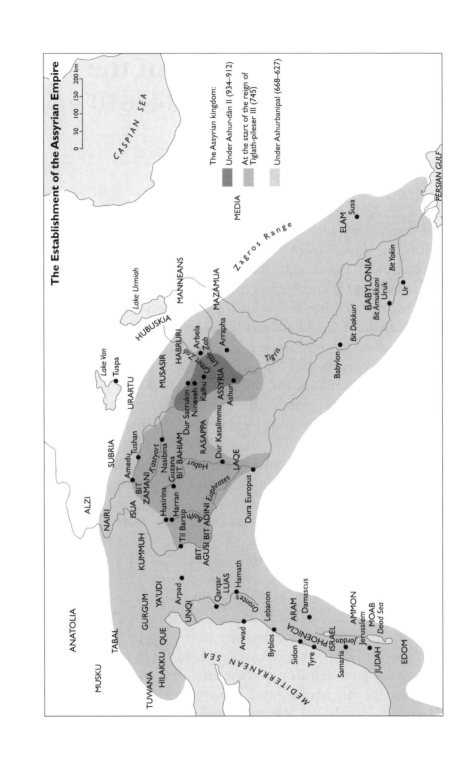

The Establishment of the Assyrian Empire

The Assyrian kingdom:

Under Ashur-dan II (934–912)

At the start of the reign of Tiglath-pileser III (745)

Under Ashurbanipal (668–627)

CASPIAN SEA

0 50 100 150 200 km

MEDIA

ANATOLIA

MUSKU

TABAL

GURGUM

TUWANA

HILAKKU QUE

MUSASIR

URARTU

Lake Van

Tuspa

Lake Urmiah

MANNEANS

HUBUSKIA

Zagros Range

SUBRIA

ALZI

NAIRI

ISUA

Amedu

Tushan

BIT
ZAMANI Kasyart

KUMMUH

YA'UDI

Arpad

UNQI

Qarqar

LUAS

Hamath

Orontes

Lebanon

Arwad

Byblos

Sidon

Tyre

PHOENICIA

ARAM

Damascus

Jordan

ISRAEL

Samaria

Jerusalem

JUDAH

AMMON

MOAB

Dead Sea

EDOM

MEDITERRANEAN SEA

Husirina

Harran

Til Barsip

BIT
AGUSI BIT ADINI

Guzana

Nasibina

BIT BAHIAM

Balih

Euphrates

Dura Europus

HABRURI

Dur Sarrukin

Nineveh

Kalhu

ASSYRIA

Ashur

Dur Katalimmu

RASAPPA

LAQE

Habur

Arbela

Little Zab

Great Zab

Zab

Arrapha

MAZAMUA

Tigris

Babylon

Bit Dakkuri

BABYLONIA

Bit Amukkani

Uruk

Bit Yakin

Ur

ELAM

Susa

PERSIAN GULF

The first expansion (934–827)

From the Tigris to the loop of the Euphrates

Virtually destroyed by the Aramaean invasions at the start of the first millennium, the state that was rebuilt in the 'Assyrian triangle', of under 13,000 km², between Ashur, Nineveh and Arbela, intended first and foremost to regain what it had regarded since the fourteenth century as its natural western frontier, the Syrian bend of the Euphrates, and to ensure its domination over the whole of Upper Mesopotamia.

Defining new frontiers

After an initial restoration of the state under Ashur-dan (934–912), in a country still suffering from famine, the real undertaking of reconquest was launched by Adad-nerari II (911–891). Its aim was to secure the eastern and northern frontiers against the mountain tribes; to regain possession of the plain of Upper Mesopotamia, which was occupied by Aramaean principalities forming Hanigalbat around Naṣîbina and the Bît-Bahiâni around Gûzâna, and repulse the Babylonians who had occupied the left bank of the Tigris as far as Arrapha. In seven campaigns (901–894), Hanigalbat was reconquered; Naṣîbina, Gûzâna and Huṣîrina came under Assyrian rule, and Assyria's western frontier was extended as far as the Habur and the Middle Euphrates. Assyria thus regained control of its means of access to Iran and western Syria. In the south, the frontier with Babylonia was stabilised and an agreement with the king of Babylon, Nabu-shum-ukin I, resulted in a peace treaty concluded in 891 between the two sovereigns, accompanied by an exchange of their daughters in marriage. The treaty was to last eighty years. Assyrian control over its new frontiers was ensured by Tukulti-Ninurta II (890–884); he crossed the barrier of the Kašiyâri mountains, present-day Tur-Abdin, to wage war in the valley of the Upper Tigris against the Bît-Zamâni and its capital Amedu. The defeated king, Amme-Ba'al, had to pay a heavy levy and promised to reserve for the Assyrians the horses that were bred in his country. Then, in 885, Tukulti-Ninurta II undertook a huge campaign to the south-west; he went down as far as Sippar, then returned up the Euphrates, levied tribute from the lands of Sûhu and Laqê, went along the Habur and came back via Upper Mesopotamia.

Access to the sea

In the course of a reign lasting a quarter of a century, Ashurnasirpal II (883–859) developed Assyrian might in spectacular fashion; his first aim was to force the Aramaean 'stopper' that blocked access to the western bend of the Euphrates, especially the states of Bît-Adini and Bît-Agûsi, at the same time securing rich booty. He also campaigned beyond the Kašiyâri mountains, in the mountainous valleys of the upper reaches of the Tigris and Euphrates. Control of the course of the Upper Tigris was ensured by founding the town of Tušhân, which was populated by Assyrian settlers. The neo-Hittite states of Carchemish, Kummuh and Gurgum, which dominated access routes between Anatolia and the bend of the Euphrates, became Assyria's allies. During these campaigns, adversaries who submitted were compelled to pay an annual tribute (*maddattu*); against those who resisted Ashurnasirpal II systematically carried out a policy of terror and scorched earth. Yet the Assyrian conquest never appears to have been a kind of blitzkrieg; it proceeded by means of campaigns that were renewed each year, wearing down foes' resistance and procuring for Assyria material resources which it needed to pursue its war effort. By proceeding in this way, from 876 onward Ashurnasirpal II made sure of having access to the Mediterranean.

Western geopolitics

The region the Assyrians discovered when reaching the Mediterranean coast was characterised by its economic prosperity and its absence of political organisation; it had burst into a multitude of states and principalities which were in constant rivalry and had been formed in several waves, since the collapse of the Hittite empire at the end of the second millennium up to the Aramaean settlements of the early first. An initial grouping gathered together Cilicia (Hilakku, Tuwanan, Que, Ya'udi) and the plain of north-west Syria (Unqi, Pattina, Arpad, Lu'aš). The kingdom of Hamath controlled access to the south by the valley of the Orontes. To the east of the Lebanon range the powerful kingdom of Aram had been formed, with Damascus for its capital, while the east coast was the domain of the Phoenician cities (Arwad, Byblos, Sidon, Tyre). On either side of the Jordan were the kingdoms of Israel and Judah, Ammon, Moab and Edom. Beyond that, Egypt's sphere of influence began, but that did not truly intervene in the region before the seventh century.

Successes and failures in the west

Ashurnasirpal II's expedition and its consequences

In 876, Ashurnasirpal reached the Mediterranean coast by way of the valley of the Orontes and the Lebanon range. When he arrived at the sea, he washed his weapons in it, resuming the symbolic practice of the earlier great Mesopotamian conquerors. His annals complacently detail the enormous tributes he extracted from these campaigns. This expedition, the fruits of which were invested in the embellishment of a palace that the king was having built in his new capital, Kalhu, did not result in true integration. The neighbouring kingdoms which had submitted became tributaries; they had to pay a regular annual contribution, and align their external politics with those of Assyria, but in return kept their local dynasty in place and maintained internal autonomy. All that was generally sanctioned by diplomatic treaty. However, this homogenised description of the relations between the king of Assyria and his vassals belongs to Assyrian inscriptions and annals, whose purpose was to establish a model of royal success, and does not necessarily reflect reality. Ashurnasirpal II's campaigns show that, although the majority of the vanquished kingdoms complied with the tributary system, areas with a tribal structure or those organised in small principalities had to be compelled by force. This difference in treatment arose from a choice: the Assyrians sought to maintain stable structures that would guarantee them security on their frontiers, an income from tribute and auxiliaries for their army. In exchange, they would give the kings the benefit of their protection, even a share in booty. Assyrian domination therefore extended over a discontinuous area, with strong back-up points and intermediate zones without privileged status. The king of Assyria wove a network of client-states, whose elites he involved in the work of enlarging Assyrian lands; but that domination was ensured only by the repeated presence of the army which the king of Assyria led on annual campaigns, with the aim not only of levying the tribute but also of renewing a sovereignty which sometimes remained very nominal. Regions that were not regularly visited swiftly resumed their autonomy, for example Sûhu on the Middle Euphrates. The Assyrians' policy of domination ultimately united the western states against them, while from the middle of the ninth century, in the east of Anatolia around Lake Van, a confederation of mountain states was formed which laid down the basis of the state of Urartu, the Assyrians' close and fearsome adversary.

Shalmaneser III's attempt at conquest

When Ashurnasirpal II's reign ended in 859, Assyria was in a powerful situation, and the new ruler, Shalmaneser III (858–824), resuming on his own account his father's

'Mediterranean dream', attempted a real conquest of the Mediterranean coast. But matters had moved on; the king of Assyria was henceforward confronted with western states which were determined to put up resistance, under the leadership of the most powerful Aramaean state at the time, the Aram of Adad-idri/Hadad-ezer. In 857, Shalmaneser III was able to carry out a fruitful first excursion in the west; but the definitive conquest of the Bît-Adini in 856, which resulted in a permanent Assyrian settlement in the town of Til-Barsip, renamed Kar-Shalmaneser, gave a fresh impetus to the mobilisation of the kingdoms of the west. Shalmaneser III confronted them in 853, in the valley of the Orontes at Qarqar, in a battle which he wanted to make decisive. Facing the Assyrian army was a coalition that had come to the aid of the king of Hamath, comprising 3,940 chariots, 1,900 horsemen, 1,000 camels and over 60,000 footsoldiers, provided by the rulers of Damascus, Israel, Ammon, Phoenician principalities (Irqanata, Arwad, Byblos, Usanata, Šianu) and more distant allies (Egypt and the Arabs of the desert). The battle went against the Assyrians and, despite Shalmaneser's claim to have made the rivers run red with the blood of his foes, he was unable to force his way through and had to backtrack.

The contingents of the Qarqar coalition (853)

'1,200 chariots, 1,200 horsemen and 20,000 soldiers from Hadad-ezer of the Land of the Donkey [Damascus], 700 chariots, 700 horsemen and 10,000 soldiers from Irhuleni of Hamat, 2,000 chariots and 10,000 men from Ahabbu of Sir'ala [= Ahab of Israel], 500 soldiers from Byblos, 1,000 soldiers from Egypt, 10 chariots and 10,000 soldiers from Irqanata, 200 soldiers from Matinuba'l of Arwad, 200 soldiers from Usanata, 30 chariots and 10,000 soldiers from Adunaba'li of Šianu, 1,000 camels from Gindibu' the Arab and [...] 000 soldiers from Ba'sa son of Ruhubi, of Ammon, these twelve kings he [= the king of Hamath Irhuleni] summoned to his aid.'

Failures and crises

The king of Assyria turned his attention for a time to other theatres of operations: for instance, in 851 and 850, at the request of king Marduk-zakir-shumi, he intervened against the Chaldaean confederations in the south of Babylonia. A fresh attempt in the Mediterranean west, in 845, with an army of 120,000 men, again ended in failure; but in 841 Shalmaneser III took advantage of the dissolution of the anti-Assyrian coalition and the conflict that accompanied it between the kingdoms of Aram, Israel and Judah, to conquer the new king of Damascus, Hazael; but he was unable to capture the capital. After a last fruitless attempt in 838, henceforward he conducted his operations around the south-east of Anatolia (Cilicia); starting in 832, he left the conduct of military operations to his general-in-chief (*turtânu*) Dayyân-ashur. For nearly thirty years there was no more Assyrian intervention south of the Orontes.

The fact that Assyrian expansion ran out of steam was also the sign of an internal crisis that was brewing, for the fruits of conquest had been badly shared out in Assyria itself, to the almost exclusive profit of the king. The royal power had to come to terms with the great houses of the Assyrian landowning nobility, which supplied the basic contingents of the army and the executives of the administrative system. Starting in 827, a large part of Assyria rose in rebellion, and Shalmaneser III died leaving his country in a state of crisis.

CRISIS AND REFOUNDATION (823–727)

Assyrian withdrawal

The general revolt of 827 weakened the country but did not strike its vital forces; it was more of a crisis in the exercise of government and social relations.

The lessening of the crisis and the loss of western territories

The civil war nevertheless lasted until 820 and affected both the large towns of old Assyria (Ashur, Nineveh, Shibaniba, Arrapha, Arbela), with the exception of the capital, Kalhu, and the provincial centres of Upper Mesopotamia and the Middle Euphrates. It chiefly revealed the hostility of the former provinces and minor nobility, led by the son of king Ashur-da'in-aplu, against his brother Shamshi-Adad V (823–811) and those holding high office in the state, especially the general-in-chief (*turtânu*), who kept for their own exclusive use the profits taken from the provinces which had emerged from the conquest.

The first effect of this rebellion was Assyria's loss of its territories in the Syrian bend of the Euphrates, and the cessation of the tribute payment by its vassals in the west. Its western frontier was thus reduced to the Habur and the Gûzâna region. Once he had finished with the rebels, Shamshi-Adad V did not resume the great Mediterranean expeditions of the preceding reigns, preferring to consolidate the country's northern frontier, until 815; so we see him intervene south of the lakes of Van and Urmiah against mountain tribes, in order to procure the horses necessary to strengthen his force of charioteers. He encountered and fought tribes of Medes and Persians, who were settling east of lake Urmiah.

Intervention in Babylonia

Still more significant were his operations southward, in Babylonia. In 824, the king of Babylon had helped Shamshi-Adad V to subdue the revolt in Assyria, but on conditions which the king of Assyria felt to be humiliating. He took advantage of a political crisis affecting his southern neighbour to intervene brutally in 814 and 813. Though he achieved a spectacular success, as henceforward there was no political power in Babylon for a period of forty-three years, the long-term result of his intervention was the shifting of Babylon's political centre of gravity to the south of the country, in the Chaldaean confederations; these would prove to be Assyria's implacable and tenacious foes for the next two centuries

The Assyria of Shamshi-ilu

The early eighth century was marked by a gradual weakening of royal power; in the reign of Adad-nerari III (810–783) there was an increase in the strong influence of his mother Sammuramat, the prototype of the legendary Semiramis and the only queen in Assyrian history in honour of whom an official stele was erected in the town of Ashur. Beginning in 796, business was mostly conducted by the general-in-chief, the *turtânu* Shamshi-ilu.

The struggle against Urartu

The first personal military campaigns of Adad-nerari III, between 806 and 803, enabled Assyrian might to be restored temporarily in the west; north-west Syria (Hatti), west Syria (Amurru), the Phoenician towns, Israel and Philistia once more recognised Assyrian sovereignty. The king of Aram, Bar-Hadad, was himself besieged in Damascus and had to pay an enormous tribute.

These successes, which were due also to a reorganisation of the system of managing the provinces, did not mean fresh expansion, however, and were swept aside by the rise in power of the state of Urartu. Having solidly established itself in eastern Anatolia, it then spilled over very widely south-westward, and revealed itself to be a redoubtable military power. From the reign of Shalmaneser IV (782–773), in the face of repeated attacks by the Urarteans, the Assyrians had to content themselves with putting up a resistance, without being able to take the initiative, and their situation ineluctably declined.

Shamshi-ilu

Shamshi-ilu, the *turtânu*, carried out his duties under four successive kings of Assyria, from Adad-nerari III to Ashur-nerari V, from 796 until the rebellion which put Tiglath-pileser III on the throne in 745. He was eponym on three occasions, in 780, 770 and 752. He was also governor of the province of Harran and exercised absolute command over all the peripheral provinces of the kingdom that were likely to suffer foreign invasion. He was *šâpiru* of Hatti (north Syria), Gutium (central north Zagros) and Namri (central south Zagros). In Bît-Adini, he virtually carved out a personal principality for himself, with Til-Barsip/Kar-Shalmaneser for its capital, where he left inscriptions celebrating himself. The diplomatic treaty in Aramaic carved on the stelae of Sfiré have enabled him to be identified with Assyria's representative: Bar Ga'ah, son or grandson of Ga'uni, king of Sarugi, a little kingdom north of Bît-Adini which was made a vassal under Shalmaneser III. Shamshi-ilu/Bar Ga'ah is thus a perfect example of the integration of the local elites of Upper Mesopotamia into the governmental structures of Assyria.

More civil wars

The reign of Ashur-dan III (772–755), Shalmaneser IV's brother, was first marked by two epidemics of plague which ravaged the heart of Assyria, and by a rebellion in the traditional religious capital, Ashur, in 763–762. The *turtânu* Shamshi-ilu kept up the Assyrian presence in north Syria and on the frontier with Urartu, but the extension of his prerogatives emphasised the weakness of the royal government, and his authoritarianism earned him the resolute enmity of the Assyrian nobility. It all resulted in a general rebellion in Assyria, lasting ten years, until Ashur-nerari V's accession to the throne (754–745). The same causes produced new upsets, staring in 756, but that crisis brought an energetic ruler to the throne, Tiglath-pileser III, perhaps a brother of

Ashur-nerari V, who had begun his career as governor of Kalhu. He assumed direct control of government, while Shamshi-ilu was finally eclipsed.

Refounding the empire

In under twenty years, from 744 to 727, Tiglath-pileser III spectacularly altered the balance of power in the Near East in Assyria's favour, and endowed his empire with a sound structure that was destined to last for more than a century. Some of the conquered regions were directly annexed and transformed into provinces, while the vassal states of the Mediterranean coast were compelled to pay a regular tribute, under the supervision of Assyrian officers. A close watch was kept on provincial governors, who no longer had the autonomy which certain high-ranking dignitaries had appropriated for themselves during preceding reigns.

The empire expands

In 744, the new king brought peace to Assyria's eastern and southern frontiers; going down the Zagros range, he went as far as eastern Babylonia, where he made the Aramaean and Chaldaean tribes and confederations toe the line. Confident of his rearguard, in 743 he was in a position to confront and crush, near Samosata in the upper valley of the Euphrates, a vast coalition combining Urarteans and the majority of the Aramaean states in Syria. The Urartean threat was henceforward under control; as for the Aramaean coalition, it fell apart and all the kingdoms of the west submitted to Tiglath-pileser III. He exploited this victory to the full, deporting 72,950 prisoners and, in 740, annexing the kingdom of Arpad to Assyria, thus providing the latter with permanent access to the Mediterranean coast.

The year 738 was devoted to obtaining the submission of all the kingdoms situated along the Mediterranean coast, from Tabal as far as Israel, and was accompanied by a fresh deportation of 30,300 people. Next, between 737 and 735, Tiglath-pileser III waged a methodical offensive eastward, first against the land of the Medes, which he went through as far as the south of the Caspian Sea, and against the Urarteans, one of whose capitals, Tushpa, on the shores of Lake Van, he besieged. But the country was still far from being conquered definitively; so the king of Assyria turned westward once again. In 734, he scattered a coalition of the king of Judah, some Philistine rulers (of Ascalon, Gaza) and some trans-Jordanian (of Ammon, Moab and Edom). In 733 and 732, when appealed to by the king of Judah, he ravaged the kingdom of Israel and laid low the state of Aram. Damascus was captured and looted, and its population deported.

Annexing Babylonia

In 728, Tiglath-pileser III achieved a master stroke; taking advantage of political troubles in Babylonia, he intervened. Since the time of Shamshi-Adad V, being placed under more or less direct supervision, the Babylonian state had seen a succession of local kings, some of whom had emerged from the Chaldaean confederations, but none had been able to keep the throne for long. Did Tiglath-pileser consider the system no longer viable? At all events, at the end of his intervention he assumed the crown of king of Babylon, which was as good as annexing Babylonia to Assyria. When his son, Shalmaneser V (726–722), succeeded him, he carried on the same principle, perhaps in the form of a personal union, with a reigning name specific to Babylonia: Ulûlayu. The new king of Assyria also achieved successes in the west; he captured and destroyed Sam'al, capital of one of the last independent Aramaean states in north Syria, Ya'udi, then in 722 applied the same treatment to the state of Israel and its capital, Samaria. But he had no time to take advantage of his success; he was overthrown in a palace revolt, to the profit of another son (?) of Tiglath-pileser III, who ascended the throne in 721 under the name Šarru-kîn, 'the legitimate king' (Sargon II), and founded the Sargonid dynasty, which was the most prestigious of the Assyrian empire.

THE SARGONID EMPIRE (721–610)

The implacable Babylonian problem

Despite an ambitious imperial policy that was crowned with success, the Assyrian kings were unable to find a satisfactory solution for incorporating Babylonia into the Assyrian empire. The Chaldaean confederations resisted them ferociously, with the support of the neighbouring kingdom of Elam, and forced Assyria to divert a large part of its forces there. In the north, the Sargonids were able to crush the might of Urartu definitively, and ensured the security of their frontier with the kingdoms of western Anatolia (Phrygia and Lydia). But two powerful states, Egypt and Elam, felt threatened by the empire's strength and kept up a resistance to Assyrian ascendancy. Sargon II and his successors were thus dragged into a series of new conquests, which gradually exhausted the country.

Quelling adversaries, and settlement in South Anatolia

Several rebellions broke out in the empire in favour of political change in Assyria, but were swiftly put down by Sargon II. The kingdom of Israel completed its transformation into an Assyrian province (721); the Aramaeans of Damascus, Arpad and Hamath were crushed, and part of their populations deported (720). The same treatment was meted out in 717 to the town of Carchemish on the Upper Euphrates, which had formed an alliance with the kingdom of Phrygia, in central Anatolia, and its king Mita (Midas). However, Sargon II could not prevent the restoration of an independent kingdom of Babylon under the leadership of the Chaldaean Merodachbaladan II, backed by the kingdom of

Elam. Not until 710–709 did he launch a decisive military campaign which cut Merodachbaladan off from his Elamite support; he pursued him as far as his southern capital of Dûr-Yakîn. Merodachbaladan II took refuge in Elam, and Sargon II had himself acknowledged as king at Babylon. The system of personal union in a double monarchy was abandoned; Babylonia was treated as a simple province of the empire. Sargon similarly led expeditions against Assyria's northern foes; he intervened among the Manneans in the north-east (715–714), and chiefly against Urartu, finally breaking its might in 714. His other great theatre of operations was southern Anatolia, where he had to reinforce the frontier that was threatened by the ambitions of Phrygia and the small kingdoms under its control (Gurgum, Tabal, Milid, Kummuh), at the same time extending his influence as far as Cyprus. The end of his reign, however, shows evidence of the difficulty of operating on fronts that were very often distant; after launching a campaign against Elam, Sargon again had to intervene in Tabal, in the north-west of the empire, in 705. There he met a sudden death in an ambush, and his body was not even found.

Continuing the work of Sargon II

Sargon II's abrupt disappearance did not place the empire in danger, however; his son Sennacherib (704–681) immediately assumed the reins of power, but he had to face the permanent resistance set up in Babylonia against its integration into the empire. In 703, after dispatching a vast coalition of the Chaldaeans, Elamites and Arab and Aramaean contingents led by Merodachbaladan II, Sennacherib installed a king in Babylon who had been raised in Assyria, Bêl-ibni. But he had to intervene yet again in 700, to crush a new Chaldaean attempt; the Assyrian army finally managed to get rid of Merodachbaladan II. Sennacherib then replaced Bêl-ibni with his own son, Ashur-nadin-shumi, appointed viceroy in Babylonia.

Meanwhile, the king of Assyria was also present in the west to stamp out the beginnings of a revolt; but he was unable to subdue the state of Judah and had to lift the siege of Jerusalem after his army had fallen victim to an epidemic (701). From 699 to 695, it was the vast northern frontier that had to be reinforced by regular expeditions.

The destruction of Babylon and the tragic end of Sennacherib

The end of his reign was entirely occupied with settling the situation in Babylonia, which had taken a dramatic turn; several large Babylonian towns rebelled, with the support of the Chaldaeans and, mainly, Elam which provided troops and a retreat base for the rebels. In 694, Ashur-nadin-shumi was handed over to the Elamites by his subjects and executed. Despite a violent Assyrian counter-attack in 693, marked by the looting and destruction of southern Babylonia, the coalition of Babylonians and Elamites was not smashed until 791, at the battle of Halulê on the Tigris. Sennacherib then gave his vengeance free rein; he besieged Babylon (690–689). The town fell after a fifteen-month siege, and was systematically pillaged and destroyed, and Sennacherib had the statue of its tutelary god, Marduk, brought to Nineveh, while personally resuming the title of king of Babylon.

The various attempts to govern Babylonia, by vassal king or through an intermediary Assyrian prince, had failed and led the king to a radical anti-Babylonian attitude; the enormity of the punishment inflicted on Babylon and its god made a deep impression on contemporaries. Sennacherib had brought down the two powers that kept up disturbances in Babylonia, the Chaldaean confederations and the kingdom of Elam, but had not been able to smash them once and for all. In Assyria itself, his choice of the youngest of his sons, Esarhaddon, to succeed him brought trouble to the royal court, and the king was assassinated in 681 at Kalhu, in the temple of the god Ninurta, by one of his supplanted sons, Arad-Mullissu.

The Sargonids

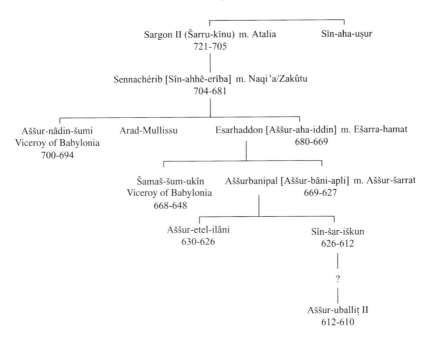

To conquer Egypt

Sennacherib's murder caused a civil war to break out, and it took Esarhaddon the whole of 680 to rid himself of his brothers and regain control of the empire.

Esarhaddon's new policy

With regard to Babylonia, he adopted a conciliatory attitude that would pay off; he embarked on the rebuilding of the town of Babylon and its temples, used the internal dissensions among Chaldaeans in order to neutralise them, and managed to contain Elamite attempts in 675–674. In the north, new forces had appeared, the Cimmerians and Scythians, who destroyed the north of Urartu. Esarhaddon left them to it and succeeded, half by force and half by diplomacy, in diverting them towards central Anatolia. This policy, less brutal than Sennacherib's, reveals a personal choice, doubtless strengthened by a fairly precarious state of health throughout his reign. But Esarhaddon too resorted to force in certain circumstances; Phoenicia, which showed leanings towards independence, was severely punished and reduced to a simple Assyrian province in 676. Tyre lost its autonomy, and the king of Sidon was beheaded. Moreover, the king of Assyria pursued the policy of expansion characteristic of the Sargonids by attacking Egypt, which had hitherto remained outside the Assyrian field of action, but had supported the anti-Assyrian agitation in Syria-Palestine. Two attempts in 674 and 671 led to the capture of Memphis, capital of Lower Egypt.

Settling the question of succession

Beginning in 673, Esarhaddon's health deteriorated, and a far from negligible part of government was carried out secretly by the queen mother, Naqi'a. In particular, she exerted her influence in the choice of the heir to the throne, which had become one of Esarhaddon's major worries, as the troubles at the end of Sennacherib's reign had left a deep mark on him. His younger son, Ashurbanipal, was the one designated, and the decision was solemnly ratified in 672 by the general swearing of an oath by the empire's vassals and allies. The eldest son, Shamash-shum-ukin, was compensated by being given personal royalty over the kingdom of Babylon. This ruling did not, however, prevent conspiracies in Assyria (670), or the hatching of rebellions in Babylonia and Egypt, which resumed its autonomy under the leadership of the pharaoh Taharqa (669). Western Media similarly escaped the Assyrian hold at the end of the reign.

The peak and decline of the Assyrian empire

On Esarhaddon's death (669), Ashurbanipal inherited the throne. His reign is often regarded as the apogee of the Assyrian empire, which brought down its last adversaries, basically Egypt and Elam, but began to recede in certain peripheral areas. Egypt was reconquered as far as Thebes between 666 and 662, and shared out among several vassal kings, but this conquest of Egypt proved no more durable than Esarhaddon's, and shows the limits of Assyria's field of action. Upper Egypt liberated itself in 660, and Lower Egypt rebelled under the leadership of Psammetichus I in 653. In the same period, we note the loss of all contact with the island of Cyprus. Meanwhile, Ashurbanipal had been occupied on the eastern frontier; in the north-east he intervened against the Manneans in the region of Lake Urmiah (660), but was unable to overcome the Cimmerians, who stepped up their incursions and carried out a spectacular raid in 657. In the south-east, Ashurbanipal had to wage a new war against Elam, whose king was defeated and killed in 653.

The rebellion of Shamash-shum-ukin and the settlement of the Elamite problem

In 652, the Babylonian problem resurfaced in all its sharpness; for fifteen years Shamash-shum-ukin had governed there, but under the tight control of the court of Nineveh and with no direct authority except over the capital and a few large towns. In the end he joined the camp of Assyria's traditional opponents in the region: Chaldaeans, Aramaeans and Elamites, and seceded. It took Ashurbanipal four years to regain control of the country. Babylon was besieged, and its inhabitants eventually capitulated in 648, while Shamash-shum-ukin perished in his burning palace. The rebels were harshly punished, but the town was not destroyed as it had been in 681, and a new viceroy, Kandalanu, was appointed there by Ashurbanipal.

The king of Assyria then decided to have done with Elam; while keeping tight control over the activities of the Chaldaeans of the Country of the Sea, in the south of Babylonia, he launched two successive expeditions against Elam (647–646), destroying its capital, Susa, from top to bottom. For nearly twenty years, nothing further seemed to disturb the rule of Ashurbanipal, who had given up his conquest of Egypt. Nevertheless, despite the glory of his reign, the deep-rooted causes of the rejection of Assyrian rule remained very much alive. Assyria itself had worn out many of its active forces in incessant military operations on increasingly distant fronts; so it is not surprising that the gigantic Assyrian empire fell apart in under fifteen years, when a civil war that set Assyria ablaze following the death of Ashurbanipal (627) was combined with an external attack by the Medes and an internal one by the Babylonians.

The civil war and its consequences

Little is known about the end of Ashurbanipal's reign. It appears that the old king withdrew to Harran, in Upper Mesopotamia, while effective government was exercised by his son Ashur-etel-ilâni from 630. On Ashurbanipal's death in 627, Ashur-etel-ilâni officially acceded to the throne, with the aid of the chief eunuch and commander of the armies, Sîn-shum-lîshir, and another of Ashurbanipal's sons, Sîn-shar-ishkun, who was supported by Babylonia. The latter found itself in an identical situation. Kandalanu died in 627, and after a period of uncertainty lasting several months a Babylonian candidate, Nabopolassar, declared himself in the south of the country, at the very moment when Sîn-shar-ishkun was claiming the throne of Assyria. So it appears that the claimants' troops first operated in Babylonia, in an often confused context. After eliminating Sîn-shum-lîshir, Sîn-shar-ishkun marched on Nineveh, where he was acknowledged as king. But when he tried to restore his authority over Babylonia, his troops were unable to bring down Nabopolassar, who had effectively become king of Babylon. This time it was the Babylonians, once more completely independent, who brought war to Assyria.

On their own the Babylonian troops would probably not have been able to overcome the Assyrians, but they received decisive reinforcements from the leader of the Medes, Cyaxarus. Since 625, he had united north-west Iran under his authority and finally driven out the Assyrians. In 615, joint action by the Babylonians and Medes caught the Assyrians in a pincer movement and resulted in the capture of Arrapha, then Ashur, the old religious capital, in 614. In 612, it was Nineveh's turn to be sacked, after a fierce attack by the Medes. Sîn-shar-ishkun disappeared at that time, and the remainder of the empire's forces fell back to western Upper Mesopotamia as far as Harran. There Ashur-uballiṭ II was proclaimed 'king of Assyria', and even received the support of an Egyptian relief army; but he was unable to prevent Medes and Babylonians from taking possession of the region in 610, sealing the end of the Assyrian empire.

DOCUMENT

One of Ashurnasirpal II's campaigns in the east of Anatolia in 865

'In the eponymate of Shamash-nûrî, on the orders of Ashur, great Lord, my Master, on the 13th of the month of Ayaru, I left the town of Kalhu, crossed the Tigris and advanced towards the land of Qipânu. I received the tribute of the princes of the land of Qipânu, in the city of Huṣirîna. While staying in the city of Huṣirîna, I received the tribute of Itti', the Azallean, and Giridadi, the Aššean: gold, small livestock and bales of wool. At the same time, I also received trunks of cedar, silver and gold: the tribute of Qatazili, the Kummuhean.

I left the city of Huṣirîna and went back up the Euphrates . . . I went in the direction of the cities of the land of Dirru. I burned the towns situated between Mounts Amadânu and Arqanaia, and took possession of the land of Mallânu which lies on Mount Arqanaia. I left the land of Mallânu, going to the towns of the land of Zamba, and burned them in passing. I crossed the river Ṣûa and halted (for the night) on the bank of the Tigris. I razed and destroyed the towns situated on either side of the Tigris on Mount Arqanaia. The entire land of Habhu was terrified and fell at my feet; I took some hostages and installed my own governor there.

From the pass of Mount Amadânu, I set out again towards the city of Barzaništun; I proceeded to the town of Damdammusa, the citadel of Ilâni of the Bît-Zamâni. I attacked the town. My soldiers, like birds of prey, fell upon their men. I put 600 of their fighters to the sword and cut off their heads. I took 400 men alive, and 3,000 prisoners. I took possession of the town. I brought the survivors and the heads to Amedu, its royal capital; I made a pile of the heads before the town gate and impaled the survivors on stakes all round the town. I did battle at its town gate, and razed its orchards. I left the town of Amedu and entered the pass of the Kašiyâri mountain and the town of Allabsia, where none of the kings, my forefathers, had ever set foot or launched an expedition. I went to the town of Udu, the citadel of Labṭuru, son of Tupusu. I swooped down on the town; with saps, siege engines and assault ramps, I took the town. I put 1,400 men to the sword, took 580 men alive and captured 3,000 prisoners. Some of the survivors I impaled on stakes all round the town; I had the eyes torn out of others. The remainder I brought to Assyria. I took possession of the town.'

This text is an extract from the annals of the king of Assyria Ashurnasirpal II (883–859), and recounts the military campaign carried out during the summer of 865 in the upper valleys of the Euphrates and Tigris, east of Anatolia. The intention was not to conquer these territories, but to make a show of Assyrian presence there. The account is given in the first person, and appears as a victorious march through wild regions; the king collects booty there, triumphs over all opposition, and complacently relates the ravages he has perpetrated: the practice of a war of terror is described here in all its aspects.

A 'tour' in the northern territories

The Assyrian army left Kalhu, the capital, in the spring (Ayâru, the second month in the Assyro-Babylonian year, corresponding to April–May). The king had called his army together, composed of professionals and part of the Assyrian population, who were mobilised just after the harvest. There, weapons had been issued and equipment checked. The campaign was not considered likely to last much longer than the summer, and had a triple objective: to collect the tribute of the vassals of Upper Syria, subdue or destroy the mountain states of the upper valley of the Tigris, which represented a permanent threat to Assyria's northern frontier, and to bring back booty that would be used to complete the building of Kalhu's great edifices.

Receiving the tribute

Upon his arrival at Huşirîna, where he stopped briefly, the king received marks of respect from his local vassals. They were accompanied by a tribute made up from local resources (wool and livestock, wood for building), and also wealth belonging to the rulers of these Aramaean or neo-Hittite states, essentially precious metals. Payment of these annual contributions was a sign of their acknowledgement of Assyrian sovereignty, and no one could escape it without being regarded as a rebel. Though heavy, payment of the tribute brought the compensation of Assyrian protection for these local kings against their rivals. For Assyria, it represented an indispensable source of income, and the king had no hesitation in journeying to collect it, at the same time displaying the might of his armed forces.

The military part of the campaign

Leaving Huşirîna, the Assyrian army went north once more and plunged into little-known territory: at first it followed the valley of the Euphrates, then, by a series of mountain passes, joined that of the Upper Tigris, which it traversed from west to east, along the entire expanse of the Bît-Zamâni which Ashurnasirpal wanted to quell. The campaign ended in the Kašiyâri mountains, separating the valley of the Tigris from Upper Mesopotamia.

The text does not spare us the cruel details of the atrocities inflicted on local populations; such treatment aimed at wiping out their ability to resist. Enemy warriors, who represented a potential danger, were put to death, and their heads used to build trophies, as in front of Amedu. Those taken prisoner were then impaled below the walls of the town, or mutilated, as at Udu. The representation of some of these scenes in palace iconography at Kalhu, or later Nineveh, led to the forming of an extremely negative judgement about Assyrian war practices in modern times; furthermore, Ashurnasirpal was one of those Assyrian kings who are thought of as truly sadistic because of the way they gloried in such behaviour. However, Ashurnasirpal kept a certain number of survivors with him, bringing them back as slaves to act as labourers in Assyria.

Covering the territory

As in other parts of the annals of the kings of Assyria, this text is especially rich in topographical and political references. Despite the very conventional aspect of the account, which makes the king almost the sole protagonist in the venture, with a first-person narration of operations (he mentions his soldiers only once), the area in which this royal 'feat' took place was not imaginary. Whenever they can, the Assyrians detail the names of towns, kings, countries and the natural features encountered, and for this reason the annals are a precious source of information. Ashurnasirpal emphasises how this whole mountainous region in the north-west of Assyria is split up; at the same time, by naming its various components, he identifies it and gives it a comprehensible order.

The edges of the known world were thus pushed farther back at each new campaign; but the details given are not all of the same kind. Whenever possible, the king names the countries and their rulers; that is the case of the vassals whose tribute he receives during his stay at Huṣirîna, or when he attacks Bît-Zamâni of the Aramaean prince Ilâni. Elsewhere, he simply mentions 'the towns' of this or that country and, when almost no information is available, indicates only the major topographical features: watercourses (Euphrates, Tigris), mountains (Amadânu, Arqanaia, Kašiyâri). In this arrangement of the landscape adopted by the annals, the fundamental references are therefore the major natural obstacles over which the king of Assyria triumphs, and the network of settlements, which are uniformly described as towns (*âlu*), though it is difficult to know whether they were real urban centres or merely villages. The number of inhabitants enables us to pinpoint important towns, such as Damdammusa in Bît-Zamâni, which must have held at least 4,000 people, or Udu, whose population is estimated as at least 4,980. Bît-Zamâni was sufficiently well known to the Assyrians for Ashurnasirpal to be able to specify that Damdammusa was a military stronghold, whereas the real capital was the town of Amedu (present-day Diyarbakir).

A policy of systematic destruction

Throughout the text, we discover that in some places destruction pure and simple is carried out; the 'towns' situated in the area of Mounts Amadânu and Arqanaia were burnt, razed, destroyed. Then the king of Assyria 'took possession' of the land. It is noteworthy that this was a constant feature of Assyrian policy, consisting in annihilating certain existing landmarks in those countries they were seeking to conquer; it was a matter of weakening their enemies, but also depriving them of the traditional structure provided by these towns. In any case, at this stage in the history of the empire, the possession claimed by Ashurnasirpal was mainly nominal; only in the land of Habhu did he install a governor (to be understood, in fact, as a vassal ruler who would recognise his authority), whose loyalty he ensured by carrying off hostages to Assyria. The remainder of the lands through which he passed were not placed under any effective control; not until the reign of Tiglath-pileser III (744–727) would vassal states be transformed into true provinces of the Assyrian empire. At this stage, it would be more appropriate to speak of a zone of influence set up by the kings of Assyria than of a real conquest.

Terror and its implications

The specific nature of an Assyrian policy of cruelty needs to be qualified; in the first place, it appears that wars in the Near East were fairly often marked by such practices, the vanquished enemy having no right to any considerate treatment. On the other hand, such cruelty was deemed to serve precise ends: it was to terrify an enemy who could not be reduced to begging for mercy, as the instance of Amedu clearly shows. Although Ashurnasirpal was able to seize Damdammusa, he could not do the same with the capital of Bît-Zamâni; he carried the battle to the gates of the town, burned the orchards in the surrounding countryside, but does not specify that he took possession of the town. The siege methods available to the Assyrian army did not allow it to undertake long sieges, and served for only one attack which was not renewed if it failed. The macabre exposure of the heads of the vanquished and the prisoners impaled around Amedu were thus intended to spread terror among the inhabitants, who had already realised that their resources had been destroyed. The memory of this treatment might make things easier in a future campaign. In the case of the town of Udu, at the close of the expedition, the principle was almost the same. We note that in this instance, as with Bît-Zamâni, Ashurnasirpal carried off a human booty of 6,000 non-combatants, whom he took back to Assyria, most probably to be assigned to the construction of the monuments in the town of Kalhu, then in its final phase. The royal palace would be inaugurated in 864. The use of terror was thus aimed at extending armed action and preparing the ground for future expeditions. It was linked with the brevity of the Assyrian campaigns in that period.

The picture of the king that emerges from this extract is of a sovereign who wages war without any feelings, identifies himself with the destructive forces of nature or of the Mesopotamian pantheon, and explores the farthest limits of the known world. There is no lack of comparisons in the royal annals, which present the king as a lion or impetuous bull, a flood or ravaging hurricane, and his soldiers as birds of prey, as in this instance. Confident of the support of the god Ashur, who, at his coronation, commanded him to make the god's supremacy known throughout the entire world, the king of Assyria triumphs over all obstacles, human or natural.

Chapter 3

Control of the imperial territory

Though all the king of Assyria's subjects were bound to give him military service, the might of the Assyrian army lay first of all in the presence of numerous professional troops, hardened to war by annual campaigns. Under the command of the king and the *turtânu* (general-in-chief), this army included a great variety of specialist corps which enabled it to adapt to every kind of terrain and capture enemy towns. In the seventh century, the cavalry was tending to supplant chariots. At first mainly Assyrian, the army subsequently became imperial, with the addition of vassal contingents. Assyrian kings did not hesitate to make use of a policy of terror against their foes, from whom they extracted booty or tribute, or whom, under the Sargonids, they deported en masse.

Assyria comprised some urban centres and a mainly rural population, spread among landed estates of fairly limited size. To make up for the gradual weakening of their active forces, accentuated by the increase in non-productive residents in their capital towns, the Assyrians sought to provide themselves with a more extensive agricultural area by exploiting the plains of Upper Mesopotamia as far as Harran. Apparently, however, that did not prevent a rise in the prices of basic products in Assyria itself.

At first the Assyrian kingdom functioned with a network of client-states on its periphery and a certain number of frontier provinces which were placed under the responsibility of high-ranking palace dignitaries. From 745, the overall zone of Assyrian domination was divided into provinces which were administered by Assyrian governors directly responsible to the king. Conquered territories were used initially in purely predatory fashion, before this gradually evolved into the regular levying of a tribute, though this did not rule out the quest for economic development of the provinces.

MILITARY ORGANISATION

A diversified army

In organisation as in action, the Assyrian army was one of conquest. To the might of its numerical strength, it allied the use of specialised corps and a familiarity with war that was maintained by virtually annual campaigns. The incorporation of vast territories into the original kingdom, then transformation into a multi-ethnic empire, starting with Tiglath-pileser III, led to the integration of local contingents and the building of an increasingly complex system of permanent garrisons.

Ashur's troops

The army (*kiṣir šarri*) was formed by recruiting Assyrian peasants, who were bound to give the king an annual military service, the *ilku*. Troops were assembled after the harvest for a summer campaign, which initially aimed at relatively close territories: the mountainous valleys of east Assyria or the plain of Upper Mesopotamia. The greater part of this army was an infantry of archers, divided into light or heavy units, complemented in the seventh century by corps of pikemen. Recruitment fell under the responsibility of the land-owning nobility and local administrative authorities, who received their instructions from the king and had to give him an account of the numbers gathered. The army was organised in hierarchised contingents of ten, fifty or one hundred men. These companies were themselves arranged in tactical units of a thousand men. The hierarchy of command combined with this numerical basis (leader of ten, fifty, one hundred men, etc.) more generally ranging titles: 'captain' (*rab kiṣir*), 'chief in charge of equipment' (*rab urâte*), who could be attached to the military households of the greatest personages in the empire.

The army of Sargon II

For a campaign in Babylonia in the reign of Sargon II, the royal army was composed of contingents raised in Assyria, comprising a corps of Aramaeans, commanded by the chief of the *ša rêš šarri*, joined by cavalry units and chariots from Babylonia, Chaldaea and Samaria, plus a unit known as 'the deportees', made up of contingents from the former kingdoms of Carchemish or Hamat, who had been incorporated into the Assyrian army. It also included corps of troops who formed the royal guard. In marching order, this army placed its contingents under the aegis of the gods: at the head came the regiments of Nergal and Adad, followed by that of Ishtar, composed of the royal bodyguard around the king, with the troops of Sîn and Shamash on his right and left.

The army had a permanent nucleus, however, in which professional soldiers served, young men of the Assyrian nobility and specialist troops. As the expeditions grew more and more long-range and it became necessary to leave troops to control territories that were distant or hard to quell, the sovereign increasingly called upon contingents that were recruited on the spot; but these had a tendency to flee conscription, forming bands of deserters (*halqûtu*). Warlike nomadic tribes such as the Itueans were used as well to strengthen the garrisons of fortresses, but they also acted as a special force sent to various parts of the empire on all kinds of missions. Under the Sargonids, the practice of integrating a proportion of foreign vassal or conquered troops, including their officers, into the Assyrian royal army is well illustrated, as are systematic attempts to rally certain Aramaean tribes of Lower Mesopotamia to the service of Assyria, by ensuring their food

supplies or, on the contrary, cutting off their sources of provisions.

The king was always the supreme commander of the army,
even if he did not take part in the expeditions. He was
assisted by the true specialist in military matters, the general-
in-chief (*turtânu*). The latter's increasingly important position in public affairs led Tiglath-pileser III to double up the
office during the last third of the seventh century, in order to
neutralise any possible personal ambitions. At the end of the
empire, it was above all the chief of the eunuchs (*rab ša rêši*)
who was in charge of the army. Each of the great dignitaries
of the court had his own military household, charged with the
safety of the frontier provinces for which they were responsible, and they were summoned back into the royal army at
times of big campaigns. Similarly, provincial governors maintained troops of local militias who could take part in large-
scale operations waged by the king.

Specialist corps

Assyrian kings attached great importance to having available
army corps that were adapted to various terrains: in the
mountains, sappers were called upon to open up roads; the
resistance of towns was crushed by a whole range of siege
equipment, thus avoiding long sieges for which the logistics
of an annual campaign did not provide. On flat terrain, in the
ninth and eighth centuries, the army used the noble weapon
of the chariot. In the eighth century, increasingly well-
equipped heavy chariots enabled up to four men to be
carried; but their effective role in battle tended to disappear
after Sargon II, in favour of a cavalry of mounted archers,
which became an essential corps in the Assyrian army. Used
at first on steep ground, then to secure roads or pursue run-
aways, the cavalry corps henceforward played an effective
role in battles, while their equipment grew heavier. The
army's movements brought the need for elaborate logistics,
for instance to prepare water reserves when deserts had to be

crossed, or to organise the transport of booty and the super-vision of prisoners or deportees. The army also included cou-riers and corps that specialised in reconnaissance operations.

The various technical corps were the object of special attention on the part of the king and top military administra-tion: war machines and stocks of weapons and equipment were kept in arsenals built in immediate proximity to the royal palace, and were under constant surveillance and main-tenance. To provide for permanent requirements for chariot-horses, then mainly for saddle-horses, the Assyrians obtained their supplies from western Iran. Scrupulous care was given to the training and upkeep of these horses in royal stud farms or on lands belonging to the local administration. For very precise requirements, foreign specialists were called in; for instance, when Sennacherib set up a river fleet intended to intervene in the marshes of southern Babylonia, he had it built in Assyria by Phoenicians who were brought specially to the site.

Strategy and tactics

The aim of a military campaign was both to destroy a certain number of objectives and to bring back booty; when it returned to Assyria, the army took on the appearance of a vast caravan, bringing back prisoners, livestock and every kind of produce, the greater part being reserved for the gods and the king.

Before the campaign

The principle of Assyrian military action was to gain perma-nent superiority over its adversaries, from the moral stand-point as well; the army was accompanied by the symbols of the great warrior gods of the country – Ashur, Ishtar, Ninurta – and every campaign was preceded by a series of oracular consultations during which the anticipated plan of action was submitted for the gods' approval. A certain number of preserved accounts, the *tamîtu*, show that the smallest details of the planned itinerary were scrutinised.

Operations

While not hesitating to launch attacks himself, accompanied only by his bodyguards, the king of Assyria most often sought to assure himself of a numerical advantage that would compensate for the absence of true tactical superiority in the field. The Assyrian army's capabilities for manoeuvring were in fact not really superior to those of most of its adversaries, although it had the benefit of genuine combat experience. In any case, the nature of the sources is such that only the king's exploits are recorded, even if it is acknowledged that his soldiers were capable of long forced marches, or of crossing rivers 'as if they were streams'. The account of operations concentrates on the irresistible pace of the royal attack and the sovereign's capacity for plunging into unknown or inhospitable regions. The description of most of the battles yielded by the royal annals is therefore heavily stereotyped, emphasising the damage inflicted on the enemy. Similarly, the majority of the military scenes sculpted on the bas-reliefs of Assyrian palaces portray the king and his army at the moment when the scale of their attack puts the enemy army to flight or forces it to hand over besieged towns. Passing from one town to the next to have the sovereignty of its king acknowledged, the Assyrian army was also capable of building fortified camps in the non-urbanised areas, marking out roads and crossing rivers on inflated skins. When the campaign ended, before returning to Assyria, the king would often leave a stele or inscription on rock intended to mark his passage for the benefit of future generations.

On the fringes of military operations

The ferocity of Assyrian war is notorious; the aim was not only to defeat foes, but also to weaken them as much as possible, if not wipe them out completely. Those who capitulated were subjected to payment of an enormous tribute, while those who offered resistance saw their crops systematically looted or destroyed, their town sacked, their elites eliminated and their populations deported.

The policy of terror

The psychological aspect of war was carefully maintained: to terrify the recalcitrant or set an example, collective mutilations were performed, or spectacular forms of torture; prisoners were impaled or flayed alive in the sight of their compatriots, towns were burnt together with their inhabitants. After the battle, the soldiers cut the hands and heads from their enemies' corpses to make into trophies which were recorded by army scribes. Defeated kings, if not executed, were brought back to Assyria to take part in the triumphal entry into the capital by the king and his troops, then to be exposed to the public gaze in humiliating conditions.

Deportations

When the conquered region proved difficult to control, the Assyrians resorted to deporting the population. If they did not invent this practice, its chief purpose being to bring back large quantities of slave labour, from the time of Tiglath-pileser III they made it an instrument in managing the empire, exchanging populations from very distant regions among one another. Sources document 157 deportations between the ninth and seventh centuries, with a total of some 1,320,000 people, but it may be estimated that in reality the number was nearer 4,500,000. If the kings of the early eighth century deported by tens of thousands, except under Shalmaneser III when more than 160,000 people were victims, the figure rose to nearly 400,000 during the reign of Tiglath-pileser III, and almost 470,000 under Sennacherib. The human cost of these deportations was enormous, since it is thought that, in certain instances, half the deportees died during the journey; moreover, when they arrived at the site of their enforced residence, they were sometimes the target of hostility from the local populace, who had to contribute to their upkeep or provide them with land. Although some groups of deportees entrenched themselves lastingly as settlers in the areas where they had been installed, such as those of Samaria in Upper Mesopotamia, the despair of others actually increased their implacable hatred of the Assyrians, and failed to render them more submissive or integrated into the empire.

Garrison and information services

Control of the frontiers, conquered zones and major communication routes became increasingly important as the imperial structure developed. On the northern and eastern frontiers, points of contact with Urartu and the Median confederations were kept under surveillance in the seventh century by resident garrisons, whose business was to levy the tribute and keep an eye on local populations, or to act as centres of colonisation in the less populated areas. These fortresses had to have enough staff and provisions, and their officers, the *rab birti*, sent regular reports to the central offices of the royal palace. Should danger threaten, they could serve as a refuge for the local people and their belongings. In the same way, the principal communication routes of the empire were supervised by relay-posts (*bît mardîti*) which acted as staging-posts for the royal couriers. In addition to their function of maintaining order, all these back-up and control points were at the same time used as a base for people who were sent among the enemy to collect information of all kinds about the local political and military situation.

AT THE HUB OF THE EMPIRE

Old Assyria

The glorious aspects of official records conveyed by royal annals and inscriptions mask a more prosaic reality. Assyria was a small country, and the motivation for its expansion was the result of a deliberate choice of a military option, born of resistance to Aramaean incursions, the need to control its outlets to neighbouring regions and secure supplies of the raw materials it lacked, and to regain the glory and might of the Middle Assyrian state of the second millennium. This expansion was supported by a demographic, economic and social dynamism which was very real until the beginning of the eighth century, but which subsequently declined. So, paradoxically, just when it was achieving imperial organisation in the seventh century, Assyria was growing weaker in men and resources.

The rural situation

With the exception of the religious and political capitals (Ashur, Arbela, Nineveh and Kalhu), Assyrian urban centres were small townships with a geographically limited horizon. The majority of the Assyrian population was composed of lowly peasants gathered into hamlets (*kapru*) that were either independent or attached to the estates of the big landed property owners, which never attained any great size, apart from the royal domains and those of the temples. The average area of individual smallholdings farmed with a biennial fallow season is estimated at some twenty hectares; as for the large properties of dignitaries in the king's service, these could reach some 2,000 hectares, but scarcely ever extended uninterruptedly. For example, the chief of Ashurbanipal's eunuchs, Nabû-šar-uṣur, owned at least 1,700 hectares of arable land, 40 vineyards, 2 orchards and over 50 families of agricultural workers. Rîmanni-Adad, the same king's equerry, bought at least 750 hectares of land. In fact, these large landowners combined medium-sized estates, sometimes spread among several provinces, in order to have at their disposal agricultural produce peculiar to various regions of the empire: in the reign of Sargon II, the governor of Damascus, Bêl-dûrî, owned 580 hectares of cereal-producing land in the district of Gûzâna, in Upper Mesopotamia. Establishing landed estates was not reserved only for the great personages of the realm; in the first half of the eighth century, the headman of a district in the province of Kalhu purchased a series of estates, several of which were situated far from his place of residence, and constituted a capital estate of at least 50 hectares for himself; at the same time, the brother of Kalhu's governor went ahead with similar purchases to a total of nearly 200 hectares. The sale of family lands among private individuals was not general practice, however. The neo-Assyrian period still maintained the system of royal edicts of *andurâru*, which did away with the transfer of family land inheritance. The land-owning power of the Assyrian nobility, which was undeniable in the ninth and early eighth centuries, declined as royal authority grew firmer. Under the Sargonids, the king could at any time rescind an office and the advantages in kind connected with it. The men who formed the closed circle of government tried to profit from their situation as quickly as possible to acquire riches, and convert into personally owned land the benefits they derived from their duties; for example, in the space of eleven years, Rîmanni-Adad proceeded with no fewer than 21 purchases of land or slave labour, in a geographical area stretching from the Transtigris to the valley of the Orontes.

In Assyria, the permanent requisitions affecting farmers, either for war or for major construction works, meant that the labour force was sparse, even at times of the empire's greatest prosperity, and explain why the sales of landed estates included with the land the families who worked it, sometimes entire villages. Some independent farmers had to resort to borrowing with interest to make up for a temporary shortfall in resources, but they would then often fall victim to an ineluctable process of impoverishment; for example, they would have to go and harvest on their creditor's land, after being requisitioned to work on the royal lands. Harvesting on their own farm would therefore be possible only at the end of the season, in less favourable conditions, which would prevent their repaying their debt. The burden of the service due to the king similarly explains why towns attached great importance to their exemptions (*kidinnûtu, zakûtu*), and gifts of land made by the king to his servitors were quite often accompanied by exemptions from taxes and unpaid labour duties. Relations between the rural population and the towns remained limited to paying their dues and the royal tax. The majority of peasants lived in a semi-autarchic regime, resorting to local urban centres only when they needed metalware.

The evolution of towns

A particular feature, due to the development of the empire, affected towns that were centres of government: their population tended to swell in terms of administrators and civil or military officials, or in artisans, which meant so many extra mouths to feed. Moreover, building requirements brought into several urban sites populations who could no longer be fed directly by the town's surrounding farmlands alone. During the construction of the royal palace at Kalhu, under Ashurnasirpal II, two-thirds of the 63,000 residents were a sort of artificial component who needed to be fed although they were producing no agricultural resources. Trade and craft activities were under the thumb of palace economy. Craft production in particular was ruled by the system of the *iškaru*: the royal administration distributed raw materials to groups of artisans, whose duty was to return the finished products within a certain time. Basically, commerce served the requirements of the court in luxury goods and, for a long time, a very large proportion of those requirements was covered by the booty from military expeditions.

An inevitable end

A fairly clear trend seems to indicate that the price of cereals was very high in the seventh century, especially in the latter half, but it is hard to gauge such 'price fluctuations'; indeed, not only was it rare for there to be a monetary equivalent of basic produce, such as cereals, but no real 'market' existed for this produce, only local situations which often differed widely, with a few constants such as the very high cost of transport. As early as the eighth century, a letter sent to the king revealed a doubling in price between barley-producing regions 'in the steppe' and the town of Nineveh. Furthermore, the simultaneous use of varying standards for units of weights and measures in the empire had repercussions on prices, which seemed to vary while the basic value did not fundamentally shift.

The value of cereals (quantity obtained for one shekel of silver, or its equivalent in copper)

Date	Quantity	Place
Eighth century	120 litres	Nineveh
	240 litres	'In the steppe' (*madbari*)
698	20 litres	Ashur (year of famine)
*c.*660–650	1,200 litres	Official inscription of Ashurbanipal
After 648	10–24 litres	Ashur
	20 litres	Huṣîrina
	0.66 litre	Kalhu (year of famine)

The available data also tend to give us documentation about extremes. Official reports are stereotyped; what worth can be given to an inscription of Ashurbanipal celebrating the prosperity of his reign by a mention of a value of cereals that is not to be found in any contemporary text? In any case, it is probable that the influx of precious metals into Assyria, the result of conquests and levying tribute, brought about a depreciation in silver. Moreover, it appears that the prices for cereals in the seventh century were mentioned because it was a period of famine and therefore they do not reflect a normal economic situation. It is still difficult to assess the fundamental reality of Assyria's economic state. An associated study of the rates of interest shows that it was scarcely favourable: loans in money carried average rates of 30 per cent, and in cereals, 50 per cent; and those rates could soar to 140 per cent or even 150 per cent.

Thus at the close of the empire, the portrait emerges of an over-developed urban Assyria, exploiting the neighbouring provinces to the maximum. And, in each of those provinces, the local centre also siphoned off a significant proportion of the agricultural production. During the seventh century, the old Assyria must have seen its population decline, as a result of losses suffered in wars, even victorious ones, removals of the workforce to colonise other regions, and the precarious situation of the peasant population, an increasing part of whose farm produce was confiscated by payments to the urban centres in the name of royal tax. The case of the village of Bît-abu-ila'a, in the province of Rasappa, in the second half of the seventh century, shows that an entire village community was forced by necessity to sell all its land to a group of buyers composed, in essence, of army officers (*rab kiṣri*).

A new kingdom of Upper Mesopotamia

On the pattern of the political organisation achieved at the beginning of the second millennium, and then when the Middle Assyrian empire drove its western frontier as far as the bend of the Euphrates, the plain of Upper Mesopotamia was regarded as a sort of natural extension of Assyria. It was the region which the early neo-Assyrian conquerors sought first to recover and then to turn to good account, as they progressed by successive advances from the Tigris to the Habur, the Balih and then the Euphrates.

The situation when the Assyrians arrived

At that time the region was sparsely populated, with the exception of a few small urban centres which were often very old (Kahat, Harran). Aramaean settlement, which had driven out the Assyrians early in the first millennium, relied mainly on a pastoral economy and a few urban principalities that served as operational bases. When Adad-nerari III marches from Naṣibîna on Gûzâna at the end of the ninth century, he mentions no village that had been looted or had paid tribute; Tukulti-Ninurta II and Ashurnasirpal II, descending the Habur in 885 and 883, had already found only a few rare townships there.

First attempts to make use of the territory

Assyria's patient policy of reconquest did not rely on massive repopulation, but on integrating the local Aramaean populations and attempting to settle Assyrian colonists. The Assyrian kings therefore established a local policy of reoccupation of the land, by constructing 'palaces', in other words, military and administrative centres; organising the farming population in 'ploughlands' in order to rationalise agricultural production; establishing grain reserves and acquiring draught animals. This undertaking aimed in the first place at developing a fixed settlement capable of resisting the Aramaeans of the steppe, then making use of the land to obtain new sources of supply. On the political plane, Assyrian kings left certain Aramean rulers *in situ* as long as they loyally fulfilled their role as vassals, but incorporating them into the Assyrian hierarchy. In his bilingual stele, discovered at Tell Fekheriye, Haddad-yis'i presents himself as both the Aramaean prince of Gûzâna and the governor of the province dependent on the town, with the Assyrian form of his name, Adad-it'i. This was also the case, in exemplary fashion, of Shamshi-ilu, *turtânu* of the king of Assyria and Aramaean prince known also as Bâr-Ga'yah, in charge of the provinces of the Balih and the Syrian bend of the Euphrates.

The region of Harran

From the mid-eighth century, the policy of development became more systematic, with the settlement of large numbers of deportees in the Habur and Balih valleys. In the view of the Assyrian kings, the region of Harran seems to have formed the western pole of the heart of the empire: the palatial centre of Hadatu, which served as Tiglath-pileser III's operational base for his campaigns in north Syria, was set up nearby. Harran was the scene of a conspiracy against Esarhaddon in 670; it would seem that Ashurbanipal came to reside there at the end of his reign; above all, it was there that the remains of the Assyrian court took refuge in 612 after the destruction of Nineveh.

The census of the families of farmworkers in the Harran region, grouping dependants of local Aramaean populations, Assyrian colonists and deported settlers installed on estates belonging to members of the court high nobility early in the reign of Sargon II, bears witness to these efforts to develop, with heavy expansion of vineyards alongside cereal-growing land. But the imbalance in the internal division of this population has quite rightly been noted: there were many fewer children than adults, a result of the difficulties of moving the deportees, or even an indication of an insurmountable demographic impoverishment in the population overall. At the same time, Upper Mesopotamia illustrates the process of fusing the Assyrian and Aramaean cultures, as evidenced by the mixed use of clay tablets for inscribing sometimes cuneiform, sometimes the Aramaic alphabet, at Dûr-Katlimmu on the Habur, Mallanâte near the Balih or Burmarina on the Euphrates.

THE PROVINCES

A complex system

Dividing up the provinces

Integration into the Assyrian empire was achieved by defining provinces whose designation was based either on the capital town (Naṣbîna, Gûzâna, Amedu), or on a broader territorial name (Rasappa, Mazamûa). They were entrusted to those loyal to the king, members of the upper nobility who, for their sole benefit, derived substantial incomes from them, a fact that led to the crisis in 827. These provinces coexisted with vassal kingdoms which were left to their traditional dynasties in return for payment of the annual tribute, supplying troops and serving Assyrian interests. A special category of province was placed under the responsibility of the holders of the highest offices in the state; with their posts they combined responsibility for a frontier area: the territories between the Euphrates and Balih were in the charge of the general-in-chief; the Tur-Abdin range and valley of the Upper Tigris in that of the chief cupbearer; the mountainous region directly to the north of Assyria was in the care of the palace head-steward, and the Habruri region, north of Arbela, in that of the palace herald. This combination of frontier marches protected northern means of access to Assyria and Upper Mesopotamia. From the time of Tiglath-pileser III, the number of provinces increased considerably, by the transformation of certain vassal states or the subdivision of former entire areas. When the office of *turtânu* was duplicated, the 'right-hand *turtânu*' kept the region of Harran, and the 'left-hand *turtânu*' took charge of the province of Kummuh, on the Upper Euphrates. This reorganisation, which was accompanied by a strengthening of the centralisation of the empire, probably extended over several reigns, and did not acquire its full force until the time of the Sargonids.

Managing the provinces involved levying the royal tribute, and its allocation was the responsibility of the governor; some of it he sent to the capital, using another portion to maintain the forces of surveillance or local defence, or to build up reserves intended for the needs of the royal army. The remainder was for his personal requirements. The division of the tribute into three parts was left to his discretion, which must have meant a difficult balance between a sense of his own interests and that of the service he owed to the king. The governor's duties also included collecting and sending in written form all information concerning his province. These reports converged on the chancellery in the capital, placed under the authority of the crown prince, before being presented to the king.

Provincial administration

It is difficult to draw up a rational picture of Assyrian government because, from the top to the bottom of the state, there was often confusion between imperial and estate administration: the palace was both the centre of government and the focal point of the king's domain, and this dual function was repeated at all the intermediate stages, in the secondary palaces and provincial centres. Moreover, important members of the royal family and high court dignitaries formed their own households around them, managing their own possessions on the one hand, but also having a finger in supplying the state. Those among them who were at the same time responsible for a province lived there only as an exception and therefore had to ensure the presence of local delegates to look after its affairs and make certain that it was properly managed. Lastly, titles were often very general in nature, such as the *qîpu*, 'trustworthy man', and sometimes covered identical realities. In the government of a province, the 'chief of the district' (*bêl pahâti*) seems to have been the equivalent of the 'official' (*šaknu*). Starting in the reign of Tiglath-pileser III, the system was reorganised and rationalised towards centralisation. Most likely to curb personal ambition, but also modelled on what happened in the army, important posts were entrusted to a group of three people: the incumbent, his assistant (*šanû*) and a 'third man' (*šalšu*).

External entities

The richest regions of the Near East in that period, both demographically and economically, lay beyond the boundaries of Assyria and its extension in Upper Mesopotamia, which explains why, despite its enormous war effort, Assyria had so much difficulty in conquering them, and then in keeping them under its yoke. We find, therefore, that it took the kings of Ashur more than one and a half centuries to overcome the kingdom of Damascus, and then to break the might of Urartu, whose final destruction, in any case, was the work of the Cimmerians and not the Assyrians. The latter were never truly able to establish a stable domination over Babylonia, and the attempts to conquer Egypt proved fairly quickly to be fruitless. Only the lack of political organisation or internal rivalries in these regions enabled the Assyrians to subjugate them. The structural change in the empire's organisation, introduced by Tiglath-pileser III from 745 onward, allowed them to be incorporated more durably, but the empire's disintegration in under five years demonstrates how fragile that construction had been.

Development and exploitation

From plunder to tribute

The relationship established by the Assyrians with conquered populations was certainly responsible for this irrefutable fact: the conquests of the ninth and eighth centuries were often akin to systematic plunder, pure and simple, which filled the stores of the palaces of Kalhu and Nineveh with precious metals and raw materials. The system of deportation also bled dry several regions of the empire and strengthened a general feeling of hostility that manifested itself in repeated rebellions when the political situation of the empire's government grew weaker. Significant echoes are to be found in several passages in the Bible, describing Nineveh as a lions' den and expressing the common sentiment of western regions that they were being used as a hunting-ground for these bloodthirsty wild beasts. Even subsequently, the regularisation of the flow of products or labour into a system of tribute that was more balanced than the raids of the preceding period continued to be a one-way affair. This imbalance, moreover, had consequences in Assyria itself, where the influx of precious metals brought in its wake a monetary depreciation and significant rise in prices.

Shalmaneser III's booty in 857

	Pattina	Amanus	Bît-Agûsi	Carchemish
Gold	90 kg	5 kg	90 kg	
Silver	3,000 kg	300 kg	180 kg	2,100 kg
Bronze	9,000 kg[a]	2,700 kg		900 kg
Iron	9,000 kg	900 kg		3,000 kg[b]
Luxury garments	1,000	300		
Purple wool	600 kg			600 kg
Cedars		200		
Other		200 litres of cedar resin		
Cattle	500	300	500	500
Sheep	5,000	3,000	5,000	5,000
People	King's daughter[c]	King's daughter[c]		King's daughter[c] and 100 noble girls

[a] + 1,000 bronze receptacles
[b] + 500 weapons
[c] With her dowry

Uniting the empire

Did the Assyrian kings have a genuine imperial conception of their domain? The first essays at conquest were aimed at recreating the great Assyria of the second millennium and stamping out the Aramaean threat. The expansion westward, beyond the Euphrates, early in the ninth century was the response to a desire to accumulate wealth and affirm Assyrian might. At that stage, the conduct of the conquests, based fundamentally on a network of vassal kings, was achieved by a development of the administrative and diplomatic practices that had been traditional in Mesopotamian kingdoms for several centuries. But from the mid-seventh century, and especially under the Sargonid dynasty, a true empire may be considered to have been established. Vassal kingdoms were given a permanent representation of the central Assyrian government, then, after the local dynasty had been eliminated, were transformed into provinces of the empire managed by an Assyrian governor. Communication routes were developed and controlled; attempts were made to turn certain economic focal points to profitable account. Recent archaeological excavations of Ekron in Palestine yielded the remains of a veritable industrial production centre of olive oil, which had been developed under Assyrian rule. By incorporating the imperial economic sphere, possibilities for development were opened up that were far from negligible: the Phoenician cities, big suppliers of luxury products demanded by the royal court, thus managed to retain their prosperity and a relative autonomy until the reign of Esarhaddon. The tribute system itself was no longer necessarily predatory; in general, it was adapted to the actual potential of the country in question. Assyria confiscated to its own profit the surpluses invested in luxury products, without imperilling the general economy of the kingdoms or provinces affected. This 'tapping' sometimes had the effect of stimulating the economy and developing a local administrative cohesiveness, by reinforcing the powers of the ruling elites; for instance, the transformation of the Median confederations into an organised state was one consequence. Also worthy of note are the attempts to colonise and restore the potential of inhabited regions, and an effort to incorporate western elites into the imperial system, which led to what has been called the Aramaicisation of the Assyrian empire.

A fair exchange?

A growing adherence to the empire seems to have developed and, on the part of local elites, a transfer of their allegiance from their own sovereign to the king of Assyria, who really became the sole point of reference. In return, Assyria appears to have opened out to external elites and external influences in cultural matters (adoption of the *bît hilâni*, a colonnaded hall of western origin, in Assyrian palaces), and even in religion (a statue of the Syrian goddess Kubaba was installed in a temple in Ashur). As a result of this direct exchange, the presence of the tributary rulers as a 'drive belt' between their population and the Assyrian government was no longer needed, as the relationship grew more direct, and they were replaced by Assyrian governors. Although this system remained delicate, it had the merit of uniting a western Near East that was already culturally homogeneous but politically disparate, with its numerous neo-Hittite, Aramaean, Phoenician and Palestinian principalities. The imperial constructions that followed the Assyrian empire (neo-Babylonian, Achaemenid, even Seleucid) would reap the benefits of this process of unification.

DOCUMENT

Extract from the *Census of Harran*

'Arnabâ, son of Se'-apla-iddin, winegrower and his mother. Total: 2. Ahabû, winegrower; Sagibu, his adolescent son; Il-abadi, his son of 4 cubits; 2

women. Total: 5. 10,000 vines; 2 houses; 10 *imêru* of personally owned agricultural land. Total of the village of Hananâ, in the district of Sarugi.

Sîn-nâ-'id, winegrower; Nusku-ila'i, same profession; Našuh-qatar, his son of 4 cubits; a woman; 2 daughters. Total: 6 (*written: 5*). Ahunu, winegrower and his mother. Total: 2. In all, 3 winegrowers, one weaned son, 2 women, 2 daughters. Total: 8. 15,000 vines, 6 *imêru* of agricultural land, one house. Total of the village of Mari-Til-Uari, in the district of Til-abnâ.

Il-nuri, winegrower; Al-se'-milki, his adolescent son; one nursing son; one woman; one daughter of 4 cubits; one of 3 cubits. Total: 6. Se'napi, winegrower; one son of 4 cubits; one woman. Total: 3. Idranu, of the cooks' group, (currently) winegrower; one woman. Total: 2. 29,000 vines; 2 houses; 2 head of cattle; 10 *imêru* of agricultural land. Total of the Village-of-the-King, near Dimmêti, in the area of Qipâni.

Nusku-ila'i, of the group of bakers, (currently) winegrower; one son of 4 cubits; one woman. Total: 3. Adi-mati-ili, winegrower; one woman; one daughter of 5 cubits; one of 4 cubits.

General total: 7. 6,000 vines. Total of the village of Bêl-abu'a, near Dumâ, in the area of Qipâni.

Se'idri, winegrower; Našuh-idri, his adolescent son; one woman, one nubile daughter. Total: 4. 5,000 vines, one house, one vegetable garden. Total of the village of Hamedê, in the area of Qipâni.

Našuh-sa [...], of the group of [...], (currently) winegrower. Našuh-[...], his son; one woman; one daughter. Total: 4. 4,000 vines, [...]. Total of the village of [...] in the area of Qipâni.

Han[...], cattleman [...]; Kankanu and Šer-dalâ: his two adolescent sons; Luba'-Našuh, son of Kankanu, of 3 cubits; 3 women; one weaned daughter. Total: 8. 61 horses and cattle. Total of the village of Yanatâ, near the town of Haurina.

Rahimâ, goatherd; Našuh-sama'ani, his adolescent son; one woman; one daughter of 3 cubits. Total: 4. 57 goats, inspected. Total of the village of Gadu'atâ, in the district of Hasam. Il-šimki, winegrower; one son of 3 cubits; one woman, one weaned daughter. Total: 4. 7,000 vines. Total of the village of Aku'anu, near Harran.

Se'aqaba, keeper of a plantation of trees; Šer-manani, his adolescent son; Kusayu, his son of 4 cubits. Total: 3. An orchard of *šaššugu* trees. Total of the village of Yanibir-Ṣuhuri, in the area of Qipâni.

General total: 37 farmworkers; 11 winegrowers.'

Here we have an extract from a series of documents discovered in the royal palace of Nineveh in Assyria, but which concern the region of Harran, in western Upper Mesopotamia. The reason for their being in the Nineveh archives has to do with the very nature of the texts; they record properties belonging to members of the court, perhaps even the royal family. The precise determination of the people involved and the period when these texts were drawn up remains under discussion. The most commonly accepted theory is that they date to the reign of Sargon II (721–705), and relate to properties of members of the royal family.

Components of the census

On the face of it, the text appears as a census and its first editor likened it to the famous Domesday Book of medieval England. Indeed, it mentions people who are classified by family, sex and age, as well as the land owned and the herds they take care of. But the locality, which is specified at the end of each entry, shows that it is only a very partial census. Within several large districts (Qipâni, Sarugi, Hasame and Harran), all situated in the region of the Upper Balih, the census-takers have recorded the composition of farms divided among ten different villages. It is therefore not a matter of a whole property belonging to one holder, but a series of scattered properties. Nor are the families recorded in the census the only occupants of the villages cited: we thus find that within each village area are agricultural lands with a special status – either royal lands in the midst of private properties or, more probably, lands belonging to the owner(s) who had financed the census.

The purpose of the operation itself is not mentioned in any of the documents. It could be simply a record of places allowing an inventory of landed property to be drawn up; but in that case it should be found in the personal archives of the owner or owners concerned. Its presence in the archives of the royal administration has led rather to the supposition that it was a dossier formed with a view to obtaining, or having exemptions applied from, taxes and obligatory labour granted by the king to the owner. Nevertheless, the whole thing provides useful data on the composition of the agricultural estate of one or more members of the Assyrian high nobility during the Sargonid period and, above all, given the rarity of this kind of text in Mesopotamian documentation, on the composition of the families of farmers who were attached to it.

Land

The landed property cited was chiefly given over to vineyards, of far from negligible size: the smallest had 4,500 vines, the most extensive 29,000. There is nothing surprising in the presence of winegrowing domains here; since the second millennium, western Upper Mesopotamia had enjoyed a reputation for producing wine, and exported it to Assyria and Babylonia. Wine was still a luxury product in the first millennium, kept for offerings to the gods and banquets of the king and high nobility. Its rarity in Mesopotamia, and the precautions to be taken for its transport, made it costly. Great Assyrian landowners therefore sought to acquire estates situated in production regions that would ensure its availability.

The other assets quoted are cereal-growing lands, measured in *imêru* (around one hectare), or orchards, or herds. The area of the land (on average, 8–10 hectares) is larger than is usually found on individual properties, and it is not certain that all the land was cultivated, unless there was a system of leaving part fallow. Lastly, one notes the mention of dwelling houses, but not always; the census-takers thus record only what does not actually belong to the families in the census. When they have their *own* properties, these are indicated, as in the first paragraph ('10 *imêru* of personally owned agricultural land'), or they are not included in the breakdown. Overall, therefore, we find contrasting situations: some of the families have personal property, others have only the farmland that is made available to them.

The farmers' families

The final total records 48 people, divided between 37 peasants and 11 winegrowers. However, the breakdown of the people recorded in the census (60) is higher. There are, in fact, 13 winegrowers, but the first two have their own lands and are thus omitted from the total (this must mean that they do not benefit from a possible tax exemption). The rest of their families (5 people) have not been taken into account, and the census-taker has not counted as 'peasants' the goatherd Rahimâ and his family (4 people). Bearing these subtractions in mind, we get a total of 38 people described as 'peasants', and not 37. Setting aside this error in calculating, we find that the families of the winegrowers (excluding the first two) are recorded as 'peasants', as are those of the cattleman and the keeper of the tree plantation.

The other interesting point of the document is that it gives the composition of the families: we see that men are listed first (adults, sons), then women (adults, girls). The latter are never named, whereas in general the men and their sons are. The classification by age is especially intriguing: distinction is made between children at the breast, or nursing (literally, 'milk children'), then those who are weaned (literally, 'children separated [from the breast]'). After that, enumeration is not by age but by size: according to this system, sons or daughters measure 3, 4 or 5 cubits. With a cubit estimated at 27–8 cm, we therefore have children of 0.82 m, 1.10 m and 1.37 m on average. It is obviously difficult to match these heights with actual ages, but it may be supposed that children between 3 and 10 years are being recorded. Beyond that, they are, in keeping with the modern equivalent, 'adolescents' or 'teenagers'. For the girls, the term *batussu* is used, meaning nubile. As is confirmed by other Mesopotamian practical texts, 'childhood' does not go beyond 10 years.

A demographic imbalance

The last point to note is the make-up of the families and the relationship between the generations. Here, we are a long way from a normal situation. There are only two (female) representatives of the generation of grandparents. Adults number 31, children (including adolescents) 27. There are 33 men for 27 women, combining all age groups. Some families are incomplete, that is, formed of a man and his mother, or a couple without children. Although the keeper of the trees, Se'-aqaba, has two sons, there is no woman in his household. Only one family – that of the cattleman Han[…] – seems to have three generations; his two sons are married, and one is the father of a boy of 3 cubits. People have remarked on the narrowness of the pyramid of ages thus formed and, overall, the very low number of children. There are many possible causes: consequences of a deportation or a recent epidemic, a general demographic stagnation, etc. But whether infant mortality was over-high, or fertility was poor, the situation recorded in the Harran census was to be found in other parts of Assyria, and demonstrates the exhaustion of the country starting from the end of the eighth century BC.

Chapter 4

The centre of Assyrian government

The king of Assyria was both the legitimate successor of a theoretically unique line, and the chosen of the gods, and was thus endowed with every quality. The transmission of power, however, was not effected without some clashes in the neo-Assyrian era, and provoked factional struggles within the court. At his coronation, the king received his authority from the god Ashur, but the strong development of royal absolutism under the Sargonids left him with great freedom of action, especially when it came to choosing the holders of the chief offices in the empire.

Placed under the gods' protection, the king was surrounded by a body of experts whose duty was to take care of him spiritually; in the eyes of his subjects, he appeared to be imbued with a semi-divine power and aura, and everyone owed him absolute obedience, backed by oaths of loyalty (*adê*) which they swore to him. To those who served him devotedly he granted his favour and the material benefits that derived from it. To the foreign kings whom he had subjected, sometimes brutally, he granted armed protection in return for the payment of a regular tribute, together with acknowledgement of his sovereignty and that of the god Ashur.

Although the royal palace was the seat of government, it was also the sovereign's residence and the model of the prosperous and harmonious world over which he reigned. The Assyrian kings multiplied these luxurious buildings as if they were so many personal exploits. They lived there surrounded by a court of dignitaries whose task was to govern the empire, and by an excessive number of serving staff. Also residing there were the royal family and wives, as well as women of the harem. The very personalised nature of relations with the king aroused rivalries in the various factions in the palace. But Assyrian kings by no means neglected the country's temples, and the exercise of religion benefited from the splendour surrounding the king.

THE KING OF ASSYRIA

Royal ideology

Royal titles

Assyrian royal ideology began from a traditional Mesopotamian model, but pushed it to hitherto unattained dimensions, as the development of royal titles bears witness. The king is presented as a warrior hero: he is always 'great' (*rabû*) and 'mighty' (*dannu*); he is the chosen of the gods, who have summoned him to the throne; if he is at first the 'king of the land of the god Ashur' (*šar māt Aššur*), his vocation is to dominate all the lands situated between the Upper Sea (the Mediterranean) and the Lower Sea (the Persian Gulf). By virtue of his qualities and might, he is in fact the only true sovereign, far above the others, and regards himself as 'king of the universe' (*šar kiššati*) and the 'king of the four regions of the world' (*šar kibrat erbetti*). The Assyrian monarch seeks to add a temporal dimension to the spatial setting of his domination, by achieving exploits that remain forever engraved in people's memory. So he does not miss the chance to mention in his annals that he has travelled through places which none of his predecessors has ever reached. Similarly, in his inscriptions, he invites posterity to admire respectfully everything that he has done.

The neo-Assyrian king is clearly a monarch with absolute power, the sole point of reference for his subjects. It was the task of official art and literature to glorify the royal personage, which means that the information they pass on needs to be decoded.

The titles of Ashurnasirpal II

'Ashurnasirpal, king of Assyria, the great king, the mighty king, the unequalled king of the universe, king of the four regions of the world, the sun of all his people, the valiant king, the chosen of the gods Enlil and Ninurta, the one who tramples on all his opponents, who opens breaches in the high mountains of distant countries which no one had never reached, the powerful male who tramples his enemies underfoot, who annihilates his foes, who destroys his enemies' fortifications, who quells those who rebel against him, who receives tributes and taxes from the four regions of the world, who captures their hostages, the conqueror of the peoples of the four regions, the son of Tukulti-Ninurta, the mighty king, king of Assyria, son of Adad-nerari, the mighty king, king of Assyria; the valiant man whose actions are upheld by the gods Ashur, Adad, Ishtar, Ninurta, his allies, and who knows no rival among the princes of the four regions of the world; the mighty king who has extended his conquests from the banks of the Tigris to Mount Lebanon and to the great sea of the land of Amurru [...].'

Royal qualities: an idealised portrait

Like his predecessors, the king was endowed with outstanding qualities in all aspects – moral, religious, political, physical – which justified the support afforded to him by the gods. Official titles always present him as the 'vicar' (*iššiakku*) of the god Ashur, and the law had it that the god was the country's only true king. But an irreversible political evolution left the neo-Assyrian king in control of running the empire, on condition that he adopted the official wording which made him the shepherd of his subjects and the destroyer of Ashur's enemies.

The exaltation of the royal person appears clearly in texts and pictures decorating the palace; they bring to the fore his qualities as a warrior, which were acquired during his princely upbringing. The king is an accomplished horseman and combatant. He is presented in the guise of a hero in the service of good, who does not hesitate to confront fearsome enemies and, between his military campaigns, practises the 'sport of kings', hunting lions, wild bulls, gazelles – even ostriches. These physical qualities are matched by exemplary moral ones; in addition to the constant piety which makes him pray and consult the great gods of the pantheon before every important decision, he is determined to treat his subjects and the vassal kings justly, once they have acknowledged his authority by prostrating themselves before him and kissing his feet. The king thus becomes the representative of order and civilisation in the face of chaos. Descriptions in the royal annals emphasise, for example, the contrast between foreign lands, notable for the wildness and roughness of their natural conditions, and the sphere of Assyrian domination, which is humanised, ordered and prosperous. So the king of Assyria puts across the idea that he reigns over the only civilised territory, surrounded by barbarian or unknown peoples. When he receives an appeal from Gugû (Gyges), king of Lydia, Ashurbanipal speaks of this kingdom as 'a distant place, whose name the kings, my forefathers, had never heard'.

Accession to the throne

The problem of succession

The dynastic uniqueness postulated by the Assyrians from the very beginnings of their state did not prevent a certain number of *coups d'état* taking place; but a clear feeling of dynastic legitimacy persisted, and present-day historiography regards Tiglath-pileser III or Sargon II as having issued from the outer circles of the royal family rather than as sheer usurpers. The problems did not lie so much there as in the multiplicity of possible claimants. In fact, there had never been any strict definition of rules setting out the order of succession; choice of the crown prince depended on the king and could be altered at any time. For instance, Sennacherib, having initially designated Ashur-nadin-shumi, subsequently made him viceroy of Babylon and, from 698, changed his choice to Arad-Mullissu. Finally, in 683–682, Esarhaddon was named crown prince. Appointment as crown prince in the Sargonid period involved the constitution of an official household and active participation in the empire's affairs. The best-known instance is that of Sennacherib; once appointed crown prince, he installed himself in the 'house of succession' (*bît redûti*) and was initiated into the affairs of the empire. It was his duty to gather every piece of information coming from the various provinces and frontiers of the empire and to pass them on to his father to help him in decision-making.

Coronation and assuming office

Accession to the throne was accompanied by a coronation ceremony, which took place in the temple of Ashur. Indeed, it was the god himself who entrusted the new sovereign with the duty, and the latter promised to ensure that the authority of 'king Ashur' would be recognised throughout the empire, and even beyond, which was the justification for his conquests. But it was a matter of political recognition, and Assyrian conquest was never akin to a religious crusade. Under the Sargonids, the start of the new king's reign also brought with it a reorganisation of all duties and offices, and their accompanying benefits, because those who were in his service were bound to him by a bond of personal loyalty. After the period of more or less open crisis in the late ninth century and first half of the eighth – when royal authority was challenged, either overtly by the towns and Assyrian nobility, or more stealthily, with the generals-in-chief (*turtânu*), Dayyan-Ashur then Shamshi-ilu, taking over the conduct of affairs – the kings of Ashur, commencing with Tiglath-pileser

III, saw to it that their power could no longer be contested: holders of high office owed their position to royal favour and not to their social standing, and could be dismissed at any time.

THE EXERCISE OF ROYAL POWER

The king was directly in charge of the empire, and the only decisions that mattered were his, which he worked out in detail with the help of a limited group of relatives and close associates.

The king and his gods

The šangû of Ashur

In addition to his military and political activities, the king of Assyria had heavy religious obligations. In fact he was the head of the clergy, since he was the chief priest (*šangû*) of the god Ashur, and regularly participated in many ceremonies whose rites were carefully prescribed: ritual purification (*bît rimki*), a meal in the presence of the gods (*tâkultu*), the ceremony of the New Year. Clearly, the king could not take part in all these rituals; the liturgical calendar of the town of Ashur alone, although incompletely known, already seems to have been well filled. He was therefore able to have himself represented symbolically by his cloak, and chiefly to delegate his office to priests locally invested with the title *šangû*. To give him support in his government, but also if he was not adequately fulfilling his religious obligations, the clergy passed on to him advice emanating from the deities themselves, by means of prophets (*raggimu*) or prophetesses (*raggintu*). The majority of the latter were attached to the temple of Ishtar, and their words give a glimpse of a practice of the worship of Ishtar which includes completely original mystical aspects.

Consulting the oracle

The very concept of royal office emphasised the sovereign's responsibility to his gods, whose favour depended on his abilities to fulfil his role. According to their own personal character, Assyrian kings showed themselves to be fairly nervous about this divine influence on the king's destiny, and resorted to oracular consultations. Sennacherib, for instance, instigated several divinatory intercessions to try to determine which sin committed by Sargon II had earned him his brutal disappearance, which even prevented his being accorded funeral honours. Esarhaddon, afflicted by the veritable family war he had to pursue in order to accede to the throne, and by his precarious state of health, also had frequent recourse to the services of his experts in divination.

The diviners, or soothsayers, formed a special category of royal servants, specialists in extispicy and astrology, who had emerged from religious circles. They ensured the spiritual care of the king in Assyria and Babylonia, interpreting signs and portents that occurred at the time of consultation, or from observation of the heavens. They also played a part in the running of the empire's affairs, since all important political or military decisions had to be validated by an oracular consultation (*têrtu*). The soothsayers who specialised in hepatoscopy often acted 'in the dark', observing in the livers of sacrificed lambs the positive or negative nature of the divine reply to a question whose content they did not know; it had been written in a document (often a papyrus) which had not been communicated to them. But the astrologers, who had to establish the political consequences of astronomical phenomena, and the exorcists, who knew the king's 'sins', found themselves in possession of state secrets and therefore had to be of unfailing loyalty. Interpretation of the sometimes ambiguous replies provided by the gods of divination, Shamash and Adad, depended on a profound knowledge of the many collections of divinatory texts. Reports on the observations were assembled in the great centres of

Assyria and Babylonia, and passed on to the king by the court seers. But the 'experts' did not always agree among themselves, and had no hesitation in denouncing the shortcomings in their colleagues' interpretations, in order to attract royal favour for themselves.

The substitute king

A particularly noteworthy case of the king's subjection to divine influences is that of the substitute, or stand-in, king (*šar puhi*). When the seers and astrologers who, throughout the empire, watched out for the appearance of favourable or unfavourable signs concerning the king, arrived at the conclusion that a particularly dangerous period lay ahead (it was often a matter of an astronomical phenomenon such as an eclipse or conjunction of planets of bad influence), the sovereign symbolically abandoned the attributes of his office, withdrew to his private apartments and lived there under the designation 'labourer' (*ikkaru*). A substitute king was then put in his place, with the duty of accumulating on his person the unlucky effects of the dangerous period. The holder of this post was not always a rebel or condemned man taken from prison, as was long believed; he could be a member of the nobility, thus proving his loyalty by sacrificing himself for his lord and master. When the dangerous period was over, the substitute was in fact disposed of, and the king resumed his position.

The king and his subjects

An absolute monarch

In theory, in the king's relationship with his people social hierarchy did not exist; from the most eminent to the humblest, all were his servants. The same Assyrian word (*urdu*) was also used for slaves. In return for the protection and prosperity which he was deemed to ensure for them, they had to be exclusively in his service and 'mount guard' (*maṣṣartu naṣâru*) for him. This tendency to absolutism, not to say despotism, was consubstantial with the setting up of the empire, and was in full force under the Sargonids. The duty to serve involved not only devotion to royal commands (*abat šarri*), which had the force of law, but also active commitment to his protection.

The duty of loyalty to the king

This is what is expressed by the term of Aramaic origin, *adê*: it was given concrete form by the swearing of an oath of loyalty which, on solemn occasions, could be performed by the entire population of the empire, but was applied especially to all who were directly in the king's service. The most famous of these declarations of *adê* are the two ceremonies which were organised to have Ashurbanipal's legitimacy as crown prince recognised: the first in 672, for the empire's vassals, the second in 669 (the oath known as 'Zakûtu's', from the name of Ashurbanipal's grandmother, who organised it) for the royal court. Capital punishment rewarded those who violated the royal *adê*, whether intentionally by treason, rebellion or conspiracy, or by omission in not revealing culpable acts of which they were aware. This system naturally encouraged suspicions and accusations, and a need for everyone to find powerful protectors who could guarantee them royal favour. Some cases may appear atypical, such as someone accused of *lèse-majesté* because he had given his sons the names Sîn-ahhê-erîba/Sennacherib and Aṣṣur-bâni-apli/Ashurbanipal, which were reserved for royalty alone. A significant part of the correspondence found at Nineveh is composed of letters or reports sent to the court, increasing protestations of loyalty or pointing out that the writer had been wrongly accused or feared being so, or on the other hand denouncing the illegal activities of a colleague. In theory, the king took every precaution, since on his orders divinatory inquiries were regularly carried out to assure himself of the loyalty of this or that great servant of the state.

Royal favour

Anyone in the king's service who fulfilled his duties with recognised assiduity and devotion attracted royal favour. This included very material aspects and could be expressed as a gift. Indeed, the Assyrian ruler made awards, most often of land from the royal estates, either to bodies such as the temples, or to individuals in gratitude for services rendered. Adad-nerari III, for example, donated several estates to the temple of Ashur, including two of at least 1,000 hectares apiece. The interest of these texts lies in the fact that they were sometimes accompanied by a detailed inventory of the landed properties, with the type of produce grown on each, the numbers of people attached to them as well as possible tax exemptions pertaining to them. Under Ashurbanipal we find a special kind of donation, basically comprising exemptions from taxes and free labour on lands already belonging to the beneficiaries.

Extract from a deed of exemption in the reign of Ashurbanipal

'Balṭaia, head of supplies to Ashurbanipal, king of Assyria, who does what is right and good, who has been devoted to his lord from the time of his appointment as crown prince until his accession to the throne, who has given up his whole heart to his lord, who has truly kept himself in my service, who succeeds in what he undertakes, who has increased in honour within my palace, who has mounted guard over my royalty, I have decided, following the impulse of my heart and my personal consideration, to treat him well and make him a gift. The fields, orchards and people he has acquired under my protection, and which form his assets, I have exempted from taxes, and have put this in writing and sealed it with my royal seal. I have made a gift of it to Balṭaia, head of supplies, who reveres my royalty.'

The king and his vassals

A protector king

From the time of the predatory campaigns of the early neo-Assyrian period to the acts of maintaining order once the empire had been definitively established, the relationship of the Assyrian king with those whose sovereign he claimed to be did not really alter. The king of Assyria imposed his weighty protection on those whose territory he passed through; on condition that they acknowledged his superiority or, more precisely, that of the god Ashur whose executive he was, they were left where they were and guaranteed against any external attack. Such a pact could take the form of a veritable diplomatic treaty, but it never placed the two parties on equal footing. The king granted his formal protection and the vassal committed himself to serving the interests of Assyria. Only Shamshi-Adad V had to treat on equal terms with Marduk-zâkir-šumi, king of Babylon, when he needed his aid to put down the rebellion of 827; but those conditions were judged to be sufficiently humiliating to justify the brutal campaign waged in Babylonia several years later. The vassal's commitment was directly to the person of the king of Assyria, unless in exceptional circumstances such as those of the Assyro-Aramaean stelae of Sfiré which record the treaty concluded between the king of Arpad and the *turtânu* Shamshi-ilu, acting under his Aramaean name Bar-Ga'ah, on behalf of the king of Ashur. Assyrian protection was not simply a matter of form, and there were several attested interventions to help a vassal king against his external foes or internal disturbances. In the ninth and eighth centuries, client-states of Assyria such as Arpad or Ya'ûdi were not obeying only a relationship imposed by force: their rallying revealed a real desire for unity and stability, in the face of designs by sovereigns like the king of Damascus that were just as imperialistic as those of the king of Assyria; or when confronted with the internal imbalances brought about by the sometimes complex ethnic composition of the Aramaean or neo-Hittite principalities. Later, under Tiglath-pileser III and the Sargonids, the king of Assyria's prime concern was to protect his empire against the invasions or political machinations of the large neighbouring states – Urartu, Phrygia, Egypt and Elam.

Paying the tribute

In exchange for this Assyrian protection, the vassal king had to give presents (*nâmurtu, tâmartu*) and pay an annual tribute (*maddattu*) which were material evidence of his country's dependency. They had to be proportionate to the value he set on the connection binding him to the Assyrian king. The vassal king's goodwill could also be encouraged by the presence in the Assyrian palace of one or more of his sons, who were answerable for their father's loyalty. If so, great care was taken to see that they were imbued with Assyrian ideas on how to run an empire, so that they could later become its loyal associates, though that policy was not always crowned with success. Halting the annual tribute payment meant rejecting Assyrian guardianship, and was interpreted as an act of rebellion liable to retaliatory measures. Official Assyrian discourse enabled undertaking such measures to be justified, and Ashurbanipal could speak of 'the bitter anger which inflamed his liver and stomach' when he learned that the king of Elam, Tammarîtu, whom he had showered with favours, had sided with his enemies.

The serene evocation of the authority of 'the king of the world' sometimes gives way, however, to a brutal reminder of his might, which allowed him to bend foreign populations 'under the yoke' of Ashur. Certain rulers, Ashurnasirpal II to the fore, seem to have taken real pleasure in having the bloodiest aspects of their military campaigns recorded in their annals. But as time went on, it is noticeable that writings by the Assyrian kings of the ninth and eighth centuries exalting their warrior strength were followed by the Sargonids' more majestic depiction of their might.

WHERE THE POWER LAY

The palace

New capitals, new palaces

After having the royal Old Palace of Ashur restored, the neo-Assyrian rulers deserted the town, which remained the religious capital and burial place of the kings. It was not neglected, however; Ashurnasirpal II had works carried out in the Old Palace, Shalmaneser III rebuilt the walls and Sennacherib had a princely residence built south of the town for one of his sons, who was appointed governor of the town. Several Assyrian kings, including Ashurnasirpal II, were buried there, in enormous stone sarcophagi. But they preferred to have new palaces built for them in fresh capitals. For more than one and a half centuries, they favoured the upper part of the town of Kalhu, at the confluence of the Tigris and Great Zab: Ashurnasirpal II surrounded it with a wall eight kilometres long, and built the 'Palace without Peer' (northwest palace), which was in use until the end of the eighth century. His son, Shalmaneser III, had a new edifice constructed there, called the south-east palace, now in a very bad state of preservation, and most importantly an ensemble of buildings gathered around three large courtyards, known as the *ekal mašarti*. It served as an arsenal to hold the booty from royal campaigns, and war equipment, and part of the administration was installed there. Adad-nerari III in his turn built a residence at Kalhu, to the east of Ashurnasirpal II's great palace. In the reign of Tiglath-pileser III yet another new palace was erected, in the centre of the acropolis, incorporating Adad-nerari III's building. After his usurpation, Sargon II lived first at Kalhu, where he had a conversion carried out on an edifice known under its present-day name of the 'Burnt Palace', dating to the ninth century and already restored by Adad-nerari III. Subsequently, the founder of the Sargonid dynasty abandoned the Kalhu site to have a new capital constructed much farther north, at Dûr-Šarrukîn. Sennacherib in fact preferred to install himself at Nineveh, on the Tigris, which had at first been used as the royal summer residence under Ashurnasirpal II and Shalmaneser III. There he had the gigantic 'Palace without Rival' (south-west palace) built. To keep the area of the palaces supplied with water, he had the river Husur channelled, and ensured its regular rate of flow by building two dams in its course and an aqueduct upstream. Nineveh was surrounded by a wall twelve kilometres long, containing a number of gates. Esarhaddon also lived at Nineveh, where he had an arsenal constructed in the south part of the town; he later had a new palace at Kalhu started (south-west palace), but it remained unfinished. Ashurbanipal stayed loyal to Nineveh; after having some rearrangements carried out in Sennacherib's palace, he had the *bît redûti* rebuilt on his own account, and this became the splendid north palace, renowned for its bas-reliefs and library.

The construction of royal residences was not confined to the empire's capitals; several edifices of the same kind were built in the western provinces: at Apqum, Hadatu and Til-Barsip. The palace on this last site served as a residence for the *turtânu* Shamshi-ilu, who adorned it with inscriptions bearing his name.

Building the palaces

Building a palace was connected with royal ideology and, like all the sovereign's actions, had to be something extraordinary. The king was directly involved in its construction, and had written progress reports on the work sent to him regularly. Sennacherib thus boasted of having invented a technical process that allowed the casting from one single block of the bronze lions, weighing 43 tonnes each, which supported the columns of one of the porticoes in his palace. The majestic dimensions, the colossal number of buildings and courtyards, the rarity and value of the materials used, together with the sumptuousness of the decoration, made them unique works, intended to be passed on to posterity. Accounts of construction or restoration, just as much as of military exploits, therefore find a place in the royal annals.

Beginning in 1840, the rediscovery of several of these palaces in the state in which they had been at the time of Assyria's fall confirmed the splendour evoked by the texts. The shell of the buildings was of brick, as throughout Mesopotamia, but the roofing was of cedar beams, and the sills and some of the panelling in alabaster. The main doors were flanked by lions and winged bulls, between three and five metres tall, and the walls of the principal rooms were decorated with vertical slabs of limestone which were entirely carved in bas-relief: majestic figures of the king and his court, genies with animal heads, the depiction of military campaigns or, as in Ashurbanipal's palace at Nineveh, of the royal hunt. All building materials had been brought to Assyria, sometimes from very far away, like the cedars of Lebanon, which were floated down the Euphrates, or the winged bulls, which were brought on rafts from the mountain quarries.

Palace lay-out

Each royal palace comprised two essential parts: the first, the *bâbânu*, was the setting for the palace administration and the king's public life; the second, the *bîtânu*, held his apartments and those of the palace's female population, in particular all his wives and very young children. A whole army of domestics, courtiers (*manzaz pâni*) and administrators, priests, scientific experts and guards peopled the palace, and were subject to a strict etiquette, doubtless taken over directly from the court and harem rules of the Middle-Assyrian era. Under Ashurbanipal, the palace staff numbered 13,000. A fair number of those in the king's direct service were eunuchs; their lack of offspring was deemed to enable them to transfer their entire loyalty to the king, without having to take family interests into account.

Library and garden

In Ashurbanipal's palace complex was stored what has been called the 'library of Nineveh', where several thousand cuneiform tablets were discovered by archaeologists. The mass of texts revealed since the nineteenth century come in fact from three collections: the north palace, the south-west palace and the temple of the god Nabû. Although attributed to Ashurbanipal, this library had started to be formed by his predecessors. In essence, it was a collection of the scientific literature of the period, intended to help the well-read and the experts in the king's service to ensure his magic protection. Most of the major works had been recopied several times, each tablet bearing a colophon inscribed by the copyist in the name of the king, which enabled it to be placed in the lexical, divinatory or ritual series to which it belonged.

Colophon of a tablet from Nineveh, in the name of Ashurbanipal

'Palace of Ashurbanipal, king of the universe, king of Assyria, whom the gods Nabû and Tašmetu have endowed with vast understanding, who possesses clear sight. I have written on tablets, checked and collated what is essential in the scribe's art, a work which none of the kings who preceded me had learnt to do, the remedies concerning the body from the forehead to the nails, non-canonical extracts, supreme medicine of the gods Ninurta and Gula, everything that can be done; to read them and have them read to me, I have had them placed within my palace.'

The king paid great attention to the continual enrichment of this fund of knowledge, and sent experts to Babylonia charged with finding for him, in the personal libraries of the well-educated, rare works which they brought back to Nineveh. The repression that followed the rebellion of Shamash-shum-ukin at Babylon was also the opportunity for a number of confiscations, as is suggested by a catalogue tablet dated 647.

Some sovereigns had sumptuous parks created around the palace, in which flora and fauna from all over the empire were assembled. The gardens of Sennacherib's palace were laid out in terraces and supplied with a sophisticated watering system, and seem to have served as a model for the 'hanging gardens' of Babylon.

The court

Palatine administration

This encompassed a certain number of great dignitaries: the grand vizier (*sukkallu dannu*), the general-in-chief (*turtânu*), the herald (*nâgiru*), the major-domo (*ša pân ekalli*), the grand cupbearer (*rab šaqê*), the chief baker (*rab nuhatimmi*), the intendant or steward (*mašennu*), the chief eunuch (*rab ša rêši*). With their administration some of these managed the crown domain, under the authority of the major-domo, and looked after the provisioning and upkeep of the vast human community that lived in the palace and its outbuildings, but also saw to the running of the military machine – men, horses and equipment – or to the centralisation of the taxes and various supplies to be made to the royal administration. Others, under the responsibility of the grand vizier, conducted the government of the empire and relations with the provinces. The correspondence and information departments were placed under the direct authority of the crown prince, and were at work in the household of the succession (*bît redûti*), an autonomous part of the palace complex. The burden of administrative tasks explains why certain offices were duplicated at the end of the eighth century. The majority of these high-ranking officials ran their courtly offices in tandem with governmental responsibilities, and with their close relatives formed the circle of the king's intimates who assisted him in running the empire.

Their importance is shown by their presence in the system of the eponymate, which from the very outset had enabled a regular computation of the years to be made in Assyria. Each year was named after an official, and the order in which they assumed the dignity of the office, after the king who took on this duty at the commencement of each reign, remained virtually unchangeable until the end of Shalmaneser V's reign (722). The Sargonids later reformed the system by introducing new dignitaries.

An example of an eponym list

753	Ashur-nerari (V)	King
752	Shamshi-ilu	General-in-chief
751	Marduk-šallimanni	Palace herald
750	Bêl-dân	Grand cupbearer
749	Shamash-kenu-dugul	Palace intendant
748	Adad-bêl-ukîn	Governor of Ashur
747	Sîn-šallimanni	Governor of Rasappa
746	Nergal-nâṣir	Governor of Naṣîbina
745	Nabû-bêl-uṣur	Governor of Arrapha
744	Bêl-dân	Governor of Kalhu
743	Tiglath-pileser (III)	King
742	Nabû-daninanni	General-in-chief
741	Bêl-Harran-bêl-uṣur	Palace herald
740	Nabû-êṭiranni	Grand cupbearer

In the late ninth century, the families of the high nobility amassed offices and the benefits that accompanied them; for instance, according to his stele which was discovered at Ashur, the *turtânu* of Shamshi-Adad V, Bêlu-balaṭ, combined with his post those of herald, steward of the temples, leader of the armies and governor of the towns of Tabîte, Harran, Huṣirîna, Dûr-Mât-Bêl-bâni, Zallu and Balihu. These high-ranking dignitaries were given the privilege of being buried in the immediate proximity of the Old Palace of Ashur, which served as a royal cemetery, and several dozen stelae bearing their names have been found there.

The women of the palace

The part of the royal palace holding the harem comprised several households: that of the queen mother, the chief wife, secondary wives and the king's sisters. These exalted ladies enjoyed relative economic independence, with landed estates of their own and autonomous management of their resources and expenditure, which were the concern of an administration that was specially appointed to them. They were present at certain religious and funerary rituals, and took part in oracular consultations. Their fairly strong influence on the king might lead them to intervene in the empire's political affairs. They certainly represented an important element of the court.

Queen Naqi'a

Of Aramaean origin (her name, Naqi'a, 'the pure', was translated into Assyrian as Zakutu), she won the favour of Sennacherib and became his most influential wife. Having obtained the appointment of her son Esarhaddon as crown prince, she exerted a direct influence on the running of affairs during his reign. It was she, again, who imposed the appointment of Ashurbanipal. To avoid any repetition of the disturbances at the start of Esarhaddon's reign, she instigated a general swearing of the oath of loyalty (*adê*) by the Assyrian population.

Not all the women in the palace enjoyed the same independence – far from it – and the majority did not even have the right to emerge from the part of the palace that was reserved for them. The recent discovery of tombs containing female skeletons under the floor of the harem in Ashurnasirpal II's palace at Kalhu confirmed that some women had thus spent their entire life there.

Life at court

The high and mighty of the empire surrounded the king and formed his court. In his likeness, they were sumptuously clothed, wore many jewels, were made-up and perfumed. Major events (inauguration of official buildings, military victories, solemn occasions in the king's life) were the opportunity for banquets to which the king invited his great dignitaries. They were governed by strict ceremonial dating back to the Middle-Assyrian era.

A royal banquet

The most gargantuan of known banquets was the one to which Ashurnasirpal invited 69,574 guests, including 16,000 inhabitants of the town of Kalhu, over a ten-day period, after the royal palace was completed. The list of food consumed, several dozen lines long, enumerated vast quantities: 1,000 fat cattle; 14,000 sheep; 1,000 lambs; several hundred animals of the deer family; poultry, including 20,000 pigeons; but also 10,000 fish, 10,000 jerboas, 10,000 eggs and thousands of pitchers of beer and goatskins of wine. Huge amounts of loaves, baskets of vegetables and fruit, as well as condiments, are similarly listed and carefully detailed, showing that all the empire's resources were called upon to contribute.

Strict etiquette was in force, too, at the royal audiences: the sovereign sat in the throne room, accompanied by eminent members of his entourage, to receive the homage and tribute of his vassals or local representatives of his people, who came to prostrate themselves at his feet. Not everyone had access to royal favour, however; after the fierce tensions between the traditional Assyrian nobility and the powerful nobles who had been made wealthy through conquest, in the ninth and eighth centuries, which sometimes jeopardised royal authority itself, the Sargonids imposed a strict relationship of personal dependence.

Factions and parties

The empire's nobility thus became one that was allied to holding office, and posts could be revoked at any time. In reality, that did not prevent the formation of powerful clans within the court, and the various cliques confronted one another fairly overtly, above all when it was a matter of appointing the future successor. Actual power could therefore be divided, and the huge influence wielded by queen Naqi'a, for example, in the reign of her son Esarhaddon, is worthy of note. The dignitaries who enjoyed the king's favour passed on the benefits to their family, but also to all those who were dependent on them. The royal court was, in addition, the place where young men from the families of dignitaries in office came to learn the business of being in the king's service.

The temples

The sacred quarter of Ashur

Assyrian political capitals were at the same time religious centres, often of very ancient origins. From this aspect, the most important town was naturally Ashur, the country's first capital which, from the time of Ashurnasirpal II, Assyrian kings left to the undivided sovereignty of the eponymous god of their land. On the steep cliff overlooking the old course of the Tigris, a sacred area had developed on either side of the royal Old Palace, dominated by the god Ashur's temple and his ziggurat. The sanctuary was considerably rearranged in Sennacherib's reign, and comprised a complex ensemble of courtyards and sacred buildings; in particular, there was a building reserved for the activities of religious artisans, the *bît mummê*, where specialist craftsmen worked who had been carefully selected for their skills. Not far away towered the double temples dedicated to Sîn and Shamash, and to Anu and Adad. The latter was framed by twin ziggurats. A temple to Nabû, and one dedicated to Ishtar *aššurîtu* ('Assyrian'), completed this sacred ensemble.

Other religious centres

On the acropolis at Kalhu, the dwellings of the kings and those of the gods cohabited. There is evidence of several large temples, for the most part built by Ashurnasirpal II, but maintained and sometimes added to by the other rulers who lived at Kalhu. Four sanctuaries have been discovered and identified: a temple to the god Ninurta, the town's chief deity, provided with a ziggurat; two to Ishtar, in the name of 'Šarrat-nipha' and 'Ishtar of the bît-Katmuri'; and one to Nabû. The goddess Ishtar was the principal deity of Assyria's other two major towns, Arbela and Nineveh. In the latter, Ishtar of Nineveh had a temple and ziggurat on the acropolis of the royal palaces. Under the Sargonids, a syncretism was effected between Ishtar and the divine figure of Mullissu, the consort of the god Ashur, who was himself assimilated to Enlil. A temple to Nabû, complete with a library, which under Sargon II became a temple to Nabû and Bêl/Marduk, rose alongside Ishtar's. Other temples dedicated to Sîn, Shamash and Adad are mentioned in written sources, but it has not been possible to pinpoint them on the Nineveh site. When Sargon II had Dûr-Šarrukîn built, sanctuaries were also constructed, directly connected to the royal palace, as was the ziggurat. Within the citadel's surrounding wall, but distinct from the palace complex, to which it was linked by a bridge, rose a temple to Nabû.

Other less important religious centres are known in Assyria, at Imgur-Bêl, Kurba'il, Šibaniba, Tarbiṭu, and major places of worship in Upper Mesopotamia had been attached to the Assyrian domain, such as those of the god Adad at Gûzâna or Sîn at Harran. All these temples benefited from constant royal attention and regular gifts of land, staff and products intended for worship. A series of royal decrees laid down the offerings to be made to the Assyrian deities, sometimes taking up older texts: for instance, under Shalmaneser III, the system of religious offerings to the gods Ashur and Šarrat-nipha was updated from when it had been established in the reign of Tukulti-Ninurta I (1244–1208).

Specific Assyrian features

While having many features in common with the religious practices of Babylonia, especially in the prescription of cere-monies or composition of the cult's personnel – officiating priests (*šangû*), lamenters (*kalû*), singers (*nâru*), sacred actors (*kurgâru*) – Assyrian religion nevertheless had some special features of its own. Some were connected with the particular aspects of the country, which were directly subject to Upper Mesopotamia's cultural influences, such as the special place occupied by Ishtar that included aspects of Hurrian and Syrian origin, notably at Arbela and Nineveh. Others derived from Assyria's gradual imperialisation and the spectacular enhancement of the royal personage. It is striking to note that, while proclaiming the eminent superior-ity of the god Ashur over his country, the clergy participated to no small degree in establishing royal absolutism and even-tually found themselves less autonomous in their relations with the sovereign than their Babylonian counterparts. But that is by no means to overlook the political weight repre-sented by their support when problems of royal succession cropped up, or to forget that the town of Ashur sought and managed to maintain a relative autonomy in the heart of a state that was entirely subject to the king. Lastly, it should be noted that the counterpart of this ideological use of religion to the advantage of royal absolutism was the process of emphasising the position of the god Ashur himself: from a simple local figure in the heart of the traditional Sumero-Akkadian pantheon, he became one of its leaders, assimilat-ing elements that belonged to the god Enlil, even replacing Marduk of Babylon. An Assyrian version of the *Epic of the Creation* thus puts Ashur on stage as hero and king of the gods, whereas another learned work, the *Ordeal of Marduk*, makes Ashur the head of a tribunal before which the god of Babylon appears. It remains difficult, however, to determine whether these ideological reconstructions, chiefly in evidence in the reign of Sennacherib, reveal the existence of a true trend of thinking in Assyria, or whether they represent no more than isolated attempts.

DOCUMENT

The king of Assyria and his servants: letter from the exorcist Adad-šum-uṣur

'To the king, my Lord, from your servant Adad-šum-uṣur. May my lord the king be in good health! May the gods Nabû and Marduk shower on my lord the king many, many blessings! Ashur, king of the gods, pronounced the name of my lord the king so that he might exercise royalty in Assyria. Shamash and Adad, by their unequivocal oracular replies, confirmed my lord the king in the exercise of royalty over all countries.

The reign is good: days of uprightness, years of justice, rain in plenty, abundance of high waters, favourable prices! The gods are friendly, piety is widespread, the temples brim over with wealth, the great gods of the sky and earth have been exalted in the reign of my lord the king.

The old dance joyously, the young sing, women and young girls are full of joy and jubilation. Men marry women and provide them with precious rings, sons and daughters are born into the world, the birth rate is good. To anyone who was guilty and condemned to death, my lord the king has granted him his life; those who have been imprisoned for many years, you have freed them. Those who had been ill for a long time have regained their health. The hungry have been filled, the dry have been anointed, and the naked covered with a garment.

Why amid all these things should Urad-Gula and I be morose and downcast? Now, my lord the king has made plain to his subjects his love for Nineveh. He has spoken thus to the heads of families: "Bring me your sons so that they may present themselves before me!" Urad-Gula is my son. He too should be with them in the entourage of my lord the king, so that with all the people we may rejoice, dance and bless my lord the king! My eyes are fixed on my lord the king. But those who are in the palace, all those people have no liking for me. There is none among them who is my friend, not one on whom I can have a present bestowed, who would accept it from me and intercede on my behalf. May my lord the king have pity on his servant, so that I among all his subjects may not perish! May those who delight in my misfortune not achieve what they wish against me!'

This is a letter sent around 668 to the new king of Assyria, Ashurbanipal (668–627), by one of the principal educated men in the court, the chief exorcist, Adad-šum-uṣur. Appointed to this post in the reign of Esarhaddon, his position was shaken at the start of Ashurbanipal's reign because the king had taken a dislike to Adad-šum-uṣur's son, Urad-Gula, and had excluded him from his learned entourage, composed of experts who 'mounted spiritual guard' to protect the king from evil influences.

The letter takes the form of a petition in which Adad-šum-uṣur displays all his literary culture to flatter the king and persuade him to look kindly upon his son and himself. It illustrates the absolute devotion owed to the king of Assyria by his servants and the terrible misfortune that the loss of royal favour means for them; at the same time, it evokes the special atmosphere of the court and the pitiless nature of the struggles for influence waged by the various cliques.

The misfortune of the faithful servant

The letter describes two diametrically opposed poles: on the one hand, a young king endowed with all the finest qualities, enjoying the favour of the gods, the source of prosperity for his country by his presence alone, and holding the most absolute power. On the opposite side, Adad-šum-uṣur and his son Urad-Gula, his 'servants' (the term used is the same as for slaves). The joy and happiness which their duties formerly afforded them have vanished, and they are 'morose and downcast' in spirit. The mere fact of working in the service of his master is indeed the source of happiness for the true servant; if he is prevented from doing so, his life loses all its point. In clear terms, Adad-šum-uṣur reminds him that his entire person is 'devoted to his lord and king', and that he only awaits royal permission to demonstrate this complete loyalty. If that should be the case, he and his son could give material evidence of their regained happiness by dancing and blessing the king's name. The picture that recurs in this kind of circumstance is one of the faithful dog which leaps for joy around its master when the latter pays it attention and allows it to fulfil its duty. Other letters from royal servants make the image more explicit by presenting their writers as devoted dogs which roll at their master's feet and live for him alone.

The misfortune currently afflicting Urad-Gula, which has repercussions on his father, is so profound that Adad-šum-uṣur can contemplate nothing less than death if the king does not at least take pity on him. The chief exorcist's argument is clear: if the king truly has no need of his son's services, his life will cease to have any direction or meaning, and nothing will remain for him but to die. If Ashurbanipal does not wish to show him special benevolence, may he at least have pity on him!

A king endowed with the gods' favour

To emphasise this contrast, Adad-šum-uṣur does not hesitate to depict in dithyrambic terms the favourable aspects of the new reign: Ashurbanipal has been 'called' by the gods, especially Ashur, the chief among them in Assyria. Indeed, at the coronation ceremony, which takes place in the temple of Ashur, the god clearly delegates his power to the new king. Although for the Sargonids the principle of royal succession was based on transmission from father to son, there were many claimants, and it was not always the eldest who was chosen. Ashurbanipal himself had received recognition to the detriment of his brother Shamash-shum-ukin, thanks to the influence wielded by his grandmother, Zakutu. But, according to the principles of royal ideology then in force, the god Ashur alone called to the throne the one he deemed most worthy.

In any case, this choice was confirmed by oracular consultations, and the patron gods of hepatoscopy indicated their consent by 'unequivocal replies'. The examination conducted by the soothsayers in the king's service had supplied only perfectly positive answers, without the slightest restriction that could have been occasioned by a dubious configuration in what the omens portended. Adad-šum-uṣur thus tactfully reminds the new king that the circle of experts in divination, to which he belongs, clearly upheld him at the time of his accession.

The reign of a miracle-working king

Divine favour had immediate repercussions on the state of the country, and the letter's central theme is devoted to a description of the happy results of a good king's reign: he will live long, obtaining order for his country in the fields of justice, agricultural economy and trade relations, scrupulously fulfilling his religious duties. Here we have the portrait of the ideal ruler according to

Mesopotamian standards: power and glory are not accentuated here so much as his abilities to ensure the happiness of his subjects. The wishes expressed in Ashurbanipal's coronation hymn are identical: 'During his years of rule may there be constant rain from the sky and waters from the underground depths! Grant our Lord Ashurbanipal, king of the country of Ashur, long days, many years, a mighty arm, a long reign, years of plenty, a good name, good renown, happiness and joy, favourable oracles and primacy over all kings!' The consequences are idyllic, and Adad-šum-uṣur enumerates in minute detail the various aspects of happiness that the king procures for the Assyrian population, by way of a certain number of stereotypes: the old are no longer weighed down by years but prance about joyfully; young men and girls meet in festive encounters, amid singing and laughter. This results in marriages that produce numerous and healthy offspring. The country thus appears to be plunged into an atmosphere of uninterrupted gaiety, where the rules of sociability produce the happiest consequences.

But the positive effects of the new reign do not end there, since they affect even the dark side of Assyrian society: the wicked are pardoned, prisoners freed (probably an allusion to a remission of debts by the new sovereign, freeing debtors from their forced labour with their creditors). Royal grace is similarly extended to the sick, who make miraculous recoveries, and to all the deprived, to whom the king guarantees the three traditional subsistence rations: bread, oil and wool. So the king is also a miracle-worker and restores the body of society, ridding it of imbalances and injustices.

The writer pleads a special case

There is therefore a striking contrast between the general euphoria and the terrible ill-fortune afflicting Adad-šum-uṣur and his son. When the king, on his accession, had invited the notables to send him their sons to serve him at court, Urad-Gula had been 'forgotten', although he dreamed of nothing other than to serve his royal master, body and soul. Worse still, neither he nor his father could count on any backing whatsoever from anyone at court to speak in their favour; on the contrary, they seem to be the target for the hostility of 'those who have no liking for them'. Overlooked by their lord, in despair because they cannot fulfil their service, abandoned by all, they are therefore launching a final cry for help before dying.

The harsh reality of a courtier's life

It is known that at every change of reign, under the Sargonids, the great dignitaries and principal courtiers had to surrender their office, together with all
the benefits that went with it. The new king would then decide whether to
restore it to them or choose new incumbents. While his father kept his post,
Urad-Gula, who also occupied an important place in the circle of educated men
who specialised in the king's spiritual protection, fell into disgrace with
Ashurbanipal, although the exact reason is not known. Behind the rapid
description given by Adad-šum-uṣur, just beneath the surface lies the reality of
a ruthless struggle between various clans to obtain royal favour. One sees that
it is necessary to ensure the support of the most influential members of the
court by making all kinds of gifts and presents, and that a strong protective
network is required to make one's career in the king's service. Anyone who
does not succeed in this is pitilessly swept aside and his rivals are not embar-
rassed to show their delight. While still maintaining the fiction of an exclusive
personal relationship between the king and his devoted slave, Adad-šum-uṣur
hints at a real mistake on Ashurbanipal's part if he cannot recognise his faithful servants and has let himself be deceived by slanderers. He thus implies that
the promising debut of an almost perfect king should not be stained by such
an injustice. As he plainly no longer has direct access to the sovereign, he has
no other recourse than this letter of entreaty.

A coded message

In fact, each of the two protagonists is well aware of what this is all about, and
Adad-šum-uṣur does not attempt to excuse his son for any possible criticisms
that have earned him his disgrace. Rather, he uses all the resources of his educated culture to present a picture of the situation, which makes direct allusion
to some of the most famous works in Mesopotamian literature, in particular
The Righteous Sufferer (*Ludlul bêl nemêqi*), which describes the undeserved mis-
fortunes that befall a righteous man. He knows that the king has received a sufficiently erudite education to be able to identify and appreciate this procedure,
thus implicitly showing that Ashurbanipal risks depriving himself of such valuable men. By making an approach to the king's personal culture, he demonstrates his ability to manipulate the most delicate flattery, and relies on the
king's intelligence to be grateful to him.

In the exclusive relationship between the absolute lord and his loyal slave
which he presents quite baldly to the king, Adad-šum-uṣur also implicitly

reminds him that the servant's total devotion to his master creates a moral obligation. If he demands complete obedience, in return he cannot abandon his servant without condemning him to certain death, and by doing so setting a remarkable example of injustice.

Adad-šum-uṣur employs a number of processes to attract the attention and interest of the king, but also to give him a lesson in morality and regain, if not his total confidence, at least his esteem. He seems to have achieved his goal only in part: Ashurbanipal agreed to have the letter read to him and had it placed in his library archives. Adad-šum-uṣur retained his position until his death a few years later, but in spite of further petitions could not get his son reintegrated into the king's service.

DOCUMENT

The setting for a royal life: Sargon II's palace at Dûr-Šarrukîn

In the second part of his reign, Sargon II (721–705) had a new capital built from scratch, 'Sargon's fortress' (*Dûr-Šarrukîn*), sixteen kilometres north of Nineveh, on the present-day site of Khorsabad. Since the time of Ashurnasirpal II, neo-Assyrian kings and sovereigns had acquired the habit of reinforcing their glory by building a royal palace. Such an accomplishment was part of the great works accompanying their reign. Dûr-Šarrukîn represents the most spectacular example of this kind of enterprise, as the ruler extended the project to an entire new town.

Its realisation mobilised the human and material resources of the whole neo-Assyrian empire, to the advantage of the one who, in his list of titles, presented himself as 'king of the universe' (*šar kiššati*) and within a few years was able to create an assembly that reproduced the fundamental elements of the world. Provided with a vast enclosing wall and the largest of the known royal palaces, the town was laid out in accordance with a strict plan and bears witness to the way in which Assyrians envisaged the royal area.

Sargon II's early demise, then the relative desertion of the town, left the site as it had been. Covered over by the dust of centuries, Dûr-Šarrukîn was the first neo-Assyrian complex discovered in the nineteenth century, and the quality of the monuments brought to light fired people's imagination.

The mobilisation of the empire

Dûr-Šarrukîn was built in the space of seven years, from 713 to 707. Until then Sargon II had resided at Kalhu, like his predecessors, where he had had the 'Burnt Palace' adapted. The relatively peaceful situation of the empire from 714, except in Babylonia, enabled him to undertake this colossal project of building a new capital out of nothing. He chose to have it erected on an almost uninhabited site, at the foot of Mount Musri and its springs, near the course of the river Husur, on the territory of a village called Magganuba, whose inhabitants were evicted. They received compensation in silver and bronze, and were resettled in the district of Nineveh.

The project included not only the creation of a palace and adjoining park, but also temples dedicated to the principal gods, which were provided with vast landed estates (4,000 hectares for the god Nabû alone), residences for the members of the court and dwellings for the population of the new capital, and canals for water supplies and irrigation; this ensemble formed an entire town which was to become the new political capital of Assyria.

The king entrusted the organisation of the work to his brother, the *sukkallu* Sîn-ah-uṣur, and all provincial governors were compelled to supply materials and labour. For instance, the town's wall was divided into sectors, each allocated to a governor charged with its construction. Deportees were also used. The enormous booty taken by Sargon II at the time of his campaign against Musasir and Urartu in 714 enabled him to cover a large part of his needs. However, in spite of requisitions and tributes, his desire to have the work carried out in a very short space of time meant that resources were sometimes lacking, and the king had to borrow the shortfall from merchants and financiers, or 'lift' certain pieces of decoration from existing royal palaces.

In 707, the statues of the gods were installed in the temples consecrated to them. A few months later, an earth tremor shook the town, apparently without any serious consequences. In the autumn, the official inauguration of the palace and town took place, marked by a gigantic banquet, and the king moved his permanent residence there. But he occupied his new capital barely two years before vanishing in a military campaign in 705. The idea of a 'sin' committed by Sargon prompted the new king, Sennacherib, to transfer the capital to Nineveh, and Dûr-Šarrukîn became a secondary palace centre.

The plan of the town

The town of Dûr-Šarrukîn is shaped like an almost square trapezium, 1,750 by 1,680 metres. Its surrounding wall includes seven monumental gates, three of which are adorned with reliefs and glazed bricks. Only a few areas were excavated in the town itself, which does not allow us to know the exact lay-out of the residential blocks and the street network. For a while this lack of vital pieces of information let it be supposed that the town had in fact remained unfinished, but the mention of governors of Dûr-Šarrukîn, and of an urban population subsequent to the reign of Sargon II, leads one to think that the urban area was actually constructed, even if the surface inside the enclosing wall was not completely built upon.

Two main building complexes have been exposed: one to the south, thought to be an arsenal, but which also includes rooms for official use, the other to the north-west, forming a collection of vast dwellings separated from the town by an internal enclosing wall and forming a sort of citadel dominated by a huge acropolis, astride the wall, on which the royal palace was erected, and a group of temples directly connected to it.

The citadel and the acropolis

The citadel was isolated from the town by an interior wall of 300 by 650 metres. Access to it was by two monumental gates, but there was a clear wish to separate this official area from the rest of the urban habitat. It included a number of large dwellings, probably intended for the most important dignitaries of the court: the east one has thus been attributed to the *sukkallu*, the king's brother Sîn-ah-uṣur. Worthy of note, too, is the presence of a huge temple, dedicated to the god Nabû, erected on a terrace and linked to the palace acropolis by a bridge.

The whole area supporting the palace and temples was built on a natural mound, which was provided with a stone facing. It rose about a dozen metres above the neighbouring ground and covered a surface of ten hectares. This acropolis had the special feature of lying astride the town wall, thus marking a clear separation from the urban complex. It was reached from the citadel by a broad ramp. The façade of the royal palace included a triple gateway adorned with winged bulls, giving access to a courtyard of 103 by 91 metres. This vast space served the sector of the temples to the west, buildings for use as stores and for administration purposes to the east, and the palace block properly speaking to the north. By a fortified gateway situated in the north-east of the great courtyard, one gained access to a second open area, the 'courtyard of honour'. Its walls were covered with sculpted slabs, and on one of its long sides the triple gateway of the throne room opened. Each of the three entrances was adorned with winged bulls and representations of a hero overcoming a lion or a genie in the act of blessing.

The throne room measured 45 by 10 metres and was decorated with bas-reliefs and paintings. The throne was set on a stone podium. On the opposite wall, a stairway gave access to an upper floor and terraces. Through an adjoining room to the west, one reached a small interior courtyard serving ceremonial apartments. The rest of the palatial complex was formed on the same model, combining interior courtyards and apartments provided with terraces, giving views over the surrounding mountainous landscape. Two external courtyards, situated to the north-west, served other apartments. The passageways were also ornamented with carved friezes. The westernmost was closed to the west by a building with a colonnaded portico, an architectural style imported from western Syria and called *bît hilâni*.

In the sector of the stores, east of the great courtyard, were rooms for the preparation of meals (kitchens and bakeries), wine stores and warehouses, where 160 tonnes of iron were discovered.

The group of temples, to the west, was dominated by a ziggurat with sides 43 metres long, probably with an equivalent height, situated cornerwise. Three temples were dedicated to Sîn, Shamash and Nikkal, and three chapels to Ea, Adad and Ninurta. They were all grouped around central areas and formed a unified architectural block.

Organised space

The town was constructed to take advantage of the environment (between the relief of Mount Musri and the course of the Husur) and the disposition of the site: in its north part, a natural elevation of the terrain was used for establishing the citadel and the palace acropolis. Through one of the town gates there was direct access to the road to Nineveh. The whole of this meticulously fortified site presented the appearance of a true fortress (moreover, it included a vast arsenal), and it has been thought that establishing Dûr-Šarrukîn in the north of Assyria showed the king's concern to turn it into a permanent base for action against the empire's most threatening danger – Urartu and the mountain principalities of the Anatolian east.

The realisation of this project, however, was chiefly characterised by its clever and symbolic implementation, modelling an almost virgin area in accordance with royal standards.

Dûr-Šarrukîn's surrounding wall was adapted to the terrain as far as possible, to form an almost square trapezium, and it has been remarked that a certain number of modules and force lines were used for the siting of the most important structures. Two fundamental reference points seem to have ordered the way the sites were laid out: the first was the junction of the diagonals resulting from the angles of the enclosing wall, marking the geometric centre of the town; the second, the palace throne room, which was its symbolic heart but was completely off-centre. This throne room was situated in the north-west third of the wall, and a symmetrical town gate was built in the enclosing wall, but it was of so little use that it was later sealed up by a brick wall. Generally speaking, with the exception of the gate through which the road from Nineveh arrived, the siting of the other gates appears to be a matter of chance and can be explained only by seeking geometrical or numerical correspondences. On the south-east side, one gate was placed half way along the wall, but another was put in the first third, symmetrical with the palace throne room in relation to the town centre.

The length in cubits of the town's enclosing wall, so the inscription tells us, matches the numerical value of Sargon's name (according to a system that no one has been able to identify). Similarly, the number of seven gates giving access to the town had a strong symbolic meaning, all the more so because each was placed under the patronage of one of the principal deities in the pantheon (Anu, Enlil, Ea, Ishtar, Shamash, Adad and Bêlet-ilâni). The town wall was pledged to the fighter god Ninurta, the wall of the citadel to the god Ashur. But above all, one passed, by way of a gradation of the various spaces, from the countryside to the town, thence to the citadel and finally to the palace acropolis, which was consecrated to the king, who, through the temples and the ziggurat, established a privileged contact with the gods.

A luxurious monument to the glory of the sovereign

The result of the archaeological excavations on the site at Khorsabad, and the data provided by the royal inscriptions, show that care was taken to ornament the palace with the most precious or rarest materials. The beams and leaves of the doors were of cedar of Lebanon, but ebony, boxwood, cypress, pistachio and fir were used as well; the sills and some panelling were made of alabaster; the gates of the town, palace and temples were decorated with colossal winged bulls inserted into the jambs. They had been carved in the quarries in the north of Assyria and transported by raft on the Tigris to near Dûr-Šarrukîn; some were 4 metres high and weighed nearly 30 tonnes. The bases of the walls in most of the courtyards were lined with bas-reliefs (orthostats) representing protective genies, episodes from royal 'exploits', often of a military nature, but also others connected with the building of the palace, such as the collection and transport of the cedars of Lebanon, or with court life, such as an official banquet. Other walls were adorned with paintings or metal plating. The *bît hilâni*, at the western end of the palace, was ornamented with four cedar-wood columns, 6 metres tall, resting on enormous bronze lions. In the park which he had laid out close to the palace, but which is known only through texts, Sargon II had 'all the fragrant trees of Syria and all the fruit trees of the mountains' collected to create a landscape 'in the image of Amanus'. So in one single space were brought together the wild world of the mountains, the organised world of the royal town and, at the summit, the palace from which the king dominated the entire world.

Chapter 5
Babylonia: from kingdom to empire (900–539 BC)

Between 900 and 813, Babylonia gradually strengthened its situation and normalised its relations with Assyria, the two kingdoms lending each other mutual support against the waves of Aramaeans. But the destructive intervention of the Assyrian king Shamshi-Adad V in 813 left the way wide open to the might of the Chaldaean confederations in the Babylonian south. For a century and a half, Babylonia was the field of combat for the rivalry between an increasingly imperialist Assyria and the Chaldaeans who henceforth embodied its aspiration to independence. From these battles an independent Babylonian state finally emerged, laying low the Assyrian empire in 610 and sharing the spoils with the Medes.

Under Nabopolassar and Nebuchadnezzar II, the Babylonians established an empire that covered the greater part of the western Near East and shattered Egypt's attempts to implant itself lastingly along the Mediterranean coast. The rewards of these conquests were invested chiefly in Babylonia, with an ambitious programme for setting the country back to rights and rebuilding the great royal and religious edifices.

The matter of the succession to Nebuchadnezzar II's throne proved difficult, with several usurpations in the space of a few years. The reign of the last independent king of Babylon, Nabonidus, was marked by a crisis in the political government. Its original religious aspirations were aimed at promoting the worship of the Moon god, Sîn, to the summit of the traditional Mesopotamian pantheon. Persian

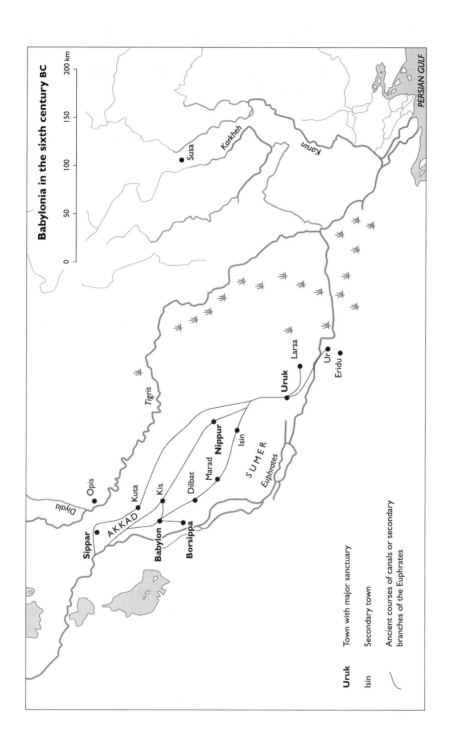

Babylonia in the sixth century BC

PERSIAN GULF

Susa

Karkheh

Karun

Tigris

Opis

Diyala

AKKAD

Kuta

Kis

Sippar

Babylon

Borsippa

Dilbat

Marad

Nippur

Isin

SUMER

Euphrates

Uruk

Larsa

Ur

Eridu

0   50   100   150   200 km

Uruk   Town with major sanctuary

Isin   Secondary town

Ancient courses of canals or secondary
branches of the Euphrates

expansion, which began with Cyrus in the middle of the sixth century, thus experienced no real difficulty in vanquishing, then incorporating, the neo-Babylonian empire into the budding Achaemenid state.

BABYLONIA FROM THE NINTH TO THE SEVENTH CENTURIES

Babylonia under external power (900–729)

The country's political state

Like its northern neighbour, Babylonia experienced Aramaean expansion at the end of the second millennium, but had greater difficulty in resisting it. While the north of Babylonia remained under permanent threat from the nomadic peoples of the desert, the Suteans, some forty Aramaean tribes firmly and permanently entrenched themselves in the east and south of the country, living in semi-independent tribal communities and concentrating on breeding livestock. Beginning in the ninth century, another population, known as the Chaldaeans, whose exact origin remains unknown, installed themselves in the marshy lands in the south of Babylonia and along the Euphrates as far as the environs of Babylon. While engaging in farming, they also controlled the trading routes with the Persian Gulf. Their social and political structure was more centralised than that of the Aramaeans: they were organised in five major confederations, and in this way managed to set up veritable principalities which infiltrated the Babylonian political fabric. This centralised organisation won them real power when they eventually united, and even allowed Chaldaean princes to occupy the throne of Babylon in the eighth and seventh centuries, but equally rendered them vulnerable to the frontal attacks of the Assyrian kings who intervened in Babylonia. The latter imposed heavy tribute, destroyed their urban centres and subjected them to several deportations. The Chaldaeans' spirit of resistance was by no means broken, however, and their hold on the marshy areas of the country made them almost impregnable in the south of Babylonia.

The rest of the country maintained its traditional organisation around the large urban areas. The most important were distinguished by the presence of a great sanctuary which played a major role in the economy of the town and its surrounding countryside. These towns had the status of holy cities (*mahâzu*), benefiting from privileges and exemptions. Babylon occupied a special position, because it was simultaneously the religious and political focus of the country. The title king of Babylon (*šar Bâbili*) thus implied authority over the entire country, though that often remained purely nominal at the start of this period, being exerted over the north and centre of Babylonia and a few towns in the south (Ururk, Larsa, Ur). The political situation was therefore unstable, marked by a succession of several dynasties, and royal continuity was far from secure. Moreover, Babylonia was hard put to it to ensure the safety of its frontiers in the face of its neighbours in the north (Assyria) and in the east (Elam), which were going through a phase of expansion starting in the ninth century.

Babylonian recovery and the first Assyrian intervention (900–812)

In the last year of his reign, king Shamash-mudammiq (?–900), who had been unable to resist the Elamite invasions in the east and the Suteans in the west, had to suffer the armed intervention of the king of Assyria, Adad-nerari II (911–891); the latter occupied the left bank of the Tigris, from Arrapha as far as Dêr and up to the Elamite borders. The frontier with Babylonia on the Middle Euphrates had been taken as far as Hit. Nabû-shum-ukîn I (899–888) began a work of national recovery, bringing the frontier with Assyria back to the region of Arrapha, and this state of affairs was supported by Adad-nerari II in 891. Assyria's growing power from then on blocked access to Babylonia by the Aramaeans, and enabled the kingdom to regain a certain vigour. The new king of Babylon, Nabû-apla-iddin (888–855), was thus able to rid the north of the country of Sutean incursions and re-establish worship at Sippar. But a new power was taking shape in the south, where the Chaldaeans had been settled for several decades, restoring the region and profiting from their strategic position on the southern trading routes to amass considerable wealth.

The situation deteriorated when Marduk-zâkir-šumi I (854–819) was threatened early in his reign with a rebellion by his brother. He appealed to the king of Assyria, Shalman-eser III, and the two armies in coalition crushed the rebels. Shalmaneser pursued his military campaign in Babylonia, where he made his devotions at the great sanctuaries, then turned southwards against the Chaldaean tribes, who from then on enjoyed quasi-autonomy. The booty he extracted shows the wealth that had already been amassed by the con-federations of the Bît-Yakîn, Bît-Dakkûri and Bît-Amukkâni. The king of Babylon was at that time sufficiently sure of his throne to be able, in his turn, to come to the assistance of the new king of Assyria, Shamshi-Adad V, who was threatened by a rebellion that had inflamed the country since 827. But the king of Assyria was not happy to find the conditions of the treaty of alliance signed on this occasion imposed upon him. In 814, Shamshi-Adad V took revenge on the king of Babylon, Marduk-balâssu-iqbi (818–813). Assyrian troops descended on Babylonia and routed the Babylonian army. The following year (813), Shamshi-Adad V waged a new campaign and captured Marduk-balâssu-iqbi. A high-ranking dignitary, Baba-ah-iddin, then ascended the throne, but was no better at resisting the Assyrian assault. The north-ern Transtigrine towns were pillaged and in 812 Shamshi-Adad V received the tribute of the leaders of the Chaldaean confederations.

The political vacuum and the Chaldaean kings (811–729)

The immediate outcome of this brutal intervention was to create a political vacuum: from 811 to 769, no true king was capable of ruling the country. In the longer term, the destruction of Babylonian power in the northern part of the country resulted in a transfer of the country's vital forces to the south. Henceforward, the Chaldaean confederations held the primacy. From the political chaos of over forty years emerged a king from the Bît-Yakîn, Erîba-Marduk (769–761), who nevertheless had difficulty in securing his government, and local disturbances are attested in his reign and that of his successor Nabû-šum-iškun (760–748), another Chaldaean, from the Bît-Dakkûri confederation.

When the new king of Babylon, Nabû-nâṭir (747–734), appealed to Tiglath-pileser III to help him re-establish order against the Aramaean tribes and the Chaldaeans, Babylonia lost the little autonomy that remained to it. The king of Assyria waged a huge campaign all along the Babylonian course of the Tigris and in the region of Nippur, right in the heart of the country. He went on to deport Aramaeans and Chaldaeans, and took it upon himself to assert Assyrian authority over the mountainous border east of the Tigris. With a close watch on it from the north and east, Babylonia was henceforward under *de facto* Assyrian control. Nabû-nâṭir was succeeded by his son Nabû-nâdin-zêri (733–732), but Babylonia was quickly plunged into political chaos again: a rebellion raised a provincial governor, Nabû-šum-ukîn II, to the throne in 732, but in his turn he was driven out by the leader of the Bît-Amukkâni Chaldaean confederation, Nabû-mukîn-zêri (731–729). The Chaldaeans' return to Babylonia unleashed a second intervention by Tiglath-pileser III. The condition of Babylonia certainly led the king of Assyria to consider its incorporation in the Assyrian empire a necessity. Assyrian diplomatic and military pressure managed to disorganise the Chaldaeans, and Nabû-mukîn-zêri disappeared in obscure circumstances. Tiglath-pileser III proclaimed himself king of Babylon in 728, and Babylonia's history entered a new phase, of direct subjection to Assyria.

Assyrian Babylonia (728–626)

A century of resistance

For a century, the history of Babylonia was linked with that of the Assyrian empire, of which it formed one of the major provinces. It none the less had a separate status, being treated sometimes as an associate kingdom whose government was entrusted to an Assyrian royal prince. Babylonian scribes preserved their own system of dating by the years of the current sovereign, even if he was king of Assyria at the same time, and only in exceptional cases used the computation by eponyms (*limmu*) customary in Assyria. The spirit of resistance to the Assyrians was particularly embodied in the Chaldaean confederations, but the population in the large towns was divided between pro- and anti-Assyrian factions. Although some were aware of the maintenance of law and order brought by the Assyrian presence, and the honours that the kings of Assyria paid to the great sanctuaries, others demanded political independence, to the point of appealing to the Chaldaeans and Elamites. During this period, the country paid heavily for this confrontational situation; Assyrian armed interventions were sometimes excessively brutal, especially in Sennacherib's reign.

The kings of Babylon from the end of the eighth to the end of the seventh century

King	Origin	Dates	Length of reign
(Nabû)-mukîn-zêri	Chaldaean	731–729	3 years
Tiglath-pileser III[a]	Assyrian	728–727	2 years
Shalmaneser V[b]	Assyrian	726–722	5 years

Merodachbaladan II	Chaldaean	721–710	12 years
Sargon II	Assyrian	709–705	5 years
Sennacherib	Assyrian	704–703	2 years
Marduk-zâkir-šumi II	Babylonian	703	1 month
Merodachbaladan II	Chaldaean	703	9 months
Bêl-ibni	Babylonian	702–700	3 years
Ashur-nadin-shumi	Assyrian	699–694	6 years
Nergal-ušêzib	Chaldaean	693	1 year
Mušêzib-Marduk	Chaldaean	692–689	4 years
Sennacherib	Assyrian	688–681	8 years
Esarhaddon	Assyrian	680–669	12 years
Shamash-shum-ukin	Assyrian	667–648	20 years
Kandalanu	Babylonian (?)	647–627	21 years
Civil war		627–626	

[a] Also attested under the name Pûlu

[b] Also attested under the name Ulûlaiu

A figure of Babylonian independence: Merodachbaladan II

In 731, Merodachbaladan II (Marduk-apla-iddin), a chief of the Bît-Yakîn, appeared as the leading Chaldaean prince. He took advantage of the unrest in Assyria that followed the death of Shalmaneser V (722) to establish his authority over the whole of the Chaldaean confederations and mount the throne of Babylon for a reign that lasted twelve years, claiming the ancestry of Eriba-Marduk, his grandfather, to justify his royalty. He brought his power to bear on the large towns in central and northern Babylonia, deporting opponents of his policy to his southern capital of Dûr-Yakîn. At the same time he followed the traditional duties of royalty, watching over the distribution and regular upkeep of the great Babylonian sanctuaries, restoring canals and roads, while the country enjoyed peace and a certain degree of prosperity. Beginning in 710, Sargon II, definitive master of the Assyrian empire, waged large-scale campaigns in Babylonia, in an attempt to dislodge the one he regarded as a usurper and blamed for his alliance with the Elamites. In his first campaign (710), he repulsed Merodachbaladan in the south, and captured one of his fortresses. In 709, he attacked the Chaldaean capital Dûr-Yakîn, which had been placed on the defensive by Merodachbaladan, seized and destroyed it, together with all the neighbouring area. Merodachbaladan managed to flee to Elam, rich booty was brought back to Assyria and part of the population of the Bît-Yakîn deported. Merodachbaladan had to wait until Sargon II was dead before he could undertake fresh action in Babylonia (703); he made sure of external allies, and in particular sent an embassy to king Hezekiah of Judah. But the vigorous reaction of Sennacherib, who intervened with his army, drove him out after only a few months. The troops sent in search of him in the south returned in embarrassment, although they had gone through and ravaged the whole of Chaldaea. A fresh campaign in 700, waged by Sennacherib against the Bît-Yakîn, resulted in another flight by Merodachbaladan, who took refuge in the marshy zone on the coast of the Persian Gulf, 'with his gods and the bones of his ancestors', at Nagite. There he died, apparently a natural death, between 700 and 695.

Good and bad times for Babylon

From 702, Babylon was governed by viceroys who were directly subject to Sennacherib: Bêl-ibni (702–700), then Ashur-nadin-shumi (699–694), the eldest son of the king of Assyria himself. In 694, the inhabitants of Babylon deposed Ashur-nadin-shumi and handed him over to the Elamites, who executed him. The king of Assyria had to wait five years to exact vengeance for this betrayal, and power was held in Babylon by two kings of Chaldaean origin in succession, Nergal-ušêzib (693) and Mušêzib-Marduk (692–689). In 689, the Babylonians saw Sennacherib's wrath fall upon them: the town was captured after a fifteen-month siege, its walls were torn down and the god's statue taken into captivity in Assyria.

The inhabitants were massacred or exiled, and Sennacherib boasted of having filled the canals within Babylon with the ruins of houses and thrown the soil of Babylon into the Euphrates. The reality of this total destruction must doubtless be taken with a pinch of salt, as the town continued to be inhabited; but it had certainly suffered terribly from this treatment, and Sennacherib's dramatic disappearance in 681 was regarded in Babylonia as a punishment sent by the god Marduk, enraged by the sacrilege.

The situation changed with the accession of Esarhaddon, who undertook the rebuilding of the Babylonian capital and dispatched envoys to the site charged with the restoration of the sanctuaries and worship. Esarhaddon reinstated the inhabitants' exemptions and brought the region back under cultivation, returning to the Babylonians the lands which the Chaldaeans of the Bît-Dakkûri had appropriated. But not until the end of his reign did Assyria consent to return the statue of Marduk to the Babylonians; in 668, the new king of Babylon, Shamash-shum-ukin, the son of Esarhaddon, brought the divine effigy back to its capital with much pomp and ceremony.

For fifteen years, Shamash-shum-ukin reigned over Babylon behaving like the traditional kings, especially with regard to the sanctuaries. But he remained strictly subordinate to his brother, Ashurbanipal, and slipped over into secession, linking with the anti-Assyrian factions that were being reborn in Babylonia, and with foreign nations that were hostile to Nineveh's rule. In 652, Shamash-shum-ukin dragged Babylon into open rebellion, in spite of letters sent by Ashurbanipal to the inhabitants, exhorting them not to break their oath of loyalty to him. This rebellion cost the capital a second siege, from 650 to 648. Contemporary texts contain mentions of famine and cannibalism, and the price of foodstuffs was multiplied by fifty. Finally, in the summer of 648, Babylon succumbed, and Shamash-shum-ukin perished in the flames of his palace, the fire having been started by his own servants. After harsh repression, though less destructive than in 689, Ashurbanipal made the surviving Babylonians swear a new oath of allegiance, and installed Kandalânu, who was probably local in origin, as their king. During his reign (648–627), the capital retrieved itself from its ruins and enjoyed a period of tranquillity.

The duration of Marduk's stay in Assyria

Sennacherib had based his actions on a divine decision condemning the town of Babylon to remain in ruins for seventy years. The process of re-establishing worship undertaken by Esarhaddon clashed with this divine decree, which, in theory, it was impossible to abolish. A manipulation in writing enabled the difficulty to be resolved. The double value of the vertical stroke as a unit in the decimal system (= 1) and in the sexagesimal system (= 60) made it possible, by reversing the order of the cuneiform signs making the figure 70 𒐏, for them to be reduced to the figure 11 𒌋, and for the first erroneous estimate to be ascribed to an 'error in reading'. In 668, the statue of Marduk had therefore well passed the duration allocated to its enforced residence in Assyria and could be handed back without contravening divine commands.

THE GLORY OF BABYLON

The conquest of the Assyrian empire (625–568)

The deaths of Kandalânu and Ashurbanipal, which occurred in the same year (627), unleashed a war between claimants to the throne, the Babylonian Nabû-apla-uṣur (Nabopolassar) profiting from it and in 626 taking the title of king of Babylon. For nearly ten years Babylonia was the scene of confrontations between Assyrian and Babylonian armies, and was not freed from them until 616. Nabopolassar took advantage of the process of the Assyrian empire's internal disintegration, but had to await the arrival of Cyaxarus' Medes before he could strike Assyria in the heart. After an initial failure against

Ashur in 615, he was able to bring his enterprise to a success-
ful conclusion in the following year.

The annihilation of Assyria

The assault on the Assyrian capitals waged by the combined
forces of the Medes and Babylonians was pitiless, probably on
a par with the harshness of the confrontations during the preceding years: the fall of Ashur in 614, Nineveh in 612 and
Harran in 610 give evidence of a systematic clearing of what
had been the Assyrian zone of habitation. The statue of the
god Ashur underwent the same fate as that of Marduk in 689;
it was taken away into captivity by the victors. Assyria became
nominally Babylonian, but none of the towns was rebuilt, and
it was not until the reign of Nabonidus (555–539) that the
temple of Sîn at Harran was restored. At Ashur, however,
some of the population were able to stay put, and a representative of the king of Babylon exercised local authority there,
reoccupying certain rooms in the Old Palace and, at an indeterminate date, having two small sanctuaries built in the courtyard of the former temple of the god Ashur, henceforth in
ruins. While the Medes secured their control over the northern parts of the former Assyrian empire, Babylonian troops
led by Nabopolassar and the crown prince Nebuchadnezzar
quelled the last pockets of resistance, at the frontier of the old
Urartu in 608–607 and the land of Kummuh (Commagene)
in 606.

Gaining control of the west

Meanwhile, Egypt had taken advantage of the political void
in the west to extend its influence along the Mediterranean
coast as far as the Syrian loop of the Euphrates, where an
Egyptian garrison took possession of Carchemish. It was dis-
lodged by Nebuchadnezzar in 605, and the Egyptians had to
evacuate the north-west of Syria after a second defeat near
Hamath. Recalled to Babylon by the death of his father,

Nebuchadnezzar reached it by forced march in twenty-three days (September 605). Once master of the throne, he resumed his military operations in the west. In 604 he had gained possession of the entire Mediterranean coast as far as Ascalon, but had not yet confronted the bulk of the Egyptian troops; when he did so, in 601, he suffered a setback. He had to return virtually every year, at least until 594, in order to achieve definitive mastery over Syria-Palestine. The vassal kings of the region at the time wavered between Egypt and Babylon, like the king of Judah, Jehoiakim. Nevertheless, a solid Babylonian garrison was installed at Riblah, in the upper valley of the Orontes, at the foot of the Lebanon range.

The sieges of Tyre and Jerusalem

The king of Judah's rejection of Babylonian sovereignty in 601 caused his young successor, Jehoiachin, to be besieged in his capital, and Jerusalem fell in 597. The town was looted, the king and elite of the kingdom were taken away in captivity to the palace of Babylon. Zedekiah, Jehoiachin's uncle, then held power in Jerusalem, where several factions confronted one another. In 589 he decided to join a coalition combining Egyptians, Ammonites and Phoenicians. Nebuchadnezzar's reaction was immediate: he laid siege to Tyre and Jerusalem. Besieged for the second time, the town resisted for two years but succumbed in 587. It was destroyed and its population deported to Babylonia. A second deportation was necessary in 582 in order to crush the last shreds of resistance, while the implacable opponents of the king of Babylon took refuge in Egypt. Tyre was harder to bring down, and it took Nebuchadnezzar fifteen years to put an end to it (588–573). The situation in Syria-Palestine finally stabilised in 568. After a last fruitless attempt by the Babylonians against Egypt, the frontier between the two powers was fixed on a line from Gaza. The neo-Babylonian empire had virtually achieved its maximum expansion; its boundaries were marked by the natural frontiers represented in the east by the Zagros range, in the north by the plain of Upper Mesopotamia and in the west by the Mediterranean. The absence of detailed historical sources prevents us from knowing whether the second part of Nebuchadnezzar's reign called for as intensive a military involvement on his part as the first. It is possible, but is not revealed by any alteration in the confines of the neo-Babylonian empire. An isolated reference to disturbances in Babylon in 593, which were harshly repressed, shows that even the heart of the empire was not exempt from forms of challenge, and enables us to understand the rifts following the death of Nebuchadnezzar II, which occurred at the very peak of the state.

The rewards of conquest

At the same time as expanding the empire, Nabopolassar and, chiefly, Nebuchadnezzar II set up a defence system for Babylonia and its capital. They also restored the majority of Babylon's great buildings and the temples in the large towns.

Access to Babylon

Immediately north of Sippar, at the point on the Mesopotamian plain where the Tigris and Euphrates are closest, the king had a long defence wall erected, then a second, farther south, going from Babylon to the Tigris. They do not appear to have been true fortified walls, but structures midway between dyke and rampart. They had a dual function: they protected the region of Babylon against the spate of the two rivers; conversely, they allowed the vast quadrilateral which they formed with the Tigris and Euphrates to be transformed into a floodable zone that would be difficult for an enemy army to penetrate. The capital itself was protected by a double fortified wall, astride the Euphrates. The one on the eastern bank, on which the two centres of power were installed (the royal palace and the sanctuary of Marduk), was duplicated by a second line, outside the town properly speaking, which guarded its farming and market gardening area.

Reconstructions and donations

Babylon had experienced a first rebuilding by Esarhaddon starting in 680, but its walls had been demolished again in 648, and the royal palace burnt. Nabopolassar and Nebuchadnezzar undertook a complete restoration of the enclosing wall and palace complex, making use of the wealth acquired in Assyria and a workforce gained from their military campaigns. The royal palace zone extended across the external wall, bordering directly on the Euphrates from which it was protected by an immense brick salient. It was also separated from the rest of the town by an internal enclosure wall, thus forming a fortified and easily isolable ensemble.

But Babylon was also the town of the god Marduk, and the grand processional way which started from the Ishtar gate in the north of the town, as well as the temple of the Esagil and the ziggurat of the Etemenanki which flanked it, were also the object of restoration and numerous embellishments. The list of the major works undertaken by the two sovereigns, to be carried on by their successors, as documented for us in royal inscriptions, is most impressive and bears witness to a determination to return all the country's great centres to their former state. The main concern was the sanctuaries, and there was no multiplication of royal palaces such as was found in Assyria. Having regained its status as the country's capital, Babylon was to keep it until the founding of Seleuceia early in the third century. The rebuilding of the great edifices was accompanied by a series of donations of land, labour and various riches to the temples, which enabled the cult's munificence to be developed on a scale never before attained in Babylonia.

The exercise of power

Relations between the king of Babylon and his subjects were apparently based on those that had been developed in Assyria, although documentation is sparse. Regular reference is made to the sworn agreements of loyalty and faithfulness to the king (*adê*), and those who violated them were put to death.

Governors of Babylonia's provinces

'High-ranking men of the land of Akkad: Ea-dayyânu, governor of the Country of the Sea; Nergal-šar-uṣur, the *simmagir*; Emuq-ahi, of Tupliaš; Bêl-šum-iškun, of the Puqudu; Bibêa, of the (Bît)-Dakkûri; Iddin-ahi, priest-(governor) of Dêr; Marduk-šar-uṣur, of the Gambulu; Marduk-šarrâni, governor of the Sumandar; Bêl-lidâr-ûmi, of the (Bît)-Amukkâni; Rîmût, governor of Zamûa; Nabû-êṭir-napšâti, governor of the Yaptûru ...'

Unlike in preceding reigns, the various ethnic communities present in Babylonia showed no perceptible opposition, and mention of Chaldaean confederations or Aramaean tribes virtually faded out, except in regard to geographical or administrative districts. The leaders of the various clans were incorporated into the machinery of the state and played a part in government. They belonged to what an official text from the palace of Nebuchadnezzar II calls the 'high-ranking men of the land of Akkad' (= Babylonia).

A few references from the Achaemenid or Seleucid era link Nabopolassar, the first neo-Babylonian king, to the dynasty of the Country of the Sea, thus to Merodachbaladan II, but it has not been possible to demonstrate this. In their inscriptions, the neo-Babylonian kings resume traditional ideology, and an entire hagiographic literature boasts of the restoration of Right and Justice in their reign.

What was the neo-Babylonian empire?

A resumption of the Assyrian empire

In other respects, in the absence of texts similar to the neo-Assyrian annals and, more generally, of official palace archives, information on the organisation and functioning of the neo-Babylonian empire is sparse. The very spirit of its creation is unclear; it was certainly not a matter of having the pre-eminence of the god of Babylon acknowledged in the rest of the Near East. All the same, the booty obtained on the capture of the Assyrian capitals allowed the kings of Babylon to follow their ambitious policy of carrying out major works without having to make periodic demands on neighbouring countries. The levies effected at the time of the campaigns in Cilicia or the capture of Jerusalem were part of the current practice of war, and had no significance by themselves. It may therefore be considered that the Babylonian empire was in essence a resumption of the existing Assyrian empire, including its territorial areas and its executives. From this point of view, the military effort to be made was less than that of the Assyrians, since the neighbouring great powers did not evince the same hostility: Elam had been seriously shaken by Ashurbanipal's campaigns, and was a kingdom in convalescence, and relations with the Medes were relatively cordial. Only Egypt presented a problem, setting its own sights on Syria-Palestine, but there was no great necessity to conquer it, and from 604 it seems more or less to have respected the Babylonian sphere of influence. The king of Babylon's acknowledged position of eminence was made clear by his diplomatic intervention, in 585, between the Medes and Lydians to define the boundaries of their respective domains in Anatolia.

The empire's provinces

The division of the empire's provinces itself remained in a state of flux: besides Babylonia's traditional provinces, it is recognised that certain districts were under the authority of Babylonian governors, such as Arpad in north-west Syria, whereas others remained vassal states, such as the Phoenician towns, which kept a status that was fairly close to the one they had enjoyed in the Assyrian empire. The kingdom of Judah also maintained its dynasty, until Nebuchadnezzar II decided to install a governor, Gedaliah, but he was of local origin. Similarly, there is mention of kings of Damascus, Moab, Ammon and Edom. The exact situation in Upper Mesopotamia and the former Assyria remains unknown, although Harran ended by coming under direct Babylonian administration, and we may note the presence of a local administrative official at Ashur. The eastern frontier was secured by a campaign by Nebuchadnezzar II in 596, and the region of Susa may have been attached to the empire for a certain time. Part of the Zagros range was under Babylonian influence, as is shown by mention of a governor of Gutium (a traditional name for the central part of the chain of mountains) in the reign of Nabonidus.

FROM THE BABYLONIAN TO THE PERSIAN EMPIRE (561–539)

Difficulties for the successors of Nebuchadnezzar II (561–556)

The first usurpation

The son of Nebuchadnezzar II, Amêl-Marduk (561–560), reigned for only two years and was swept away by a palace revolution. It seems that a latent conflict had developed between the new king and a group led by one of the court's great dignitaries, the *simmagir* Neriglissar. He had taken part in Nebuchadnezzar II's conquests, been present at the siege of Jerusalem, and made himself the spokesman for those who wanted to pursue the policy of conquest with all its accompanying advantages. Amêl-Marduk held less warlike views; so he put an end to the captivity of Jehoiachin, king of Judah. But Neriglissar carried considerable political clout; he was in charge of a large part of the frontier province of the east, along the Tigris, known as 'the province of the *simmagir*'. He also controlled a major part of the military system and, through his marriage to Kaššaia, Amêl-Marduk's sister, belonged to the royal family. From this tension between the king and the military leaders, Neriglissar emerged the victor: he had Amêl-Marduk assassinated, and took his place in 559. His reign was marked by the resumption of military operations, chiefly in Cilicia, in the south of Anatolia, and by new major works of restoration of sanctuaries. But Neriglissar belonged to a generation that was already old, and he was king of Babylon for only four years. The problem of succession arose anew on his death (556), for he passed on the throne to his son, Lâbâši-Marduk, whose youth, inexperience and lack of authority are agreed upon by our sources. The neo-Babylonian empire had scarcely more than half a century of real existence and its dynastic tradition had not been sufficiently established.

Nabonidus' accession to the throne

A new palace rebellion occurred only a few months after Lâbâši-Marduk's enthronement. Those responsible for his elimination belonged to a court faction, though it is difficult to ascertain on the basis of what interests it was formed, but it was clearly competing with the group who had supported Neriglissar. Its leaders, Nabonidus and his son Bêl-šar-uṣur (Belshazzar), were outside the royal family, but none the less members of the circle of palace dignitaries. The father, Nabonidus, was chosen as king, while Belshazzar took possession of the inheritance and staff of Neriglissar's family.

The neo-Babylonian kings

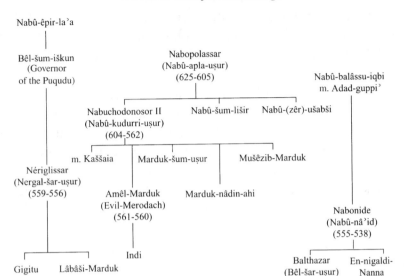

The overt usurpation by Nabonidus, who, unlike Neriglissar, had no official connection with the royal family, caused no trouble at all, however, in Babylonia or the empire. The internal rifts that characterise this period remained within the setting of the royal palace.

Nabonidus, an enigmatic king (555–539)

The individual

On his accession to the throne, Nabonidus was certainly getting on in years: his son, Belshazzar, was old enough to participate fully in political matters; in any case, the official autobiography of Nabonidus' mother, Adad-guppi', which ascribes exceptional longevity to her, since she seems to have been a centenarian when she died, proves that she had had her son at the very start of Nebuchadnezzar II's reign, perhaps even before. As for his father, nothing is known of him apart from his name, Nabû-balâssu-iqbi, and his title of governor. Nabonidus' origin itself poses a problem, since his mother had at first lived at Harran, in western Upper Mesopotamia, in the reign of Ashurbanipal and up to the end of the Assyrian empire. From there, she had been taken to Babylon at the time of the town's capture by the neo-Babylonian army, and lived in the royal palace, though it is not known precisely in what capacity. Nabonidus' links with Harran, which would subsequently exert a strong influence on his religious policy, led to his having Aramaean ancestors attributed to him on his mother's side, though this cannot be clearly demonstrated. The first part of his reign, however, was that of a king of Babylon, obedient to the strict tradition of the sovereigns of South Mesopotamia. In his first year, he undertook to set right the management of the sanctuaries in order to bring them back to traditional standards, and embarked on a series of temple restorations. The inscriptions relating to these works emphasise the extreme care paid by the king to respecting the most ancient architectural and religious features, which earned him the historiographical description of 'archaeologist-king', so clearly expressed was his attention to the past. Lastly, he did not neglect the military aspect of his office, leading a military expedition in Cilicia at the start of his reign.

Transmission of an order from Nabonidus concerning the regulations for cult offerings at Uruk

'Make the payments in keeping with the order given to us by the king as follows:

"The religious deliveries of the Eanna (the temple of the goddess Ishtar) must be made in accordance with the old system of the time of Nebuchadnezzar, king of Babylon."

The priests of the sacred college and the scribes of the Eanna have therefore consulted the records and documents of the Eanna of the time of Nebuchadnezzar.'

Relations with Belshazzar and the stay at Temâ

The choice of an elderly ruler lay perhaps in Nabonidus' personal charisma, but certainly also in a political calculation in which his son Belshazzar had a hand. The growing part played by the latter in the conduct of affairs of state is notable, and it may be that he envisaged his father's reign as a transitory phase, intended to facilitate his own accession to the throne. This calculation was thwarted by Nabonidus' longevity and his deep involvement with this royal office. It is very difficult to determine whether there was in fact a conflict of interests between Nabonidus and his son, but it is noteworthy that in the fifth year of his reign, after taking a large expedition which, on leaving Palestine, plunged into the Arabian desert as far as the oasis of Temâ, Nabonidus set up his royal residence in Arabia for ten years. In the king's absence, from 551 to 541, the conduct of government in Babylonia fell on Belshazzar's shoulders.

The precise reasons for Nabonidus' sojourn at Temâ remain a mystery: did he distance himself deliberately, or was it an exile? The Biblical account of Nebuchadnezzar spending seven years in the wilderness because of an illness that made him unclean has been advanced as a parallel; economic reasons have also been proposed (a desire to ensure control of the trade flow from south Arabia), and religious ones. Like Harran, the homeland of Nabonidus' mother, and like Ur, where he installed his daughter as high priestess, Temâ was a great religious centre of the god of the Moon, and the rest of Nabonidus' reign proves that he had a very special relationship with that deity. It is possible that all these were all contributory elements, not forgetting the political aspect that Nabonidus may have been elbowed aside by the group who had raised him to the throne but preferred to see Belshazzar conduct affairs at Babylon.

The religious problem

We know about the deeds of Nabonidus both from his own inscriptions and from a pamphlet written after Cyrus' arrival at Babylon. In both instances the accounts are polemical and must be interpreted cautiously. It emerges plainly that, during his ten-year stay at Temâ, Nabonidus directed his religious thinking towards according an increasingly important place to the Moon god, Sîn, to the point of wanting to make him chief of the pantheon. This called into question the most traditional religious system, and must naturally have provoked negative reactions on the part of the Babylonian clergy. But their opposition must not be over-estimated; indeed it is possible that its cause was not so much the religious reform introduced by Nabonidus as the tight control over their management under which he had placed the sanctuaries right at the start of his reign, in the name of respect for royal prerogatives. He thus clashed with the interests of part of the urban nobility, who derived benefits from their involvement in the management of the temples' resources. Behind the strictly religious conflict lay hidden a conflict of interests, first and foremost. It is therefore difficult to make an objective evaluation of Nabonidus' reign if one keeps only to what is said of him by his opponents.

The Persian conquest

The return of Nabonidus

When at the end of ten years he returned to Babylon in 541, Nabonidus proceeded to take the administration in hand personally, installing new officials in place of those appointed by Belshazzar. He also had the temple of Sîn at Harran rebuilt, thus realising a project which in fact dated from the start of his reign. He seems, moreover, to have introduced important alterations into the service of the cult at Babylon itself, putting Sîn into Marduk's temple and giving him a major place. But his attention was soon drawn to what was happening beyond Babylonia's eastern frontier. Profound political changes were taking place on the Iranian plateau: a new king of Persian origin, Cyrus (Kuraš), was in the act of substituting his own supremacy for that of the king of the Medes, Astyagus (Ištumegu), over the confederations of tribes of the Medes and Persians. Having united the Iranians of the west under his authority, he undertook a series of conquests which brought him to western Anatolia, then dominated by the powerful kingdom of Lydia and its king, Croesus. In 541, the Lydian capital Sardis fell to Cyrus. Nabonidus then put Babylonia on the defensive, but part of the frontier line with Iran, Gutium, seceded and its governor Gobryas (Ugbaru) rallied to Cyrus' side. Early in 539, Nabonidus had the statues of the country's chief deities brought to Babylon to avoid their being captured by a foreign attack, and perhaps to strengthen the capital's spiritual defences. But his precautions were in vain; the Persian troops entered Babylon by way of the Diyala Valley at the end of summer 539.

Cyrus' conquest

After heavy fighting, the region of Sippar fell into Persian hands. Cyrus then marched on Babylon in October 539, and the town surrendered without resistance. It may be that, according to the tradition of classical writers and the Bible, the capital was taken by an audacious surprise attack by the Persians. At all events, Belshazzar disappeared, and Nabonidus was deposed and sent to reside in an eastern province (Carmania?) of the budding Persian empire. This victory gave Cyrus not only Babylonia, but its entire empire. It was the end of the country's political autonomy, although Babylon maintained its status as capital. This fundamental political change was clearly not perceived by contemporaries, and there was virtually no interruption in Babylonia's administrative and economic practice between the neo-Babylonian period and the beginning of the Persian era. Acceptance of Cyrus as the new sovereign was accompanied by the writing of texts legitimising his taking power in the name of the Babylonian gods, and contrariwise transforming Nabonidus' reign into an example of bad kingship. Furthermore, uniting Babylonia with a power whose political weight lay in Iran was nothing new in Mesopotamia's long history, so it was easy to legitimise Cyrus' reign by examples drawn from the most ancient historical tradition. For the people of Babylonia, they were not departing from the traditional setting of their country's cycle of history. This virtually universal acceptance of the new rule also showed the weakness of the allegiance to the local dynasty, all the more so because Cyrus took the title 'king of Babylon and the lands' (*šâr Bâbili u matâti*) and preserved the links between royal power and the temples.

Babylonia's new status

Babylonia's incorporation into the Persian empire obviously meant a transfer of the centres of decision-making to Iran. In other respects, there was a remarkable continuity between this initial period of the Achaemenid empire and the one that preceded it. Local authorities in Babylonia were not altered, and the geopolitical framework itself of the former neo-Babylonian empire remained in place. Cyrus had first envisaged making it into a sort of vice-kingdom, at the head of which he placed his son Cambyses, and for just over a year the latter held the title of king of Babylon, while Cyrus kept that of king of the lands. Then responsibility for this huge area was entrusted to a governor (*bêl pihati*), Gubaru, assisted by his son Nabugu. This enormous province combined Mesopotamia and the western Near East, within the boundaries of the former neo-Babylonian empire, under the name 'province of Babylon and Transeuphrates' (*pihat Bâbili u Ebir nâri*), and that definition was to last until the end of Darius I's reign. It appears that not until the reign of Xerxes was a separation made between the two blocs, and the province of

Babylon reduced to Mesopotamia in the strict sense. It was therefore by a process that stretched across the entire end of the sixth century that the transition was made from the ancient Babylonian kingdom to the Achaemenid province of Babylonia, with a very gradual establishment of new administrative arrangements. Not until the death of Cambyses (522) did a nationalist aspiration emerge in Babylonia, and that occurred, too, at a time of general destabilisation and a power struggle at the summit of the Persian empire.

One cannot help but be struck by the contrast between the vigour of Babylonia's resistance to attachment to the neo-Assyrian empire in the seventh century, and the feeble echo met by nationalist attempts in the late sixth century. The first to lead a revolt in Babylon, taking advantage of the political vacuum left by Cambyses' death and the usurpation of Gaumata in Persia in 522, was in fact a Babylonian named Nidinti-Bêl; he presented himself as a son of Nabonidus and adopted the name Nebuchadnezzar III. Did this connection with the last Babylonian monarch, who had left a far from positive memory behind, mean that the dynasty had preserved solid support seventeen years after its fall? Although he was recognised in the majority of the large Babylonian towns, his 'reign' lasted no more than a few months, and he was defeated by an army of Darius I and executed in December 522. The cause of the second 'pretender' is even more atypical, since he took power at Babylon under the name Nebuchadnezzar IV, but was of Armenian origin, according to Darius I's inscription at Behistun. He was swiftly vanquished by Darius I's generals after four months (August–November) and died impaled. Here we have matters of personal adventurism, rather than national Babylonian rebellions, and their importance must be put in perspective.

DOCUMENT

The dreams of king Nabonidus

'In a dream I saw the conjunction of the Great Star and the Moon, and deliberated within myself. Then a man came and stood at my side and spoke to me, saying: "There is no bad omen connected with this conjunction!" In the same dream there appeared to me king Nebuchadnezzar, my predecessor, with one of his loyal men, both standing on the royal chariot. The servant spoke to Nebuchadnezzar, saying: "Speak to Nabonidus, so that I can report to you the dream he has seen." Nebuchadnezzar listened to him and spoke to me thus: "Tell me what good omens you have seen!" Then I answered him, saying: "In my dream, the Great Star, the Moon and the planet Jupiter rose in the firmament; I looked at them with gladness, they called me by name ... [lacuna] ..."

... I arranged [altars for] the planet Venus, the planet Saturn, the Star ŠU-PA, the Star X [not identified], the Great Star, inhabitants of the heavens, the principal witnesses of my dream, and addressed my prayers to them that my life might be long, my throne firm, my reign lasting and my words favourably received by my Lord Marduk.

Then I returned to my bed and during the night saw in a dream the goddess Baba, my Lady, she who restores the dying to life and grants a long life. Then I prayed to her to grant me a long existence and to turn her face towards me. And she turned her face towards me and looked steadily at me, her face radiant with benevolence, thus signifying her affection for me. Then I entered the Eniggidarkalamma temple, in the presence of Nabû, the god who makes my reign lasting, and he placed in my hands the sceptre of justice and the staff of command which justifies the expansion of the kingdom; I then turned my gaze to the chapel of Tašmetum who, like Gula, grants life, and she acted as intercessor with Marduk, the Lord, in my request for a long life, the fullness of days and the annihilation of my enemies.

The heart of Marduk, my Lord, was appeased. With the utmost reverence I concentrated my attention on him, and with fervent prayers made plain my regard. I addressed my supplication to him from the depths of my heart, as follows: "May I be the sovereign for whom your heart wishes, although I had no desire to reign, I who had no knowledge of your intentions, and in whose hands, O Lord of Lords, you have placed a royalty greater than that of the

kings you have appointed in the past and who formerly exercised power!
May my days be long, my years of life continue, so that I may continually keep
the sanctuaries of the great gods provided with offerings."'

This royal inscription is carved on a stele discovered during the archaeological excavations of Babylon; its entire upper part had been destroyed and only
eleven columns of text had survived. It was written in the literary style called
'standard Babylonian', but the cuneiform signs have an archaic form, a frequent
occurrence in inscriptions on stone. It is the first inscription of Nabonidus
(555–539), and internal criteria have enabled it to be dated to the middle of
year I of his reign. After reference to his call to the throne by the Babylonians,
who were not satisfied with the royalty of Lâbâši-Marduk, Neriglissar's young
successor, Nabonidus recounts how, through a dream, he received the assurance of Nebuchadnezzar II, his most illustrious predecessor, and of the god
Marduk, king of the gods, that his taking power was legitimate.

Nabonidus' *coup d'état* does not seem to have met any strong opposition,
but posed the problem of the legitimacy of the new sovereign, who was not
related to Nebuchadnezzar's dynasty. Nabonidus seems to have felt some dis-
quiet about this, and in the course of his account of assuming power tells of a
series of dreams which allowed him to enter into direct contact with the world
of the gods and receive assurance of their support.

The first dream: Nabonidus before Nebuchadnezzar

The first dream describes an astronomical configuration marked by an astral
conjunction: in the astrology of the period, this type of phenomenon in itself
was the equivalent of an omen. We are therefore in a learned construction
which inserts one divinatory phenomenon (the conjunction) within another
(the royal dream). The meaning of the astrological omen is immediately
explained as favourable by an interpreter who appears in the dream.

The continuation of the account then shows the new king and his predecessor, Nebuchadnezzar, in a scene of royal audience. The former king appears
in majesty, on his chariot and, in keeping with royal etiquette, does not receive
Nabonidus directly: the latter has to make contact through Nebuchadnezzar's
companion, who draws his attention to the sleeper and invites him to question
him. Nabonidus is then led to tell of his vision and describes the stars which
rose in the firmament and 'called him by name'. The rest of the text is broken,
but it is probable that Nebuchadnezzar confirmed the new king in a positive

interpretation and acknowledged his right to take his place in the line of the kings of Babylon.

Having awoken, Nabonidus proceeds with a ceremony of offerings to the astral forms of the gods: the stars he mentions are only partly those he has seen, and the presence of the others is not explained. They nevertheless clearly play the role of guarantors of the positive meaning of his dream. The prayers he addresses to them are archetypal of what a king asks of the gods: a long life and a stable reign, but he urges them also to intercede in his favour to gain access to the king of the gods, Marduk, and receive a second confirmation from him, after that of Nebuchadnezzar.

The second dream: Nabonidus before Marduk

Access to the king of the gods is also achieved by a dream approach, but it is less immediate than with Nebuchadnezzar, and requires four stages. Nabonidus first finds himself in the presence of the goddess Baba (the old name for Gula, goddess of medicine). He begs her to spare him the physical ills that could afflict him and show him her benevolence, a sign that the gods are ready to receive him.

The journey continues by way of the temple of Nabû known as the E-nig-gidar-kalamma, which has been identified as the temple called 'of Nabû-ša-harê', situated in Babylon, to the north-east of the Esagil complex. The importance of this little temple has to do with the fact that it was one of the places where the coronation ceremony was held: there the god Nabû invested the new king with the insignia of his power: the sceptre and staff of command. In his dream, Nabonidus takes part in this ceremony, which may indicate that it had not yet actually taken place.

Once enthroned by Nabû, son of Marduk, Nabonidus has to confront the king of the gods himself. As in the case of the royal audience, he cannot address Marduk straight away and has to go through an intermediary. She, the goddess Tašmetum, divine wife of Nabû and daughter-in-law of Marduk, will therefore intercede with the latter to dispose him favourably towards Nabonidus.

Access to Marduk proves all the more perilous because the god, like every supreme deity, is naturally touchy; so it is necessary to soothe his heart, and address fervent prayers to him which will enable Nabonidus to pose the vital question: has Marduk, in full possession of the facts, truly appointed him to the royalty of Babylon? The rest of the text is broken and does not allow us to know the exact tenor of the god's words, which of course one supposes must have been favourable.

An anxious king?

We know that when Nabonidus came to the throne he was getting on in years; moreover, he never concealed the fact that he did not belong to the royal family. In this inscription from the beginning of his reign, he therefore lets his doubts show through about his ability to take up the office that has been given to him. Hence the recurrence of prayers to ensure a long and illness-free life, which he offers to the stars, the goddess Baba and the god Marduk. Furthermore, he needs to know if his accession to the throne is truly the result of a divine decision. His apostrophe to the king of the gods reveals this anxiety and a faith in the omnipotence of the god, whose plans are impenetrable for a human. In each episode, whether before Nebuchadnezzar or Marduk, Nabonidus presents himself as a simple private individual; he does not hesitate to confess that he 'had no desire to reign', and seems almost crushed by the burden of the honour that has been paid to him.

An initiatory route?

In the account he gives of his dream, Nabonidus is not static; he follows a cod- ified itinerary which brings him to meet Nebuchadnezzar on his chariot. Virtually in the same era, the Biblical prophet Ezekiel, exiled in Babylonia, had a vision of God's chariot, surrounded by his cherubim, which would feed part of the esoteric elaboration of the Kabbala. Other Babylonian texts recording dreams also reconstruct veritable itineraries of journeys. It is equally likely that, in his visits to the temple of Baba, then of Nabû, to the chapel of Tašmetum, and lastly to the Esagil where he finds himself in the presence of Marduk, Nabonidus is following a precise route within his capital, the one followed by each new legitimate king of Babylon at the time of his coronation.

If the astrological section of the dream remains impossible to decode com- pletely, it is still probable that it refers to a very exact configuration, with the value of a favourable omen for a new king. The fact of having seen it in a dream gives it as much worth as if it had actually happened, provided one admits that the royal word is genuine.

Clever official wording

The sincere and spontaneous side of this account is no more than superficial, however; in fact, the theme of the 'royal dream' was not a novelty in Mesopotamian tradition. By reporting it, it was not a matter of stressing the tormented psychology of the sovereign, but bearing witness that he had had direct access to the world of the gods and knowledge of the past. In similar vein, the Sumerian prince of Lagash, Gudea, in the late third millennium BC, received in a very detailed dream the command from the god Ningirsu to build his temple. In a later inscription, Nabonidus again uses the procedure of the dream when he has to justify the restoration of Sîn's temple at Harran, which Marduk is also supposed to have commanded.

By receiving reassurance on the legitimacy of his claim directly from Nebuchadnezzar, then Nabû and Marduk, Nabonidus got round the obligations of official ideology, which had been carefully worked out by the religious and educated circles. Although here he was still in an 'orthodox' phase, respecting the divine hierarchy, at the end of his reign he no longer hesitated to base the exaltation of Sîn on his convictions alone, thus provoking the clergy's opposition. They reproached him vehemently, in a pamphlet written at the start of Cyrus' reign, presenting him as prey to anti-religious madness. For the time being, Nabonidus takes on the role of 'seer', having direct access to the divine world and being able immediately to propose an interpretation of the astronomical presages he observes or the coronation scenes in which he takes part. The aim therefore is not so much to present the king's anxieties as to proclaim his legitimacy in unchallengeable fashion.

Here we have a fine example of the creation of an official discourse, showing how themes of royal ideology are manipulated to result, after a destabilising episode in political life, in restoring to order the normal course of events. But by appropriating the role traditionally assigned to the experts in divination and establishing such a personalised relationship with the world of the gods, Nabonidus strayed outside the royal norm. Straight away, in this first inscription, a very personal behaviour is revealed, which increasingly asserted itself during the rest of his reign and led clerical circles to class him eventually in the tradition of impious kings.

Chapter 6
Society and economy in the neo-Babylonian period

Babylonian society was decidedly hierarchised, with a base formed of slaves and dependent workers, chiefly rural. The apex of the social pyramid, with its royal court and the nobility, remains little known because of the lack of sources. But the particular feature of Babylonia appears in the existence of a class of urban worthies, who enjoyed a patrimony that was passed down from one generation to the next, its management being in the hands of the head of the family, and giving rise to a great many contracts which were preserved in the family archives. These notables ensured their economic growth by having a hand in the running of the temples or managing the assets of the great families in the court, and profiting from the economic boom that accompanied the expansion of the neo-Babylonian and Achaemenid empires.

Babylonian economy was basically agricultural and relied on a carefully regulated practice of irrigating the land used for the cultivation of cereal crops and date-palms. The cost of the necessary equipment and labour, the constraints of the farming calendar and the inequality in the sharing of ownership of land led the different types of growers to adopt diversified strategies in order to ensure maximum profitability. The same economic dynamism can be observed in trade, which private individuals practised on a regional scale by forming commercial companies, while the larger organisations had no hesitation in sending their businessmen as far afield as the Mediterranean west.

Virtually nothing is known about the running of the royal palace; conversely, the temples left rich administrative archives which give evidence of the complexity of their economic structures and the wealth of their heritage and revenues. Direct beneficiaries of royal piety, they were, however, placed under the control of the royal agents, who sought to increase their profitability, whereas certain notables took advantage of the economic might of these large organisations to associate themselves with them to their own benefit.

SOCIAL AND ECONOMIC STRATA

Legally, Babylonian society was divided into two categories: free and slaves. Socio-economic reality introduced a further split between those who enjoyed true autonomy, in other words, who had their own means of providing for their needs, and those who did not have such autonomy and were dependent on a superior, whether it was a structure such as a palace or temple or a private person, to ensure their existence. There were further distinctions, between the urban population and those who lived outside the towns, farming or raising livestock, or between people who were attached to a family-type system and those who were ruled by tribal relations, or even those who lived on the fringes of normal social life. The nature of the available sources is such that all these categories are fairly well represented; though the urban notables left us many private archives, members of the Aramaean or Chaldaean tribes occur only occasionally in the available documentation. Special attention must also be paid, since the determination of their role marked the historiography of this period, to the respective weight of influence of private fortunes and those of what are called the great organisations, such as palace or sanctuary, as well as the relations that were maintained between these two categories. Here again, available documentation is not homogeneous, and determination of the power of palace economy, unlike in Assyria, comes up against the almost total absence of state archives; conversely, the temples have left us a wealth of documentation.

Slaves and dependants

Slaves belonging to private persons

Slaves were present everywhere in Babylonia, without in any way representing a major component of the population. Slavery through debt no longer existed as such, but it was still common practice to place as a form of pledge to a creditor someone whose labour covered the current interest on a loan. The sale of children by their parents was a practice not looked on with favour, and was justified only in extreme circumstances – war or famine. Slaves owned by private individuals came essentially from the existing slave population, and in the main carried out domestic tasks in the setting of the family; the number of slaves per family was therefore quite low, a few units in proportion to the level of wealth of their owners. The more comfortably off families might take advantage of a special qualification of their slaves to have them carry out artisan's or commercial tasks, or install them on farming estates in the place of families of farmworkers. The slave thus placed brought in a profit known as the *mandattu*.

Slaves could be sold, but for the most part were handed over, in the same way as other components of a patrimony, by inheritance, gift or to form part of a daughter's dowry. Enfranchisements were rare, often accompanied by precise stipulations, such as the upkeep of the former owner by the new freedman. If those conditions were not met or the deed of enfranchisement had not been put in writing and carefully kept, the procedure could be revoked.

Slaves of the temples and palace

The situation changed with regard to the sanctuaries, where there were many more slaves who came either from individual, and chiefly royal, gift, or from among needy people to whom the temples guaranteed minimum upkeep in exchange for their labour (widows and orphans, for instance, but also illegitimate children who had been rejected by their family). They were known as oblates (*širku*) and could not quit this status once it had been imposed on them. Despite the minimum subsistence it afforded them, many oblates tried to escape the temple's clutches, either by fleeing or by integrating themselves into the staff of a private person. Some of the more able oblates could, however, achieve real careers within the temple administration and attain relatively important positions, but the vast majority were first and foremost a labour force used for manual work alone. The situation of the royal slaves must have been fairly similar to that of the oblates, but concrete data about them are lacking.

Dependants

The situation of the free but not economically autonomous population was not very different from that of the slaves. For the most part, they were agricultural, settled on privately owned lands or those belonging to the temples and the palace. In families, these small farmers worked the estates that were entrusted to them against payment of dues formed of part of the harvest. Some had at their disposal, at the same time, land that belonged to them personally, but it was never of a large enough area to provide for their needs. While they were not sold together with the estate when property was transferred, as in Assyria, their freedom of movement was restricted, and they formed the basis of the dependants attached to the crown lands or those of the temples (*šušânu*, *gardu*). As such, they could be mobilised for all major works as a *corvée*, or obligation to perform unpaid labour, but could also hire out their labour and obtain a supplementary income from it.

The urban notables

The concept of a notable

The social qualification of 'notable' emerges from the presence of archives linked to the possession of a family heritage and the civil status of members of this social group: they are identified by their name, followed by that of their father and that of an ancestor. The last may be a personal name or, fairly frequently, the name of an occupation serving as a personal name. The professional qualification evoked by this occupational name may have been held in the family, but it is far from being the norm. For instance, some archives from Borsippa document a person called Rîmût-Nabû, son of Nabû-mukîn-zêri, a descendant of the Herdsman of the Cattle, and this man really did hold a prebend as being responsible for cattle intended for offerings in the temple of the god Nabû. But at Babylon we find one Iddin-nabû, son of Nabû-bân-zêri, descendant of the Blacksmith, who held the prebend of butcher in one of the capital's secondary temples. This connection to an ancestor involves vast family groups who sometimes manage their heritage communally. Some of the more prestigious ancestral names are to be found in several large Babylonian towns, without any kind of kinship existing between the various family groups. Such is the case of the so-called descendants of Egibi, attested at Babylon, Borsippa and Uruk, but only one of whose Babylon branches left very important archives. Also characteristic of these groups of notables is their frequently very close liaison with the economic activities of the sanctuaries. The most prominent families of notables occupy leading positions in the administration of the temples and of the towns; thus most of the governors of large towns come from this milieu.

The social group of urban notables is therefore characterised as composed of 'well-to-do people' (*mâr bâni*), who provide the executives of the local administration and belong to the circle of the well educated. But they formed only part of the country's social elite. Babylonian nobility, who governed the provinces or performed duties at the royal court, made up another social milieu, about which we have very little information, but which must not be confused with that of the urban notables. Economic or even family relationships could be established among them: for instance, the Egibi family of Babylon built its fortune by acting as businessmen to the family of Neriglissar and then Nabonidus; similarly, at the start of her father's reign we find Neriglissar's daughter, Gigitu, marrying a great dignitary of the god Nabû's temple at Borsippa. But this did not result in the formation of a unified social group. Some of the more active royal agents did not belong to the circle of the notables in the towns where they carried on their activities. The first farmer-general of the agricultural lands of Ishtar's temple in Uruk, appointed by Nabonidus himself, Šum-ukîn the descendant of Basiya, did not originate from the class of notables of Uruk. What might be termed the milieu of urban notables thus chiefly represents a local economic and sometimes political power, and at the same time reveals the reality of an urban 'bourgeoisie' which, in that period, was interposed between the mass of the dependent population and the ruling classes.

The structure of family archives

The numerous private archives left to us by the Babylonia of that era vary in origin, size, quality and interest, but their general structure is always more or less the same. They comprise family legal contracts such as marriage agreements and the documents relating to them – arrangements about dowries, adoption contracts, numerous texts on the division of inheritance and various contracts concerning gifts, from father or mother to child, or between husband and wife. There are also deeds of ownership, allowing a legal document to be produced in the event of any contest, and these were often preserved for several generations; they have to do with sales of real estate and movable property, chiefly of prebends or slaves, and sales of draught or pack animals. In the same category belong the verdicts in lawsuits, guaranteeing ownership of disputed property, and the elements of the judgement are recalled in the course of the text. The category most frequently represented is that of proofs of debt, which assemble IOUs (*u'iltu*) and a whole range of kindred deeds that often adopt the same outline: promises to pay, part payment, intervention by an intermediary, receipts, etc. As the skilful summary of an acknowledgement of debt was the basis of the training of the scribes who drew up agreements, it is to be found in other areas, such as trading partnerships (contracts *ana harrâni*, lit. 'for the journey'), or the contractual estimates of crops, which were used to calculate the portion to be paid by the tenant farmer (*imittu*). Acknowledgements of debts concern a variety of products, silver, most often cereals or dates, with an occasional reference to an interest, the making of a pledge or the guarantee supplied by someone on behalf of the debtor. Also included may be management contracts, which are similarly very often present in private archives: rent contracts for farming land for cereal crops or a palm-grove between an owner and one or more farmers, hire contracts concerning houses and slaves but also personal movable property. This category may include work contracts, for the fulfilment of the effective service of a prebend, for example. Less frequently we find administrative deeds, when the private individual holds an office that involves him with the administration of a temple or civil authorities, and correspondence.

The contracts making up family archives may extend over several generations, and relate to close family, but may also concern larger groups which then include family branches connected by direct bonds of kinship, marriages or business relations. The instance of archives built up communally by an extended family occurs chiefly when the method of managing the patrimony involves multiple rights of ownership and when the assets are managed in joint possession.

The role of head of the family

These archives testify to the fundamental position and role of the head of the family: indeed, in each generation one of the family members found himself entrusted with managing the patrimony; it was as a representative of their common interests that he would go ahead with the acquisition of real estate or movable property, issuing lease contracts, drawing up contractual estimates and carrying out financial deals. He also certainly had responsibility for matrimonial alliances. When the older man died, this function was passed on to his son; but when the latter was not yet old enough to shoulder such duties, or if there were only daughters to take on the management, the task fell to the brother of the head of the family. One of the characteristics of this function was that it involved keeping a significant part of the family archives. The process of passing the archives on from one generation to the next thus follows a line we can reconstruct by following family events.

Preserving the patrimony

The main concern for each generation seems to have been to maintain an average level of wealth, and this safeguarding policy took the form of a series of small purchases of land, attempts to bring together well-knit groups, and interfamily marriages whose aim was to keep the dowries brought by brides within the same family, and compensate for the outgoings represented by the dowries of daughters who married outside the family.

In practice, we discover a quest for a certain balance between property and financial activities and the use of slaves: it seems possible to estimate the annual income in relation to the capital invested provided by each of these activities at around 14 per cent for land, 20 per cent for loans and 20 per cent for slaves. Land and slaves, however, required a period of amortisation of the purchase price after their acquisition, which always covered several years. Furthermore, loans were fairly limited, and only women used them as a main income, to make their dowry bear interest. But the social status that the different generations sought to maintain was threatened by each change if external profits failed to renew the family inheritance. This explains the massive participation by the notables in the affairs of the temples, as administrators, prebendaries or artisans in certain very specialised fields, or the role of intermediaries played by families like the Egibi or the Murašû in levying taxes or managing crown estates.

Another point to be stressed is that these families sailed fairly smoothly through the various historical episodes experienced by Babylonia from the seventh to the fifth century: the rebellion of Shamash-shum-ukin, the anti-Assyrian emancipation, the Persian conquest and the revolts early in the reign of Darius I do not appear to have affected their socio-economic position to any great extent. Despite the internal threats that weighed on it, these family groups managed to preserve their possessions and social status without too many apparent difficulties, until the start of Xerxes' reign, which marked the end of most private archives, although the precise cause of this rupture has not yet been determined.

The intermediaries

Several private archives illustrate the role played by certain individuals or families who managed the interests of important personages or were associated with the economic activities of the sanctuaries. The activities of these 'middlemen' between the great landowners and the sphere of production or trade were typical of Babylonia up to the Achaemenid empire. Quite a few people thus built up their fortune not by developing their own resources, for example by creating their own personal landed estates, but by taking charge of management which the official administration or the houses of the upper crust themselves were unable or unwilling to undertake. These intermediaries have sometimes been described as bankers, but rather they were businessmen, having a finger in a variety of pies. Some specialised in taking a hand in the agricultural production of the sanctuaries by means of leases to date or barley growers; others formed fruitful relations with the royal administration: for instance, Iddin-Marduk, a descendant of Nûr-Sîn, set up agreements with the officials in charge of farming the royal lands in the region south-west of Babylon by providing them with the means of transporting the harvested crops to Babylon, which allowed him exemption from paying the river taxes on transport carried out on his own account, and to increase the profits he derived from marketing the fruit and vegetable produce purchased from the rural farmers and brought to town.

The Egibi family

The best-known example is a group of descendants of the Egibi family, whose archives cover virtually the whole of the sixth century, across five generations. Probably originating from Borsippa, they developed their business in Babylon, first acting as businessmen for Neriglissar. They continued their activities in the service of Belshazzar and then Cambyses. Starting in Nabonidus' reign, they were thus clearly involved in the interests of what may be called the crown prince's house, and managed part of his estates and his interests in general. We see them form a kind of parallel administrative structure and, for example, look after the collection of certain taxes in the service of the official administration. At the same time, the profits they reaped from their business were invested in the purchase and farming of agricultural land in the immediate proximity of Babylon, and the management of several dozen slaves to whom they entrusted small craft enterprises.

The heirs of Itti-Marduk-balâṭu

The state of the family fortune is illustrated by an allocation among the heirs on the death of Itti-Marduk-balâṭu, the head of the family, in year 14 of the reign of Darius I: his three sons divided his assets according to the inheritance system then in force, which allocated to the eldest double the share of his brothers. The eldest, Marduk-nâṣir-apli, received six houses and an empty plot at Babylon, two houses and an empty plot at Borsippa, six minas of silver and at least forty-four slaves; his two brothers received jointly four houses at Babylon and two houses at Borsippa, as well as six minas of silver and fifty-one slaves. They had to pay Marduk-nâṣir-apli compensation of six minas of silver, because one of the houses at Borsippa was bigger than the average of those that had been divided between the three brothers. There still remained, in joint ownership of all three, all the farmland, flocks of sheep, donkeys, escaped slaves (of whom they thus had ownership in name if not in practice), a slave with his family and his shop, a house at Kish, and shares in a business association set up by their father with a man named Kalbaia. Provision was also made for Marduk-nâṭir-apli and Nergal-ušêzib to recoup the dowries of their respective wives, which had been incorporated into the patrimony managed by Itti-Marduk-balâṭu. Added to this patrimony must be parts which had previously been appropriated by Itti-Marduk-balâṭu to endow his daughters on their marriage: ten minas of silver, four slaves and furniture for the marriage of his daughter Amti-Nanaia; a palm-grove, three slaves and furniture for the marriage of his daughter Ina-Esagil-belit; ten minas of silver, five slaves and furniture for the marriage of his daughter Tašmetum-tabni. Itti-Marduk-balâṭu's own wife had brought him as dowry goods to the value of thirty-four minas of silver. This resulted in a total inheritance of sixty-six minas of silver, sixteen houses, two empty plots at Babylon, over 100 slaves, land, animals and pieces of furniture of indeterminate number.

ECONOMIC ACTIVITIES

Farming and livestock breeding

Factors of profitability

Babylonian agriculture relied on irrigation and two basic products: barley and dates. The two crops had their own specific features and created a rural landscape that was appropriate to them: fields, in strips, often ran alongside waterways; the palm-groves were situated on the banks of the irrigation channels or formed enclosed orchards just outside and also within the towns. A palm-grove's production was twofold, because in addition to a certain number of trees the shade they provided enabled often quite sizeable market-garden crops to be grown at their foot. Barley and dates were considered to have an equivalent value, and the ideal standard price was 1 *kurru* (around 180 litres) of dates or 1 *kurru* of barley for 1 shekel (8.33 g) of silver. In practice, the cultivation of barley required a heavier investment in material, draught animals and labour than dates, which were the affair of specialist arboriculturist-gardeners. Date-growing was therefore more profitable than barley-growing, and there was a distinct tendency among private landowners to transform their barley-growing lands into palm-groves as far as possible. Whoever the owners were (great organisations, notables or small rural landowners), the conditions for making a profit from farming relied on an actual equilibrium between the extent of the cultivable area, the existing irrigation system, potential workforce, animals and equipment that could be allocated to it, and the produce it supplied. A certain degree of tension therefore existed with regard to ownership of land in immediate proximity to the towns, which generally speaking was better irrigated and whose produce could be brought to town without too heavy a transport cost: the administration of the temples and urban landowners argued over the matter, and in the sixth century the royal authority had to intervene on several occasions to restore to the temples lands that had been misappropriated by private landowners. But there is no comparison between the estates included in private heritages, which were often very productive though of modest size, and the immense properties belonging to sanctuaries. In any case, there were important differences between the great organisations themselves; although for lack of documentation it is still virtually impossible to evaluate the production on crown lands, comparisons may be drawn between certain temples: that of Shamash at Sippar, for instance, had at its disposal an agricultural area one-eighth that of Ishtar's temple at Uruk (almost 2,000 hectares, as against 17,000). Moreover, the extent of the sanctuaries' landed estates did not mean that the sanctuaries were actually capable of using them totally. The greater the means required to work them, the more restricted was the profit realised. The land's productivity depended less on its acreage than on the resources in personnel and material that it was possible to allocate to it. Although the royal authority fixed standards of yield, the temples did not necessarily get the best out of their land, and when the sovereign, above all in Nabonidus' reign, sought to rationalise and optimise the management of the sanctuaries' farmlands, an appeal was made to private entrepreneurs with whom the temple shared the expenses of investment. Babylonia's agricultural wealth was undeniable, however, and the quantities produced, which we have been able to reconstruct thanks to the archives, appear to have been considerable overall.

Farming practices

The agricultural calendar remained the same as in the preceding periods, with autumn sowing, winter irrigation and a harvest in April–May. A close connection was established between the timetable of the Euphrates and the farming calendar: the harvest had to be finished before the river's spate at the end of spring, as it could submerge the fields. The rise in the water level then enabled the canals to be used as transport routes to bring the crops to the storage centres. Recultivating the land in the autumn was accompanied by soaking soil that had been burnt and hardened by summer heat, but relied closely on the availability of water at a time when the rivers were at low-water mark. It is obvious, therefore, that the distribution of irrigation water was crucial, and the government entrusted responsibility for it to officials called *gugallu*, who oversaw an equitable distribution so that neither overflow nor dearth occurred. Most of the cereal-growing land was worked by a system of leaving it fallow in alternate years, to offset the salinisation of the soil connected with an over-intensive practice of irrigation. Each year, it was the landowners' custom to make a blanket estimate of the crops (*imittu*), which enabled them to fix the sum to be paid by the farmers. The latter were notified of the total and conditions of payment by documents akin to IOUs. Farming the palm-groves was a different matter: they were entrusted to arboriculturist-gardeners, whose job was the artificial fertilisation and maintenance of the palm-trees, and cultivating the market-garden crops raised in the palm-groves. The arboriculturists also had to enclose the palm-grove and protect it from the incursions of animals. They were paid a fixed salary, and not a share of the crop. Farming the palm-groves was therefore less costly in labour than farming the cereal farms, but had to take into account that palm-trees did not achieve regular production until some ten years old, and old trees had to be replaced regularly by young plants.

Breeding livestock

Raising livestock was the country's other major activity: cattle to supply working animals, and chiefly sheep. Although each family had a few animals, the great religious organisations, which required an intensive consumption for purposes of worship, numbered their sheep in tens of thousands. Local

grazing was rarely adequate at that time, whether in unculti-
vated areas or land lying fallow, and a system of distant
pasturage was developed by sending flocks to Upper
Mesopotamia. Animals selected for religious use generally
spent a fattening period inside temple sheds, in the charge of
men called 'the shepherds of regular offerings' (*rê'î sattukki*),
while contracts and annual balance sheets were set up with
outside shepherds, often of Aramaean origin to judge by their
names. Managing these huge flocks gave rise to a special
administration, with a pyramidal hierarchy of responsibilities, and the composition of a great many management texts.

Commerce

Though many families lived almost self-sufficient lives, a
retail trade also existed that allowed direct sale of part of the
agricultural production. Furthermore, some private entrepreneurs set up trading companies in order to profit from
opportunities connected with Babylon's urban development.
But all that remained relatively local. No regional sort of
trade is discernible inside Babylonia itself, with the exception
of a few special cases. The large organisations provided for
their needs in another way: either by ownership of properties
in places that produced the goods they needed, or by sending
out caravans whose mission was to search for those necessary
goods abroad.

Private trading operations

The most directly identifiable structure is the trading
company formed by contracts *ana harrâni*, which combined
two or several people in a whole range of scenarios: contribution of capital could be made by one person or shared
among several investors, and trading operations could be
effected by an agent or by one of the backers. The scope of
these associations went well beyond the commercial framework in the strict sense; it was concerned just as much with

production activities as with financial or commercial operations. If their aim remains relatively indeterminate, it is the legal nature itself of these contracts that is in fact the essential. It was primarily a matter of setting out precisely the methods of investment and profit-sharing.

In the second half of the sixth century, Iddin-Marduk, of the Nûr-Sîn family of Babylon, built his fortune on the transport and marketing of farm produce: dates, barley and, chiefly, onions. He took the role of intermediary between the small producers on the banks of Borsippa's canal, which linked this town with the southern district of Babylon, and the capital's population, which tended to increase from the time of the rebuilding, expansion and embellishment of the town by Nebuchadnezzar II. This population growth went hand in hand with a stagnation, if not a decline, in areas given over to farming within the town itself and its immediate environs. As the small producers did not have sufficient personal resources at their disposal to be able to cope on their own with the transport and marketing of their produce, Iddin-Marduk, at first by means of partnership trading associations, then independently, profited from the situation to secure an outlet for the farmers and supply the capital's market. In this period we thus see the appearance of the prototype of a businessman who builds his wealth on the existence of a relatively large market for farm produce, which he is in a position to transport and deliver because he has a set-up (half transport, half workforce) quite beyond the reach of the small rural producers.

The sanctuaries' commercial operations

The commercial activities of the sanctuaries were of two kinds: on the one hand, marketing certain surpluses, especially those arising from farming and livestock breeding, and on the other, satisfying needs for rare or exotic goods that royal donations were not enough to cover. Precious metals seem to have been the most sought after by temples, both as a means of payment and as raw materials for the manufacture of precious objects and jewels used in the cult. We may therefore note transactions between the temple and real merchants, who had the title *tamkâru* and appear to have enjoyed a privileged status in having a hand in the marketing procedures of the temples or royal palace. Their field of activity was not confined to this official circle, however, but also extended into the domain of private transactions. At Uruk, these commercial agents received from Ishtar's temple a certain sum in precious metal and a list of products to be bought. They travelled as far as the Mediterranean to procure them and brought them back to Uruk. On final delivery, the accounts were audited in order, on the one hand, to match the initial outlay with the actual expenditure and, on the other, to check that the prices of the products or objects had not been exaggerated. Lastly, the merchants proffered a symbolic personal contribution to the deity in gratitude for the success of the venture. Alongside the sum intended for the temple purchases, the merchants had available a cash fund subject to interest placed at their disposal by the sanctuary, and could use it for their personal operations. This implies that the profit gained from a trading expedition to the west was well above the 20 per cent interest to be paid and the costs of transport, and explains that they were dealing with products that were generally rare.

MANAGEMENT OF THE LARGE ORGANISATIONS

Palace and temples

The real motive force of the Babylonian economy was not to be found in the mass of more or less dependent workers or in the urban notables, but in what are described as the 'great organisations', in other words, the royal palace and the sanctuaries. This duality had been characteristic of South Mesopotamia since the third millennium, and explains why royal power had a less strong hold over the country, contrary to the situation in Assyria, and also the longevity of the large urban centres that were the site of a major sanctuary.

A double structure

The king and the gods were owners of immense landed properties, which were run with the use of a considerable slave or dependent labour force and a powerful administration. The two structures were interdependent: in fact, the king was deemed to be the chief dispenser of the produce which the sanctuary was charged with converting into offerings to its deities. He could meet these needs either by direct deliveries or by allocating land or labour to the temples. The maintenance of the sacred buildings was also his responsibility, as is shown by the numerous restoration or rebuilding undertakings carried out by the neo-Babylonian kings. The control thus exercised by the sovereign over the sanctuaries' material resources is revealed as early as the neo-Assyrian period by the restitution of the temples' landed properties, some of whose farmlands had been seized by Aramaeans and Chaldaeans, but also by the local urban bourgeoisie. It is equally revealed, especially in Nabonidus' reign, by supervision of the temples' administrations themselves and the establishment of royal officials (*ša rêš šarri*) within their management structures, or even by resorting to private businesses to get the most out of the sanctuaries' farms. In return, the sanctuaries were required to put their workforce at their sovereign's disposal to carry out major public works, and they also paid him back a significant share of the food offerings, which were incorporated into palace circulation for the upkeep of the palace staff.

Administrative grades

The way in which neo-Babylonian temples were administered is relatively well known to us through the archives of Sippar and Uruk. With local variations, a few major common principles were obeyed: religious personnel were placed under the authority of the high priest (*ahu rabû*) and comprised the cult's officiants, who were the only ones authorised to enter the sacred area where the deity dwelt (*êrib bîti*). These members of the religious staff, as such, appear only rarely in the sanctuaries' administrative archives but, together with those in charge of the administration, composed the sacred college of the temple (*kiništu*). The summit of the temple administration was collegial, led by two who were accountable: the temple's chief steward (*šatammu* or *šangû*) and the chief delegate (*qîpu*), who are to be found in all the great sanctuaries. At Uruk, they were assisted by 'the scribe of the Eanna' (*ṭupšar Eanna*), who had supreme control over the college of temple scribes until Nabonidus' reign; from 555, the scribe of the Eanna was set aside from the higher administration and replaced by a direct representative of the king, 'the royal officer, head of the administration' (*ša rêš šarri bêl piqitti*), while another royal officer had particular responsibility for the management of the royal treasury in the temple (*ša rêš šarri ša ina muhhi quppi ša šarri*). At Sippar, scribes and royal officers were both present in the running of the Ebabbar of Shamash, but at a lower grade of the administrative hierarchy. The top administration had the task of managing the temple's possessions and personnel, its income and expenditure; it organised and supervised major works, agricultural and craft production, the purchase of items not available on the spot, and the sale of surpluses. The royal administrators who were present saw to it that the division of supplies carried out on the king's behalf was done in accordance with his best interests.

Subordinate to this top-level administration were those responsible for the temple's various sectors of activity: the heads of the two largest categories of prebendaries, the chief brewer (*šâpir sirašê*) and chief baker (*šâpir nuhatimmî*), those in charge of external stockbreeding (*rab bûli*) and of animals for fattening (*rê'î sattukki*), heads of the farming staff (*rab ikkari*), head of the oblate personnel (*rab širki*). Management of the outstanding amounts due to the temple was entrusted to an official in charge of debtors (*ša muhhi rehâni*), and that of people put to forced labour to the head of the prison (*rab bît kîli*). Local management of temple lands was partly the concern of those responsible for irrigation (*gugallu*), while entrepreneurs, sometimes drawn from the staff of the temple itself, shouldered responsibility for the working of the farm-lands (*ša muhhi sûti*), with the system that has been described as lease farming.

Specific systems

Craft activities

For the requirements of worship, but also for the upkeep of the sanctuary and its staff, a certain number of artisans prac-tised their trade in heart of the temple. They were bound to it by a special oath, an example of which was found in the archives of the Eanna: a text from year 4 of Cyrus' reign puts an obligation on artisans in woodwork (*nagâru*), jewellers (*kabsâru*) and goldsmiths (*kutimmu*) of the temple to carry out their work within the Eanna, and bans them from enter-ing the service of another sanctuary without the consent of the Eanna administrators for any work or repair on objects in silver, gold, bronze, precious metals or wood. As in the pacts of allegiance known as *adê* in the neo-Assyrian era, artisans also had to bring to the administration's attention any infrac-tion of this rule that might be committed by their colleagues and known to them. The trades represented cover a good part of the traditional handicrafts of that period, with a dis-tinction between the religious domain (jewels, cult objects, deities' robes) and that of the daily life of the sanctuary. It was the task of the temple's specialist artisans to 'finish' pur-chased products or materials, either from the sanctuary's own output (farm products and wool) or from goods acquired at Babylon or in the west. These products were stocked in the temple's stores and warehouses, and distributed to the artisans, when an 'outgoings' slip was drawn up showing the quantity handed over, the purpose of the work and the artisan's name. The artisan subsequently delivered the result of his labours, which necessitated the writing of a new accounting document. Lastly, the temple drew up a summary of its outgoings and returns for a period that could cover several years. In parallel, the administration kept an up-to-date list of materials supplied to its workers for large-scale operations, such as digging canals, land clearance and certain kinds of agricultural work.

Managing the agricultural domain

The temple used part of its agricultural estates in direct development of land; in other words it assigned them to farmers whose job was to get the best out of it and deliver almost the entire crop in the form of rent (*sûtu*). Such was the case of the *ikkaru* (labourers/farmers) on the cereal-crop land and the *nukurribu* (gardeners) in the palm-groves. The former were paid by subsistence rations during the work period; the latter received the traditional wage of palm-grove farmers, the *sissinnu*. The *ikkaru* belonged for the most part to the category of temple dependants, were placed under the administrative responsibility of a *rab ikkarî*, and were grouped in teams who were allocated a plough and draught animals – hence the term 'plough' (*epinnu*) used to designate the whole lot – under a foreman known as *rab epinni*. The temple also called on independent farmers, the *errêšu*, whose activities were far from being merely a complement to the farming of the sanctuary's lands. Indeed, at Sippar the *errêšu* were present on two-thirds of the total amount of arable land, the temple directly farming only one-third. If the Sippar temple limited direct farming of its estate to one-third of its area, it was because by so doing it achieved the most stable return between the cost of investment and the profit obtained. By granting the remainder to *errêšu*, the Ebabbar ensured an income of 50 per cent of their output, which was not much less than the net profit it realised on its own lands.

The system of leasing farms

Starting in the reign of Nabonidus, temples also established on their directly farmed estates a system known as lease farming. The basic idea was to give responsibility for cultivation to one man alone, providing him with land, animals, ploughs and the necessary workforce to farm. In return, he undertook to provide an overall rent of an amount fixed beforehand. This system relieved the temple administration of the material concerns of organising plantings and harvests, and also allowed the royal administration a right of inspection over the situation of temple lands, since the first general lease farmer of the Eanna of Uruk, for instance, had begun his career as an agent of the royal estate in the reigns of Amêl-Marduk and Neriglissar. The lease farmer alone was responsible for bringing land under cultivation, but the temple administration took a hand when it came to estimating harvests for the purposes of the *imittu*. One of the benefits of the leasing system used from the time of Nabonidus over the cereal-growing area being farmed directly was to allow the temple the advantage of an addition to its farming capital contributed by the lease farmer himself. There was moreover the simplification of management represented by the farmer's taking charge of the organisation and setting-up of crop cultivation on the estate he was leasing out. In fact, the system of lease farming was applied, at Sippar as at Uruk, initially for the production of dates, and in both towns the system was established in the wake of a royal initiative. The development seems to have been fairly similar: at Uruk, leasing of date farms was taken up by members of the temple staff; at Sippar, the system was abandoned in the reign of Cyrus, to come under the control of the *gugallu*, before reappearing early in the reign of Darius I.

DOCUMENT

The life of Babylonian notables: Lurindu's marriage

'Ahušunu, son of Nabû-mušêtiq-ṣêti, descendant of Nanâhu, spoke in these terms to Amti-Sutîti, daughter of Dâdiya, descendant of Ilî-bâni: "Give me Lurindu, your nubile daughter, daughter of Mušêzib-Bêl, descendant of Ea-ilûta-bâni, [so that] she may be my wife." Amti-Sutîti agreed to the request of Ahušunu and gave him her nubile daughter Lurindu in marriage.

Amti-Sutîti, in the joy of her heart, gave Ahušunu, together with Lurindu her daughter, two minae of white silver of standard quality, five kanehs of the south house – to be made up to the value of five kanehs – in the kanehs belonging to Amti-Sutîti, next door to the house of Rêmût-Bêl, son of Iddinaia, descendant of Ilu-šu-abu-šu, and the house of Iddinaia, son of Marduk-šâkin-šumi, descendant of Nûr-Papsukkal, it being understood that they will put no obstacle between the passage [of the one] or the passage [of the other]; Amti-Sutîti will receive the rent for the shop; a willow-wood bed, a chest in *musukkannu*-wood with a gazelle's-head front, a *musukkannu*-wood lamp, two bronze goblets, a *baṭu*-pot in bronze, two outer garments, two dresses in tufted wool, four over-blouses, a table, three willow-wood chairs.

Each has taken a copy [of the contract].

[Present] at the sealing of this deed were: Nidintu-Bêl, son of Bêl-ahhê-iddin, descendant of Bêl-êṭeru; Itti-Nabû-balâṭu, son of Rêmût, descendant of the Boatman; Nabû-ahhê-iddin, son of Nabû-šum-ibni, descendant of Nanâhu; Ardiya, son of Bulṭaia, descendant of Nabû-šême; Bêl-apla-iddin, son of Kudur-rânu, descendant of Ilî-bâni. Scribe: Nabû-šum-uṣur, son of Ardi-Gula, descendant of Ir'ani. Borsippa, the 7th Tebêtu of year 28 of Darius I, king of Babylon and the Lands (493 BC). The deed sealed on the 26th Arahšamnu of year 28 of Darius I, king of Babylon and the Lands, is annulled.'

This marriage contract is characteristic of the documents relating to Babylonian family law; some fifty texts of this type are known. It comes from the private archives of a family of notables of Borsippa, descendants of Ea-ilûta-bâni, and supplies biographical information on the principal female representative of the last known generation, a girl named Lurindu. This document belongs to the category of 'verbal agreements', in which one of the parties addresses a request to the other. This type of contract was not reserved for marriages alone, as it is also to be found in cases of leasing land, for example. The party solicited agrees to the petitioner's request, repeating its exact terms. It is generally specified that each is acting of his or her own free will (literally: 'in the joy of his heart').

The marriage proposal

If, in the case of a marriage contract, the fundamental aim is to determine precisely the financial and material transfers to be made between the two families, the text also includes the solemn aspect of the 'marriage proposal' and emphasises the importance still retained by 'word of mouth' in legal relations of that period. The spoken words are the equivalent of commitment, and it is noticeable that it is not the young girl, Lurindu, who agrees to the offer, but the one in authority over her – in this instance, her mother. Normally, the father or older brother would accept the proposal, but this situation is rather special because Lurindu's mother is a widow and does not have a son old enough to assume the role of head of the family. There are certain very rare cases attested where a woman arranges her own marriage, but these belong to a particular situation in which legal authority has been transferred to the future wife herself: it concerns widows, who have already left their original family background by virtue of a first marriage. Being no longer subject to the legal authority of their natural parents, then of their first husband, these women were allowed to dispose of their rights themselves. Besides, the text makes no mention of the emotional ties between the future husband and wife; the only precise fact concerning Lurindu is that she is nubile (*nu'artu*), in other words old enough to bear children, which determines the legal marriageable age. It is possible that a real inclination existed between them, and may have influenced their choice, but that does not enter the formal framework of the marriage contract, which is concerned first and foremost with the transfer of legal authority over the girl, and the transfer of the assets that accompany her.

The dowry

The second part of the text relates to the dowry (*nidittu*) which the mother, Amti-Sutîti, provides for her daughter. Legally, the dowry is part of the inheritance that the girl receives from her parents. Fixing its amount is left to the assessment of the head of the family and, although it is always present, it is often far from really corresponding to an effective share of the family patrimony. The concern to preserve the latter had the effect of favouring not only the eldest

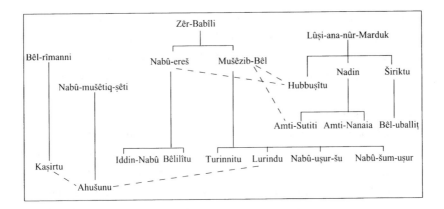

brother, but also brothers as compared with sisters. The complex history of Lurindu's family shows, too, that she receives by way of dowry only possessions that come from her mother. Her father's have been kept in favour of the male members of the family.

Money and real estate

As often occurred in the families of notables, the dowry comprised money, landed property and furniture. The sum of money (two minae, or 1 kg of silver) was not negligible since, by a contract drawn up the following year between the couple, it allowed Lurindu to acquire two slaves from her husband. The property is the main body of a building within a house, though it is not the whole building that is granted to Lurindu, but a surface area of 5 kanehs (about 45 m²) in a property belonging to her mother. The remainder continues to belong to the latter, and the contract provides for an amicable determination of rights of access and circulation between the different parts of the buildings: 'they will put no obstacle between the passage [of the one] or the passage [of the other]'. Similarly, Amti-Sutîti will continue to receive the income from renting a shop (*bît kâri*) included in this building, probably rented out for artisans' or traders' use. In total, this gift appears to be not very practical or valuable.

Furniture and clothing

The furniture includes drinking vessels (goblets and a pot in bronze), furniture for having meals (a table – that is, a tray with its support – and chairs) and a 'bedroom suite' (bed, chest and lamp). This is high-quality furniture, with ornamentation (mention of a gazelle's head) and made of cabinet-maker's wood. In addition, there is the young bride's personal wardrobe, including two high-quality garments in tufted wool. The dowry thus comprises some valuable pieces and others that have little interest: Amti-Sutîti seems to have collected everything for which she had no essential use to make up her daughter's dowry.

The witnesses and the date

The third and last part of the document is customary, too: it is stated that two copies of the deed have been made (one for each spouse) in the presence of witnesses, who are listed. This presence is obligatory if the contract is to be fully valid. In Mesopotamia, even though since Hammurabi (eighteenth century BC) the law stated that a marriage must be the subject of a written contract, legal practice had always given a higher value to oral proof, based on witnesses, than to written proof alone, which was liable to falsification and required a knowledge of writing to enable it to be checked properly. A number of witnesses (here, five) and their worthiness (they all have a nameable ancestor, thus belong to the urban notability) were deemed to prevent any sort of manipulation.

A rider

The marriage contract makes it clear that an initial arrangement made a month and a half earlier is null and void, and that the document has been destroyed. Generally speaking, the need to draw up a second contract resulted from alterations in the material arrangements: the dowry has been either increased or decreased before the definitive agreement was concluded. The transfer of possessions was in fact always effected after the marriage contract had been drawn up, and the time lapse could be of several months. If the transfer was contested, the parties were brought together to negotiate according to new terms, as in this case, or to take the matter to law should disagreement persist.

As well as being a good example of a legal deed, this text is an important element in the archives of the Ea-ilûta-bâni family and the families who are connected to it. It includes certain special features that are explained by the personal history of the family members present here.

The husband's interest

The husband, Ahušunu, descendant of Nanâhu, has a large patrimony. At this time, he is a childless widower and has for some years looked after the running of his farm estates, fields and palm-groves situated between Babylon and

Borsippa, at the same time carrying on financial business, lending and borrowing money in fairly large amounts. The contract of his first marriage, which has been preserved, shows that ten years earlier he had married the daughter of a noble family, Kaşirtu, daughter of Bêl-rîmanni, descendant of Ahhêa, whose dowry had been far larger than the one provided for Lurindu. So Ahušunu's interest in his second marriage is not for material gain: the young girl he is marrying is provided with a mediocre dowry according to the criteria of the time, but she is of an age to produce children and can ensure that he will have descendants, above all male ones, which he needs. From his point of view, the reproductive function of the marriage is the bottom line.

The bride's interest

On the other side, the terms are reversed: Lurindu is making what could be termed 'a good marriage', with a manifestly well-off notable, but one who is a widower and probably much older than she. But she has no other choice: her father, Mušêzib-Bêl, is dead and she has two younger brothers. Moreover, all three are the issue of a remarriage by Mušêzib-Bêl with Amti-Sutîti, the niece of his first wife. By marrying Ahušunu, Lurindu is making sure of her material situation, but with a dowry that does not match the true level of her own family's wealth.

The family interest

From his first marriage, Mušêzib-Bêl had had only one daughter, who had married before his death. This first marriage had been quite special in itself, since Mušêzib-Bêl had wed his eldest brother's widow, who was already the mother of a boy named Iddin-Nabû. On Mušêzib-Bêl's death, the function of head of the family, with its accompanying rights of managing the inheritance, passed to his nephew Iddin-Nabû, the son of his brother and the woman who had later become his first wife. Although this close family interweaving, so typical of the families of neo-Babylonian urban notables, may be explained by the permanent concern to restrict the number of those 'outsiders' who were eligible for the patrimony, it resulted in situations of remarkable complexity; actually, children had unequal access to an inheritance: to the inequality between sons and daughters was added that between children of a first and second marriage. Lurindu was a child of her father's remarriage, certainly the eldest – but a girl. She therefore came only in fourth place in rights to the family inheritance, after her cousin Iddin-Nabû and her two brothers, sons of

Mušêzib-Bêl and Amti-Sutîti, receiving merely an average sort of dowry, taken from her mother's personal possessions. From the family's point of view, the contract offered the great benefit of reducing to a minimum the transfer of part of the patrimony to an outside member, not a descendant of the Ea-ilûta-bâni family branch.

DOCUMENT

Land management: leasing contract

'Šum-ukîn, son of Bêl-zêri, descendant of Bâsiya, and Kalbaia, son of Iqîšaia, have addressed a petition to Nabonidus, king of Babylon, the king their lord, in these terms: "May the king our lord grant us 6,000 *kurru* of arable land, excluding the palm-grove, 400 labourers, 400 oxen and 100 cows to replace losses among the 400 oxen and, each year, we will deliver to the lady of Uruk 25,000 *kurru* of barley in full and 10,000 *kurru* of dates in full on the canal banks."

Nabonidus, king of Babylon, the king their lord, has granted their petition: he has given to Šum-ukîn, son of Bêl-zêri, descendant of Basiya, and Kalbaia, son of Iqîšaia, 6,000 *kurru* of arable land, including the fallow areas that let half the land rest each year, 400 labourers, 400 oxen and 100 cows to replace losses among the 400 oxen. The oxen and cattle must not disappear; as many calves as shall be born shall be shown to the king's administrators and shall be branded with the mark of the lady of Uruk, and shall then be returned to Šum-ukîn and Kalbaia. Broken ploughs must be repaired.

Each year, Šum-ukîn and Kalbaia must deliver to the lady of Uruk 25,000 *kurru* of barley in full and 10,000 *kurru* of dates in full, that is, 35,000 *kurru* of barley and dates, on the canal banks, in accordance with the *mašihu*-measure of the lady of Uruk. In the first year, the Eanna will supply them with 3,000 *kurru* of barley for sowing and 10 talents of iron. As for the lands of the Hallat Garden of the lady of Uruk, which are at the disposal of the *rab banî* gardeners, Šum-ukîn and Kalbaia will not apply an inclusive estimate to them and will have no right over them. Šum-ukîn and Kalbaia are joint guarantors for everything they undertake.

In the presence of Terik-šarussu, governor; Nabû-šulum-šarri, commander of the guard; Nabû-enatanu, governor of the province of the Bît-Ada; Nabû-dîni-epuš, chancellor; Mušêzib-Bêl, general; Bît-ili-dala', head of the troops; Nabû-bêlšunu, son of Šamaš-erîba; Marduk-mušallim, son of Zêriya; Marduk-šum-iddin, governor of Uruk; Nabû-šar-uṣur, royal administrator. Scribe: Aplaia, son of Bêl-iddin, descendant of Egibi. Larsa, the 28th Nisan, year 1 of Nabonidus, king of Babylon.'

This document, drawn up in the spring of 555, is a leasing contract between two individuals, Šum-ukîn, son of Bêl-zêri, and his nephew Kalbaia, son of Iqîšaia, and the Eanna, temple of the goddess Ishtar, here referred to as the lady of Uruk. In fact, it is the king Nabonidus, who was on a tour of inspection in the south of Babylonia at that time, who replaces the temple authorities to grant the petition presented by the two lease farmers.

While resuming the formal outline of the verbal contract and the clauses of individual leasing agreements, this text is of a special kind because it sets up the first leasing arrangement on the Eanna's cereal-growing land.

What the two lease farmers want

Šum-ukîn and Kalbaia, who are already responsible at this time for managing the Eanna's palm-groves, present a petition to the king which would put at their disposal a very large area of cereal-growing lands (6,000 *kurru*, or about 9,000 hectares) and the necessary equipment to cultivate them. This is not the whole of the temple of Ishtar's agricultural domain, which, as far as can be reconstructed, covered at least 17,000 hectares; but the concession represents over half of it, and comprises medium-quality land. The remainder is farmed directly by the Eanna's administration, as regards the better-quality land, or has been let out to other individual farmers.

The portion allotted to Šum-ukîn and Kalbaia will be farmed with a fallow period every other year: in fact, a surface area of only 3,000 *kurru* (4,500 hectares) will therefore be sown each year. In order to go ahead with cultivation, the two farmers obtain 100 'ploughs' from the temple, that is, working units composed of one iron ploughshare, four draught animals and one 'spare', and a team of four labourers. The temple is pledged to supply the seed in the first year: 1 *kurru* of barley (or 180 litres) for 1 *kurru* (1.5 hectares) of cultivated land, and enough iron for the blade of each plough, namely, 3 kg per plough. In subsequent years, these allocations will be up to the lease farmers, who will have to finance them out of their profits.

Calculating yield and results

The two farmers pledge to pay an annual overall rent of 25,000 *kurru* of barley (45,000 hectolitres) for working with 100 ploughs 3,000 *kurru* of land, the remainder being left fallow. In other terms, each of the ploughs is deemed to cultivate a unit area of 30 *kurru* (45 hectares) and extract from it a rent of 250 *kurru* of barley (450 hectolitres), or a ratio of 8.33:1. This is of course not the actual yield of the land, but only the part paid as rent. In the same way, a ruling decreed seven years later in the name of Nabonidus' son, Belshazzar, lays down that lease farmers of the temple of Marduk at Babylon, the Esagil, owe a rent corresponding to a ratio of 10:1 in relation to the land cultivated, and the true yield is calculated at 20:1. Applied to Uruk, this system implies a yield on the land granted by the Eanna of 16.6:1, which is not very high for the region and the period.

Other obligations

To this payment in cereals is added a rent in dates, provided by the palm-groves already conceded to Šum-ukîn and Kalbaia by virtue of an earlier contract that has not been preserved. This rent amounts to 10,000 *kurru,* or 18,000 hecto-litres. The contract also makes provision that the farmers will look after the livestock entrusted to them for farm work: at their own expense they will have to replace losses in animals, and have increase (by breeding) checked by the temple administration, who will brand the calves and return them until they are weaned.

Šum-ukîn and Kalbaia will also take charge of collecting the harvest and sup-plying their dues on the canal banks: the barley and dates are then recorded using the temple's official measure, the *mašihu*, a basket of 30 litres' capacity, before being transported on the Eanna's barges to its warehouses. The conces-sion excludes the land known as the Hallat Garden, situated in the neighbour-hood of the rural temple of the goddess Ishtar, which is used for the festivals of the *Akîtu* (see p. 184). This estate is cultivated by the temple prebendaries, the *rab bânî*, in individual plots, and remains under the thumb of the sanctuary's administration.

Prestigious witnesses

Like every contract, this one has a list of witnesses; but in this instance they are not mere notables – we are talking about high-ranking court dignitaries and royal regional governors. The only administrative representative of the temple is the last-named, Nabû-šar-uṣur, and he is the king's delegate placed at the head of the temple administration. The date (28th Nisan of year 1 = 27 April 555) shows that it was the end of the agricultural cycle, just before the harvests, and it was the next cultivation period that was at issue.

The sovereign's intervention for a planned economy

The journey undertaken by Nabonidus in the south of his kingdom was with the intention of making offerings at the great sanctuaries in this region and at the same time checking up on their situation. It found expression in the restoration of the temple of Shamash at Larsa, and that of Sîn at Ur, then by the appointment of the king's daughter as this god's high priestess. But the journey also included a certain amount of inspection of the ways in which these sanctuaries were run. For the Eanna of Uruk, this led to a reorganisation of the temple administration and the introduction of a new system of managing the landed property. The king had considered that the Eanna was not getting the best out of its immense agricultural estates, and he compelled it to place a proportion of it under the responsibility of private entrepreneurs, one of whom, Šum-ukîn, had spent part of his career in the royal administration.

The Eanna remained owner of its land and farming equipment, but had to put them at the disposal of the two leasing farmers named by the king by means of this contract. So here we have an interesting combination of the economic practices of the large organisations and the initiatives of private businessmen associated with the sovereign's entourage.

The issues of lease farming

Several clauses in the contract reveal that the lands granted by the temple were of average quality: they could be cultivated only in alternate years, whereas good farmland could support an annual crop. Heavy equipment was needed, with iron-bladed ploughs and a team of four oxen to pull them; the expected yield (16.66:1 for the harvest, half for the rent) was not very high. Proposed estimates for the same region in the third millennium BC, at the apogee of the land of Sumer, had been of the order of 40 or 50:1. Although, in the middle of the sixth century BC, the south of Babylonia was beginning to emerge from a long period of devastation and wars against the Assyrian presence, the meagre yield was not so much to do with poor-quality soil as with a scarcity of people and animals. On its best lands, the Eanna received far higher returns; but the temple did not have an adequate human and animal workforce available to farm the whole of its estates intensively, and had to content itself with mediocre yields from medium-quality land.

The lease farming system gave the Eanna two advantages: on the one hand, its administration was relieved of direct farming activities, and intervened only in order to make an overall estimate of the harvests and take care of the payment of the dues; on the other, it was assured of a minimum annual payment, to which the two lease farmers had committed themselves.

From the standpoint of Šum-ukîn and Kalbaia, the interest was different: provided they invested their own capital to complement what was provided by the temple, they could intensify the cultivation and had available a certain margin for increasing the yield of the land rented to them. With the principle of a fixed rent, they were sure of being able to keep for themselves the profits of any increase in the quantity of barley obtained on their land.

The royal intervention thus aimed at revitalising farming practices on the temple's lands, resorting to private interests to contribute the investment that was essential to an intensification of farming. We therefore perceive in Nabonidus a genuine concern for developing the management of the great religious organisations, but by means of resorting to the circle of private businessmen.

How the system evolved

The contract made by Šum-ukîn and Kalbaia with the Eanna was found, in triplicate, in the temple archives; it had therefore served as a reference and standard for drawing up other subsequent leasing contracts. The system is also attested on the estates of the god Shamash at Sippar and those of Marduk at Babylon. After a period of success and expansion, the system ran up against some problems of imbalance: at Uruk, Šum-ukîn and Kalbaia were unable to fulfil their annual obligations, a probable indication that their own investment capabilities were inadequate. On their side, the sanctuaries tried to claw back rather quickly the management of estates whose yields became more interesting and, while maintaining the principle of leasing over certain parts, entrusted their functioning to members of their own staff. After a pronounced eclipse early in Cyrus' reign, the leasing system experienced a second upsurge under Cambyses, before finally disappearing under Darius I.

Chapter 7

Religion and culture in Babylonia in the first millennium BC

The Babylonian pantheon, which was fundamentally polytheistic, combined elements inherited from a long tradition and was characterised by the primacy of Marduk, the god of Babylon. In the second part of the first millennium, however, this primacy appears less clear cut, when local traditions seem to have emerged afresh, for instance the worship of the god Anu at Uruk. The divine presence manifested itself in various ways, in astral and symbolic form, but above all in the religious statues, whose material upkeep was scrupulously attended to by the Babylonian clergy.

Each deity resided in a sanctuary that was considered to be his or her principal dwelling place, and its organisation more or less reproduced that of the royal palace. The clergy comprised officiants, the *êrib bîti*, who formed a sacred college placed under the authority of the high priest. They were assisted by specialists who took part in the liturgy or in the preparation and presentation of the food offerings. The Babylonian clergy as a whole formed a closed circle, and the people's participation in worship was expressed only when certain ceremonies were held, such as the festivals of the *Akîtu*, peculiar to each holy town.

Several levels of the practice of cuneiform writing co-existed in Babylonia. After a long period of training, certain scribes attained the status of man of letters, which implied a knowledge of a multiform science in which culture and religion were closely interwoven. The systematic copying of canonical works provided an impressive corpus of learned, divinatory and religious literature, though it did not escape a certain formalism.

THE PANTHEON AND RELIGIOUS CONCEPTS

The organisation of the pantheon

A complicated ensemble

In the neo-Babylonian era the pantheon was characterised by the supremacy of the god Marduk of Babylon, also known as Bêl, 'the Lord'. The fact that Babylon's political and religious primacy coincided was obviously not fortuitous, but emerged from the prolongation of a development which had begun in the course of the second millennium. This did not prevent the eminent role of the other deities from being maintained in their traditional towns, or the continuation of the Sumero-Akkadian stratum of the pantheon, in which supreme power over the other gods was deemed to be exerted by the triad Anu, Enlil and Ea. Equally noteworthy is the important place occupied by the deities associated with a natural entity: Shamash (Sun), Sîn (Moon), Adad (Storm), and the rank held by Ishtar as the major female figure in the Babylonian pantheon. Her main sanctuary was at Uruk, where she was worshipped under the name of 'the Urukean lady' (*Aška'itu*) or the 'lady of Uruk', associated with the goddess Nanaia, but other forms are equally well attested at Babylon, Agade, Sippar, Kish and Nippur. It is noticeable, however, that the goddess Gula, patron of medicine, seems to have avoided this syncretist movement in favour of Ishtar. But the Babylonian pantheon cannot be reduced to these major figures of gods and goddesses, sovereigns of the large urban centres that became holy towns; on the contrary, the vitality of tradition and the stoutly maintained concern of the well-read and religious milieu to adhere to it made the complete pantheon, as it is illustrated by the lexical list in Sumerian and Akkadian called 'An' = *Anum*, seem like a profusion of deities, some of whom harked back to extremely ancient times.

Relations between the deities

Each of the great gods was usually provided with a consort, who served as mediator between humans and the god, and with a 'vizier' (*sukkallu*), who also served as a relay point with the terrestrial world. Divine families were created, without in any way resulting in a completely hierarchised system that would have called into question some of the aspects inherited from tradition. One of the manifestations of the close relationship between certain gods was the expression of their name by a numerical system, handed down from the second millennium and frequently used in the writing of names. Onomastics partly reproduced the local nature of the deities: names formed with Shamash and Aia were most frequent at Sippar and Larsa, those with Ishtar and Nanaia, then Anu, at Uruk, those with Sîn at Ur and those with Enlil at Nippur. Marduk's national quality made his name widely used beyond the town of Babylon itself, in the form of Marduk or Bêl. Similarly, the use of the name Nabû was far from restricted to his town, Borsippa, but is confirmed as the most frequently used divine name in the whole of Babylonian onomastics. This was a particular phenomenon which reveals the increasingly important role played by the god who, theologically, was Marduk's son. The special part he played at the time of the New Year celebrations at Babylon show that devotion to Nabû was very widespread among the populace, and that popular piety did not necessarily favour the same gods as those enthroned at the summit of the official pantheon.

The divine presence

Although the conception of the major gods was often anthropomorphic, expressed by the presence of religious statues in human form in the sanctuaries, and by the very real material upkeep that was ensured for them, they none the less assumed many other guises. Their figured representation often made them appear in a symbolic form that was still very much in evidence in the Babylonia of the early first millennium, on inscribed stelae known as *kudurru*, and later chiefly illustrated on cylinder-seals. The ancient great Sumerian gods, Anu, Enlil and Ea, are represented by horned tiaras, Marduk by a spade, Nabû by a scribe's stylus. Some of the symbols also refer to the other major form of incarnation of the Babylonian gods – their astral form. So Shamash has the solar disc as his symbol, Sîn the lunar crescent and Ishtar the planet Venus, in the form of an eight-pointed star inscribed in a circle. The presence of the gods of the pantheon in celestial form therefore involved some religious practices that were addressed directly to the night stars; here again was a development of an ancient tradition, but one which gained its full strength with the emergence of astronomy and astrology as a means of knowing the divine world and its manifestations.

The principal Babylonian gods in the seventh and sixth centuries and their associated features

Deity	Consort	Number, symbol and associated animal	Main temple and town
Adad	Šala	Lightning, bull	
Anu	Antu	60, horned tiara	Bît Rês (Uruk)
Ea	Damkina	40, horned tiara, sceptre with ram's head, goat-fish	
Enlil	Mullissu	50, horned tiara	Ekur (Nippur)
Ishtar		15, star, lion	Eanna (Uruk
Marduk	Zarpanitu	10, spade, dragon	Esagil (Babylon)
Nabû	Tašmetu	Stylus, dragon	Ezida (Borsippa)
Nergal	Ereškigal	Sceptre with lion's head	Emeslam (Kuta)

Sîn	Nikkal	30, lunar crescent	Ekišnugal (Ur)
Shamash	Aia	20, solar disc	Ebabbar (Sippar, Larsa)
Uraš	Ninegal		Eimbianu (Dilbat)
Zababa	Ishtar of Kish	Sceptre with eagle	Ekišibba (Kish)

Evolutions

Marduk's rivals

Marduk's primacy was not, however, as absolute as the official discourse of religious texts would have us believe. We note first that, during the seventh century in Assyria, a section of the religious circles had attempted to substitute the figure of Ashur for that of Marduk in certain of his royal aspects. At the same time, in Babylonia, the old rivalry between the god Enlil of Nippur, who embodied royalty in the Sumero-Akkadian pantheon, and Marduk, king-god of Babylon, had not completely vanished and could have been one of the causes of the lack of interest from which the old Sumerian city seems to have suffered on the part of the neo-Babylonian kings. Nor can Nabonidus' attempt to promote the god Sîn as the pre-eminent deity be ignored, even if it lasted only a few years. Although it had been started by royal authority itself, it had run up against definite resistance by the clergy. Once Babylonia had been incorporated into the Achaemenid empire, the less important position held thereafter by Babylon and its god seems to have provoked a resurgence of local traditions, especially in the south of the country. This occurrence may explain the re-emergence of the worship of Anu at Uruk from the end of the fifth century, as a kind of return to the sources of the ancient land of Sumer. These various trends, however, did not result in Marduk's primacy being challenged in the region of Babylon itself, as it is well documented throughout the second half of the first millennium, but in their way they bear witness to the strength of local traditions and Babylonia's age-old resistance to any form of over-exaggerated centralisation.

Relations with the outside world

The introduction of deities of non-Babylonian origin was entirely marginal: although it is probable that foreign communities who were settled in the country, voluntarily or compulsorily, preserved their religious system, by no means did it spread. There is mention of a 'Sutean' goddess (*Sutîtu*) in the Borsippa region, and an Aramaean Ishtar (*Ahlamîtu*); rare identifications seem to have been established between the western and Babylonian gods: for instance, the same ideogram represents the god Enlil and the god Amurru, of western origin. Similarly, the Aramaean lunar god Se' could be likened to the Sîn of Babylonia. It is equally probable that the term Bêl attached to Marduk corresponds to the various Ba'als of the Mediterranean west. But these syncretist occurrences cannot be reduced to the neo-Babylonian period alone, and – except apparently during Nabonidus' reign – never resulted in a major alteration of the Babylonian pantheon and organisation of religion. It is symptomatic to note that even in the period when Babylonia was most closely connected with external centres of power, no great sanctuary to a 'foreign' god was built in Babylonia's great traditional urban centres. Not until some time around the dawn of Christianity did things begin to evolve, for example with the building of a temple dedicated to the god Gareus at Uruk, the introduction of new cults into Babylonian sanctuaries (for instance, apparently, the Ebabbar at Larsa), even the complete deconsecration of some religious edifices that were transformed by the local Arsacid authorities into military installations (like the ziggurat at Uruk) or official residences (like the Ekur at Nippur). Conversely, certain Babylonian deities seem to have spread well beyond the geographical limits of Babylonia at the end of the first millennium, as evidenced by the expansion of the cult of Nanaia as far as eastern Iran, or the building of a temple to Nabû at Palmyra.

HOW RELIGION WAS ORGANISED

The temple, residence of the deity

The largest temples were complex structures, combining with the deity's residence many chapels dedicated to the secondary gods and goddesses who formed the divine court, and also external secondary sanctuaries, in the holy town or even in neighbouring townships. Although there was a single management body, worship strictly speaking appears to have been remarkable for the diversity of its sites.

The divine apartments

The statue of the god (or sometimes the symbol) was placed in a room entirely devoted to it (*papâhu*). When it was enthroned as an object of worship, special ceremonies took place, called 'washing the mouth' (*mîs pî*) and 'opening the mouth' (*pît pî*), which enabled the divine spirit to enter its representation and transform it into a sacred object. The deity sat on a throne, itself placed on a kind of pedestal, the *parakku*. Several times a day, the officiants of the cult came to address prayers to him or her and present offerings in the form of a meal. Rituals of the Seleucid era show that cloth screens were arranged around tables while the statue consumed these offerings. At times of ceremonies, the statue was taken out of its *papâhu* and joined other statues of resident deities of the temple to form the divine assembly (*ubšukkinakku*) in the main courtyard, or was taken to places connected with particular rituals: a chamber for the rites of the sacred marriage, the temple garden on other occasions. The statue might even be persuaded to leave its sanctuary in order to take part in processions in the town or go to the external temple of the Akîtu, or even a more distant destination. At the festival of the New

Year, the statues of the principal Babylonian deities thus proceeded to Babylon, to assist the king of the gods, Marduk, at the ceremonies. These journeys were effected by chariot, but also often by boat, both richly decorated and kept for the exclusive use of the divine statue. A ritual of Babylon shows the movements of the statues of Marduk, Zarpanitu and Ishtar of Babylon through the whole town, following a meticulously regulated route. These were the rare occasions when the populace had contact with the religious representations of their gods; the rest of the time, the statues were inaccessible, remaining in the holy part of the temple, access to which was authorised to the sacred personnel, the *êrib bîti*. The *papâhu* of several great gods was often preceded by an antechamber where a secondary god was enthroned, acting as guardian: for instance, in the Esagil, access to Marduk's *papâhu* was under the command of a divine spirit called the *Karibu*, prototype of the biblical Cherubim.

Food for the gods?

The bulk of the deities' upkeep in the temples was food. Every day throughout the entire year they were served four meals, divided into a main (*naptânu rabû*) and secondary meal (*naptânu tardênu*) in the morning, and a main and secondary meal in the evening. These formed what were called the regular food offerings (*sattukku* or *ginû*). In addition, there were meals on feast days (*guqqu* and *sellu*), whose periodicity was linked to the liturgical calendar peculiar to each sanctuary, and a host of special ceremonies: nocturnal, purification of the temple, opening of the gates, ceremony of incense-burning, of the stoves, of the sacred marriage, etc. On each of these occasions veritable feasts were presented before the deified statues or symbols, including bread and pastries, mutton, beef and poultry, and various alcoholic drinks, mirroring the menus of royal banquets and consumed by the deity in symbolic fashion. Some food offerings were made directly to the astral forms of the gods. Everything was subsequently redistributed among a certain number of beneficiaries, in a highly regulated way and in proportion to their rank in the religious hierarchy. The foremost and most important of the beneficiaries was at the same time the principal dispenser of the offerings, in other words, the king. Consumption of the remainder of the divine meals was in fact a royal prerogative, and even during Nabonidus' stay at Temâ, journeys were made from Uruk to Arabia to bring him certain items from these meals. The rest was divided among the *êrib bîti* and some prebendaries, and was both an honorific privilege and a source of income.

Regulations for the division of a sheep offering in the temple of Ishtar of Uruk in the seventh century

From the regular daily offering of one sheep to Ishtar of Uruk and Nanaia:

- a shoulder, the tail and a side of ribs: the king's ration
- the heart, a kidney, the 'crucible', the choice of a shoulder: the high priest
- a shoulder, a side of ribs, the breast, the *harmil*: the *êrib bîti*
- a choice of shoulder, a kidney, the spleen: the *êrib bîti*
- a leg – this is the gift made by Nabû-apla-iddin, king of Babylon, to Nabû-kuzbi-ilî, son of Nabû-mukîn-zêri, the conjurer – and the hindquarters: the king
- half a leg: the *šatammu*
- half a leg: the *êrib bîti*
- the 'penis'(?): those in charge of the offerings tables
- the 'gate': the priest of the sacred chariot

The neo-Babylonian empire's wealth enabled rulers to dispense an enormous amount of food to the gods of Babylonia, to a degree rarely attained until then. In the reign of Nebuchadnezzar II, the goddess Ishtar of Uruk thus received in a single day, in the form of bread, semolina or pastries, 360 litres of barley and 66 of wheat, or virtually the equivalent of the basic food ration for 100 people.

Garments and jewels

The deities' statues were adorned with jewels of both ornamental and magical value. Each principal goddess of the Eanna of Uruk owned finery comprising several necklaces, bracelets and rings, the composition of which is known to us piece by piece; these items were regularly cleaned and repaired, and an exact inventory of them was kept up to date. Precious dishes and vessels were also available for the requirements of the cult, and these were stored in a special room. Ishtar's temple possessed a service of 99 pieces of silver and gold ware.

The subject of the gods' clothing is also richly represented in the temples' economic documentation, and enables us to reconstruct in precise detail the wardrobe attributed to each deity. For instance, the statue of Shamash at Sippar was clad in a linen tunic held by a belt, over which a veil of fine wool was arranged, together with some embroidered scarves. All the fabrics were finished with dyes, enhanced with braids and embroideries in precious metal, as well as ornaments in gold and silver sewn or appliquéd on the fabric. The statues of the goddesses were arrayed like those of the gods; they had more elaborate headgear, however, made up of a composite headdress in which both jewels and pieces of material were included.

The ceremony of the Akîtu

The sanctuary's most important ceremony was that of the *Akîtu*. Every great deity had his or her own festival of *Akîtu*, marked by the cult statue's emergence from the temple, then from the town, and its sojourn in an external temple situated in the countryside. At the end of this period of absence, during which the urban temple and the town were the subject of a purification, the divine statue returned to its urban residence in a solemn procession. The most famous *Akîtu* festival was that of Babylon, because at the spring equinox it combined several festivals in one single ceremony, lasting ten days: Marduk's own *Akîtu*, but also that of his son Nabû, god of Borsippa, and chiefly the celebration of the Babylonian New Year, which began at that time.

For this major festival, the statues of Babylonia's chief deities converged on the capital; they accompanied Marduk during his 'retreat' in his country temple of the *Akîtu*, and took part in his solemn re-enthronement as king of the gods, a ceremony during which the *Epic of the Creation* was recited, and perhaps mimed, recounting how Marduk attained the supreme rank. Meanwhile, the Esagil and town of Babylon were purified. During the New Year festival, Marduk summoned the king of Babylon to appear before him; the king had to confess any sins he might have committed and receive pardon from the god, who then handed over to him the insignia of power for a fresh year's reign. The king's presence was absolutely essential for this ceremony, and the chronicles of the temple's history kept by the scribes of the Esagil scrupulously record the occasions when this rule could not be observed. One of the grievances held by the clergy of Babylon against Nabonidus was that because of his stay in Arabia he had for ten years prevented the celebration of the *Akîtu* and the New Year.

The temple clergy

The designations of the temple's religious staff reveal the particular nature of their status. Besides the qualification *êrib bîti* which described the cult's officiants in general, we find titles specific to certain liturgical specialities and a series of functions lumped under the denomination of prebendaries.

The êrib bîti

The term *êrib bîti* was applied to several categories of people. Etymologically, it applied to those who had the right to enter the sacred part of the temple, and understanding the system becomes clearer by drawing a parallel with the royal palace: in their thinking, the religious personnel behaved like the palace employees. Indeed, there was a distinction between those who were directly concerned with the 'person' of the god because they had access to the private part of the sanctuary, in the same way as the palace staff of the *ša rêši* had the right to move about within the private part (*bîtânu*) of the palace. This status implied a certain ritual purity, and made its holders the god's table companions, with a right to a share of the cult's direct income, especially the food offerings, unlike those who worked for the temple but without being attached by a personal bond to the god or goddess, and who were paid with their board rations (*kurummâtu*) or with wages (*idû*). In the neo-Babylonian era, holding the title of *êrib bîti* was a prebend, and was a requisite in order to exercise the office of chief administrator of the sanctuary (the *šatammu* or, as at Sippar and Dilbat, the *šangû* of the town), as well as the main religious functions and some artisanal posts which caused their holder regularly to enter the sacred part of the temple. But there was also a narrower sense, which at that time designated only the cult's personnel, who formed the sacred college (*kiništu*) of the sanctuary. An absolutely strict definition therefore proves illusory, all the more so because local variations existed, connected with the size of the temples, and because this system evolved with time throughout the entire first millennium. Furthermore, holding several posts concurrently was a common occurrence, and some people could simultaneously hold administrative and religious positions together with the food offering service to the deity. In complex structures such as the Ebabbar of Sippar or the Eanna of Uruk, the cult's administrative responsibility was shared between the *šangu* of the sanctuary and other *šangu*s, who were more particularly attached to this or that deity of the temple, or to this or that building. So we find the *šangu* of Gula or Annunîtu. Religious activities properly speaking were performed by the *êrib bîti*, under the authority of a 'great brother', the *ahu rabû*, who held the office of high priest.

The specialists

Religious practice was of course not confined to the simple upkeep of the deity; but the basically administrative nature of the archives discovered in sanctuaries means that liturgical aspects were little or poorly documented; various members of staff appear to have been responsible for prayers, with specialisations depending on the type of prayer: hymns were the preserve of the singers or cantors, who were at the same time musicians (*narû*), petitions were the concern of lamenters (*kalû*). The latter accompanied themselves on musical instruments particular to them, such as the *balakku* or the *lillissu*, and used a special liturgical language, Emesal-Sumerian, for their lamentations. Other categories of religious 'technicians' were also known, like the conjurer-exorcists (*âšipu*), soothsayers (*barû*), ecstatics (*mahhû*) and astronomer-astrologers (*ṭupšar enuma Anu Enlil*). Rituals peculiar to each temple regularly attest the enduring qualities of often very ancient offices, both male and female, like that of *nadîtu* of Marduk (the god's secondary wife) at Babylon or *kurgarru* (sacred actor) at Uruk.

The prebendaries

The prebendaries operated the divine service. The oldest and most eminent part of this body was formed by the *êrib bîti*, but also included were those who prepared the various items of the meals served to the gods, and the ones who took part in the material upkeep of the statues or places of worship. Some of them needed to enter the sanctuary's sacred area and then joined the category of the *êrib bîti*, but the majority worked outside, sometimes even outside the urban site.

Prebendaries in the neo-Babylonian era

Religious service

Exorcist	*âšipu*
'Priest'	*êrib bîti*
Singer/cantor	*narû*

Food service

Baker	*nuhatimmu*
Brewer	*sirâšu*
Butcher	*ṭâbihu*
Fisherman	*bâ'iru*
Gardener	*rab bânî*
In charge of preparing milk products	*rê'û ša šizbi*
In charge of beef offerings	*rê'î alpê*
In charge of sheep offerings	*rê'î sattukki*
In charge of the offering tables	*mubannû*
Measurer	*mâdidu*
Oil presser	*ṣâhitu*

Other services

Boatman	*malâhu*
Doorkeeper	*atû*
Goldsmith	*kutimmu*
Laundry worker	*ašlâku*
Master mason	*itinnu*
Potter	*pahâru*
Weaver	*išparu*

Tenure of a prebend assured its holder of a certain income, in return for the regular execution of the work to which he was bound. The system was clear enough in the case of those whose responsibility was the preparation of food products, who in any event formed the numerically most important category, the bakers (*nuhatimmu*) and brewers (*sirâšu*): they

received from the temple an overall consignment of foodstuffs (the *maššartu*), part of which they prepared for the
regular food offerings (*sattukku*), the remainder being their
recompense (*pappasu*). This could also be given to them in
the form of precious metal and thus constituted the
prebend's regular income. Holders of prebends either exercised them themselves or delegated their execution to
colleagues or 'subcontractors' (*epišânu*), who then shared the
profits with them. When the category of prebendaries
reached large numbers, organisation of the *maššartu* distribution was supervised by a chief official, the *šâpiru*.
Membership of the body of prebendaries had to have the
backing of the temple administration and the group of existing prebendaries, and was shown by inscription in an official
register. Allocation of duties was effected on the principle of
a period of service (*manzaltu*), determined by the number of
days, or sometimes months, the prebendary possessed.
Moreover, the prebend acted as a kind of asset, to be passed
on to heirs or transferable in return for money. The organisation of the prebend system in neo-Babylonian temples is a
typical example of the participation of private interests in the
management of the sanctuaries' possessions. When the prebendary was an *êrib bîti* he obtained a double income: on the
one hand, the *pappasu* on the initial supply of the product by
the temple, and on the other, participation in the circuit of
redistribution of the food offerings after their 'consumption'
by the deities. One of the more astounding aspects of the
prebend system was the splitting of periods of service as a
result of divisions through inheritance or partial sales, the
effects of which were particularly in evidence in the Seleucid
era, when some prebendaries found themselves the owners of
periods of service expressed in fractions of an hour. The
actual preparation of the foodstuffs was then entrusted to
specialists, who were paid by their prebendaries on a pro rata
basis for their period of service. The treatment of prebend as
assets had the result that some women were the owners of
prebends, whereas normally women would not belong to the

almost exclusively masculine category of prebendaries. The outcome of all this was to separate the actual duty connected with the prebend, which had become the concern of a specialist paid by the prebendary, from the income it earned as an asset belonging to a lay person. Nevertheless, the possession of prebends remained in the hands of a relatively tight circle of notables, and that, together with the supervision which the temple continued to exercise, ensured that the duties relating to the cult were effectively carried out.

BABYLON, CULTURAL CAPITAL

The scribes

Although the presence of scribes writing on parchment (*sêpiru*) in Aramaic is attested, including within the large organisations, the majority of texts concerning management, contracts and tradition continued to be inscribed in cuneiform on clay tablets by *ṭupšarru*-scribes.

Scribes' initial training

This was given by direct transmission from a teacher to a few pupils. Even the idea of a collective school must be discarded; apprentice scribes learned their trade in their teacher's home. Depending on his social origin, abilities and ambitions, the scribe would confine himself to writing everyday documents, or work in the administrative departments of a palace or temple, and might perhaps end by attaining the caste of the literary and well-read, combining mastery of science and writing. Young scribes first learned lists of signs with their Akkadian phonetic equivalent, and this phase of apprenticeship has left us tablets known as 'school' tablets, on which we find the sign drawn by the teacher and its fairly clumsy reproduction by the pupil. Once the apprenticeship stage of writing was passed, the young scribes proceeded to memorise the most common phrases and formulae to be found in the contracts used in daily life. These phrases formed an adequate basis for practising scribes, those who acted to some extent as public writers. They complemented this elementary training by memorising ideograms used to render people's names. It is noteworthy that certain members of notables' families were capable of drawing up their contracts by themselves, and at all events possessed sufficient mastery of reading to be able to classify their archives and organise them personally.

Literary scribes

At a higher level, we approach the domain of specialist scribes, those belonging to a category of owners of an elaborate technique, who are known as *ummânu*. They have mastered Akkadian, but also Sumerian, and often hold a religious office or one linked with the religious field, which leads them to have recourse to the written word in order to learn and pass on their knowledge. So they copy the great series of lexical lists, lists of hepatoscopic and astrological omens, religious, literary and historical texts. The training of these scribes is obviously much longer and more arduous. Throughout its final phase they make copies of works pertaining to their field of competence, and this work is thought of both as contributing to their apprenticeship and as a means of preserving and looking after the wealth of documents belonging to temples or certain private libraries. When their studies are completed, they place as an ex voto a tablet executed by themselves in a special spot in the temple of Nabû, the *gigunnu*, such as have been documented by excavations of the small temple of Nabû-ša-harê at Babylon. The urban centres that were the seat of great sanctuaries were careful to maintain this tradition, as at Sippar, Nippur, Uruk and, of course, Babylon.

Learned literature

The gigantic corpus of Babylonian learned literature of the first millennium was based on a tradition several centuries old that had survived the political vicissitudes undergone by Mesopotamia and was then experiencing a process of unification and standardisation. The enormous task of collecting learned and religious documents undertaken by the Sargonid Assyrian kings resulted in the discovery, in the ruins of Nineveh, of the most complete and best-defined corpus, composed chiefly of texts from Babylonian tradition. Other neo-Assyrian centres (Ashur, Kalhu, Huṣirîna in Upper Mesopotamia) also possessed rich collections, and texts of the same kind came from Babylonia, where the recent discovery of a library-room in the ruins of Sippar confirms the existence of collections identical to those of Nineveh, not forgetting the personal libraries which some well-read Babylonians had assembled.

Lexical lists

The first millennium witnessed the setting up of the organisation of knowledge in canonical series which might group several dozen tablets, each containing around 100 lines. We thus know several syllabary and vocabulary lists that provide phonetic and ideogrammatic values for the cuneiform signs and their pronunciation (lists Sa and Sb), as well as the meaning in Akkadian of Sumerian ideograms, sometimes accompanied by an explanatory commentary (lists Ea, Aa, Diri). These syllabaries and vocabularies were not only used by apprentice scribes but also provided the well-read with the foundations for their commentaries based on the versatility of cuneiform signs.

Example of the arrangement of the Ea lexical list

Pronunciation of the ideogram	Form of the sign	Explanation	Akkadian translation
še-eš	A x IGI	*ša a-a-ku i-gi-i i*-gub 'inside A lies IGI'	= *bakû* 'to weep'
ir	A x IGI	*ša a-a-ku i-gi-i i*-gub 'inside A lies IGI'	= *dimtu* 'tear'
i-siš	A x IGI	*ša a-a-ku i-gi-i i*-gub 'inside A lies IGI'	= *ṣihtu* 'tear of joy'
a-ga-am	A x BAD	*ša a-a-ku ba-ad-da-i*-gub 'inside A lies BAD'	= *agammu* 'marsh'

Other lexical lists gather the Sumero-Akkadian vocabulary according to subject and aim to assemble all the material aspects of the world in a standardised version. The most famous is the list known as Ur₅-ra = *Hubullu*, after its introduction, which groups in twenty-four tablets the names of trees, objects made in wood, reed, clay and metal, the names of animals, stones, plants, place names and the names of foods. Similar compilations record the names of office (Lú list); others reveal a concern for etymological organisation (*Nabnîtu*) or provide lists of Akkadian synonyms (*Malku = Šarru*). Specialised lists were also drawn up to record plants (Uruanna, *Šammu šikinšu*), stones (Dub Na₄-há, *Abnu šikinšu*) and their therapeutic or magical value. Further lists are topographical descriptions, including that of Babylon (Tin-tir), catalogues of stars (Mul apin) or names of deities (An = *Anum*).

The divinatory series

The list system culminates in the great divinatory series, which record the various configurations of hepatoscopy (*Bârûtu*), astronomy (*Enûma Anu Enlil*), teratology (*Šumma izbu*), the value of the events of everyday life as portents (*Šumma âlu*); others are used for the interpretation of dreams or to establish a connection between the observations made by the exorcist when he visits a sick person's home and the nature or outcome of the illness (*Treatise on medical diagnosis and prognosis*). This literature concerning omens works according to the system peculiar to Mesopotamian divination, which establishes a correspondence between the appearance of a phenomenon (protasis) and an event, often of a political nature, which takes place simultaneously (apodosis). The process of unification that resulted in these series had the effect that, from originally diverse traditions and following the internal logic of their construction, they underwent an autonomous development. For example, the teratological list *Šumma izbu*, which gathers the omens connected with the births of monstrously deformed animals, starts out from true cases to end up with possible occurrences in accordance with the internal logic of the series, but which are actually no more than wild fantasies. Well-read Babylonians were therefore supposed to have an encyclopaedic knowledge.

The *Exorcist's Manual*

The *Exorcist's Manual* alone includes more than eighty works covering the entire field of diagnosis, conjuration, prayers and rituals in which an exorcist might have a hand, and which are listed according to an ordered plan: dealing with the official liturgy (fourteen works), dealing with protection against demons and maleficent forces (twenty titles), the abolition of evils and the search for good (thiry-five works), and auxiliary knowledge (five titles). But the exorcist had a duty also to know the great divinatory series enumerated afterwards: at least the astrological series (seventy tablets) and *Šumma alu* (107 tablets).

Myths and literary works

A detailed examination of what is known as Ashurbanipal's library at Nineveh has shown that the proportion of properly literary or mythological texts was in the end very restricted. It may therefore be assumed that a good part of what is called Mesopotamian literature was still being passed on orally in the first millennium. If this is valid for both the neo-Assyrian and neo-Babylonian periods, the fact remains that the majority of the official or private libraries included ample extracts, if not the entirety, of the great works of Babylonian mythological literature: the *Epic of the Creation* (*Enûma eliš*), the *Epic of Gilgamesh* (*Ša nagba îmuru*), the *Epic of Erra* (*Šar gimir dadmê*), *Ishtar's Descent into Hell*, *Atra-hasîs* (*Enûma ilû amêlu*), even Sumerian, most often in a bilingual Sumerian and Akkadian version, like the Ninurta myth (Lugal-e). Most of these literary works had been put into writing as early as the second millennium, and thus do not represent contemporary creativity, with the exception of the *Epic of Erra*, which evokes the catastrophic situation of Babylon at the time of the Sutean and Aramaean raids early in the first millennium, and was probably written in the reign of Nabû-apla-iddin (see p. 116). Moreover, it is one of the rare works whose author (Kabti-ilî-Marduk) is known, in the same way as the standard form of the *Epic of Gilgamesh* is attributed to the man of letters Sîn-leqe-unnîni. Learned literature is also to be found in *The Righteous Sufferer* (*Ludlul bêl nemêqi*), the *Theodicy*, the *Dialogue of the Pessimist*, the *Counsels of Wisdom*, some series of satirical fables and stories (*The Poor Man of Nippur*), and sometimes also works of political literature, such as *Advice to a Prince in the Form of an Omen*, the *Vision of Hell of an Assyrian Crown Prince*, the *Ordeal of Marduk* and the *Pamphlet against Nabonidus*. Some *Royal Epics* (of Nabopolassar and Amêl-Marduk) have been preserved, but in very fragmentary form, together with collections of *Love Songs*, which were part of one of Babylon's rituals.

Commentaries and games with writing

The multiple values of cuneiform signs, recorded in the lexical lists, enabled games of interpretation to be developed based on this variety of possible meanings. The clearest example is without doubt that of the seventh tablet of the *Epic of the Creation*, enumerating the fifty names of the god Marduk and giving a gloss on the value drawn from each of the signs that compose them. Commentaries were added to most of the great series of learned texts, explaining the meaning of certain words or establishing links of causality taken from their various values.

Example of a commentary on an extract from the medical series 'When the exorcist visits the home of a sick person'

'*If he sees a black pig.* (Commentary:) this can have both a good and a bad meaning: with the pronunciation SUL, the sign for PIG has the sense of FEVER; the sick man will die; secondly: with the same pronunciation, it signifies MAN IN THE PRIME OF LIFE; THAT MEANS HE WILL LIVE. If the exorcist notes that the illness is serious, the sick man will live, but if he does not consider the illness to be serious, the sick man will die.'

The latter half of the first millennium seems to have been marked by a tendency to esotericism in the use of learned texts, as shown for instance by resorting to a coded writing in certain colophons and seeking correspondences between some parts of the liver (hepatoscopy) and certain stars or constellations (astrology).

Association between portentous elements, deities and calendar in a Seleucid text from Uruk

Part of the liver	Deity	Month	Star/Constellation
Stance	Enlil	I	Aries
Path	Shamash	II	Taurus
Mouth	Nusku	III	Orion
Strength	Uraš	IV	Cancer; the Plough
Palace gate	Ninegal	V	Regulus
Well-being	Adad	VI	Raven (Corvus)
Gall bladder	Anu	VII	Scales (Libra)
Finger	[...]	VIII	Capricorn

Religious literature

This literature, too, rests on a long tradition. It reflects fundamental concepts held by the Mesopotamian people about their relations with the gods; it celebrates their glory in a certain number of hymns, the most famous being those addressed to Shamash, Marduk and Ishtar; it calls for their pardon for sins committed, in penitential prayers characterised as *eršahunga*, 'to appease the angered heart (of the gods)'; and it implores their aid in lamentations inherited from the Sumerian literary collection. It is still difficult to evaluate the degree of individual fervour transmitted by this literature, since it appears to be very codified; it is chiefly the corpus of prayers incorporated in the official liturgy of the temples that has been preserved, and shows evidence of the highly ritualised participation of congregations of singers (*narû*) and lamenters (*kalû*) in the worship. A kind of weakening of expression has been observed in the lamentations, which were originally linked with the destruction of the great Sumerian towns by the enemy or natural elements, but which become litanies in a style that is both bombastic and repetitive, multiplying the number of divine epithets. Their creation in a special form of the Sumerian language, Emesal, turned it into a language of prayer whose exact meaning was sometimes no longer perceived by those reciting it, who coupled the original text with approximate Akkadian translations. This collection of lamentations, for the most part addressed to the god Enlil, to whom Marduk is sometimes added, and recited with the musical accompaniment of the *balakku*, a kind of drum, nevertheless persisted until the early first century BC, thereby proving its importance in official religious practice. At that time it was reserved for rituals for the rebuilding of temples, and was then incorporated rather mechanically into the liturgical calendar: thus the lamentation entitled *a-ab-ba hu-luh-ha*, 'O Angry Sea!', was recited at Uruk in the Seleucid era on the mornings of the 2nd and 5th of the month of Nisân and the 8th of the month of Arahšamnu before the statue of the god Anu, because these days were regarded as favourable in contemporary hemerologies for undertakings of demolition and reconstruction of sacred buildings.

The same stilted nature is evident in the various versions of the *Prayers to the Gods of the Night*, Old Babylonian in origin (early second millennium), which became a simple component of the rituals of nocturnal extispicy (divination from entrails) to be recited by the diviner before proceeding with his consultation. The different texts of neo-Assyrian and neo-Babylonian rituals are characterised also by the extreme codification of gestures and words which were subsequently recorded, forbidding any personal variation or initiative which would risk nullifying the meaning and effect of the religious act. Use of a special cultic language and clergy who alone knew the liturgies therefore restricted part of religious expression to a fairly esoteric practice, and the religious literature reflects only partially the religious convictions of the population of Assyria and Babylonia.

DOCUMENT

An extract from the fourth tablet of the *Epic of Erra*

'You, Erra the Valiant, showed no respect for the renown [even] of Prince Marduk! You have undone the bond of Dim-kur-kur-ra, city of the king of the gods, bond of all the earth, after changing your divine [appearance] and making yourself like a man, having girded on your weapons you entered it [Babylon].

[Once] in Babylon, like one who would be master of a town, you spoke like a troublemaker [?], [and] the Babylonians, with no more leader than the reeds in the beds, thronged round you.

He who knew nothing of weapons unsheathed his sword; he who knew nothing of arrows filled his quiver; he who knew nothing of fighting threw himself into combat; he who knew nothing of running darted like a bird. The weak sought to outdo the strong, the cripples to outrun the swift-footed.

Against the[ir] governor, provisioner of their sanctuaries, they poured out gross insults. With their own hands they blocked up the gates of Babylon and the canals of their prosperity. Like foreign looters, they burned the sacred buildings of Babylon!

[Now] it was you their ringleader, [you] who were at their head! The *Imgur-Enlil*, at which you aimed your spear, begged for mercy. You steeped in the blood of men and women the seat of the god *Muhrâ*, keeper of its gates! [And these] Babylonians – they, the birds and you, the decoy – after trapping them in your net, Erra the Valiant, you seized and destroyed [them].

[For] leaving the town and going outside it, you took on the appearance of a lion and entered the palace: as soon as they saw you the troops took up their weapons, and the heart of the governor, the avenger of Babylon, was kindled with rage.

He despatched his soldiers, as if to despoil an enemy, urging the captain of the army to do his worst [and saying to him]: "This town to which I send you, man, respects [no] god, fears no one: [there] put to death the lowly and the great, and do not spare [a single] baby, [even] those still at the breast! [After this] loot all the amassed treasures of Babylon!" The king's army, gathered together, thus entered the town, their arrows aflame, their swords unsheathed. You [even] made those under special protection, sacred to Anu and Dagan, draw weapons; you shed their blood, like water, in the town drains; you opened their veins to have [their contents] flushed away to the river!

At this spectacle, Marduk, the Great Lord, cried "Woe!" and his heart tightened; an implacable curse issued from his lips: he swore never more to drink of the river's water and, from disgust at the spilt blood, never again to enter the Esagil!

"Alas!" [he cried], "Babylon whose branches I had made as luxuriant as a palm-tree, but which the wind has withered! Alas! Babylon that I had filled with seeds like a pine-cone, without tasting its fruits! Alas! Babylon that I had planted like a garden of plenty, but did not take of its yield! Alas! Babylon that I had placed around the neck of Anu, like a seal of yellow amber! Alas! Babylon that I had held in my hands like the Tablet of Destinies, handing her over to nobody else!'"

The literary text traditionally called the *Epic of Erra*, from the name of its main protagonist, the god Erra, another name for Nergal, the god of epidemics and massacres, is the epic setting of historical events that had been particularly grievous to Babylonia: the series of ravages that had accompanied the incursions of the Suteans and Aramaeans into the country from the reign of Adad-apla-iddin (1067–1046) up to the reign of Nabû-apla-iddin (888–855). As Jean Bottéro has pointed out, the literary and mythological treatment of events is based on real happenings.

The misdeeds of the god Erra

In the extract quoted above, the god Išum is addressing Erra to recall the deeds perpetrated by the latter after he had managed to trick Marduk, Babylon's protector, into momentarily leaving his town and the sanctuary of the Esagil. Erra had entered the capital in disguise and spurred the people on to rebellion. Everything then turned topsy-turvy and the natural order of things was reversed. The unrest unleashed by Erra resulted in an attack on the political, economic and even religious order: as wavering as the reeds in the reed-bed, the people of Babylon allowed themselves to question the authority of their governor (= the king), close gates and canals to any help from outside and set fire to the temples. The town itself, quoted at the beginning under one of its Sumerian names (Dim-kur-kur-ra: the bond [?] of all the countries) was stricken, and the wall Imgur-Enlil cried out in pain under the attack of Erra and the Babylonians, while the chapel of the god of hospitality, Muhrâ, was filled with the blood of murdered people.

Then Erra left Babylon to go to the royal palace (as the traces of the neo-Babylonian era show, the palace was in fact isolated by an internal wall from the rest of the town). Erra's appearance in the guise of a lion assuredly enters the series of dire predictions linked with the appearance of certain wild animals in the urbanised setting. He next set the governor against his town, causing him to launch his troops against Babylon, where they proceeded to carry out a general massacre. Babylonian blood flowed in rivers, making Babylon a defiled place. Marduk came to hear about all these excesses, and he then cursed his own town and bewailed it, echoing Sumerian lamentations over destroyed towns, or certain biblical passages: for instance, in Jeremiah 51:7–8, 'Babylon was a golden cup in the Lord's hand, making all the earth drunken: the nations drank of her wine; therefore the nations went mad. Suddenly Babylon has fallen and been broken.'

The gods' relationship with humankind

The account thus constructed raises several questions: why did Marduk not protect his town? Why did Erra/Nergal turn against his own country? More generally, why was Babylon smitten by the gods, when it was commonly believed that it was the sins committed by humans which earned divine punishment? The aim pursued by the author of the *Epic of Erra* was therefore not only to give a legitimate and sensible explanation for the unhappy events in the history of his town. He was posing the problem of the relations between humans and gods and the justification for evil when it was of divine origin. The account of Babylon's rebellion against its king nevertheless clearly shows that the townspeople transgressed the natural order of things at Erra's instigation.

Whether it was to punish or, like Erra seized with destructive fury, simply to exert their power to the full, the gods appear here as the sole possessors of the destinies of human beings, who must therefore expect to suffer their violence as well as enjoy their favours. The end of the epic shows, moreover, that Išum succeeds in restoring Erra to reason, and that the ravaged country and Babylon drained of its lifeblood are reborn to prosperity. But this optimistic view of Mesopotamian history does not exonerate humans of every fault: certainly they were deceived by Erra, but in agreeing to rebel, and then, for the king, inciting his troops to massacre, they themselves were involved in upsetting world order, in the first case reaping the fruits of their insolence and, in the second, the results of his inability to behave like a good king.

Literary qualities

Finally, the quality of the literary development is worthy of note. The text teems with metaphors, constantly linked with nature. Marduk's ultimate lamentations compare the town to a paradise garden, a precious jewel, a unique tablet. It is interesting to see how the man of letters, Kabti-ilî- Marduk, conceives his town: as an oasis in the surrounding desert and as the source of knowledge.

Chapter 8

Achaemenid Babylonia
(539–331 BC)

Between 539 and 331, Babylonia experienced two centuries of calm and economic development. Up to the end of the sixth century it formed a province defined by the boundaries of the former neo-Babylonian empire. Beginning in the reign of Xerxes (485–465), it was restricted to Mesopotamia alone, and local authorities were reorganised on the basis of new districts, the *haṭru*, incorporating a good part of those dependent on the traditional large organisations. Two other happenings accompanied this movement: the formation of vast estates allotted to the empire's nobility, and the settlement of new immigrants drawn by the administrative and military requirements of the Achaemenid empire.

The Achaemenid period was marked by the installation in central Babylonia of military colonists, often of foreign origin, on land tenures proportionate to the type of armed service they were expected to provide: archers, cavalry or war chariots. Mainly occupying royal lands, or lands granted by the crown to the royal family and higher echelons of nobility, they formed communities administered by royal agents in the setting of the *haṭru*. Their settlement was not due to a need to maintain order in Babylonia, but to make use of the country's agricultural capacities and because of the king's concern to have available a reserve army in keeping with the size of his empire.

For its central position and agricultural wealth, Babylonia was an economically important zone for the Achaemenids, and they proceeded to get the most out of it, which resulted in the development of rural centres while the large towns declined in importance. It does not seem, as one might have thought, that this development was accompanied by a massive rise in the prices of farm produce. Certainly, part of the output was taken by the central Persian government by way of taxes, but the possibilities of acquiring personal wealth remained for intermediaries working in the service of the authorities, as is perfectly illustrated by the archives of the Murašû family of Nippur.

A CENTRAL PROVINCE OF THE PERSIAN EMPIRE

A stable political situation

The brief episode of the usurpations of Nebuchadnezzar III in 522 and Nebuchadnezzar IV in 521 did not challenge Babylonia's place in the Persian empire; it even became one of the central provinces, among the most prosperous, and the city of Babylon was part of the limited group of capitals in which the Achaemenid court stayed from time to time.

Differing sources

Although two revolts are attested in the first years of Xerxes' reign (485–465), led by local usurpers Bêl-šimanni and then Shamash-erîba, they lasted only a few months and were confined to Babylon and its immediate surroundings. In any case there is nothing to bear witness to the reality of the destruction and pillage ascribed by Greek historians to the Persian kings – above all, Xerxes – in Babylon: worship continued to be performed in the temple of Marduk, and Artaxerxes II (404–359) had a building in Achaemenid style constructed in the enclosure of the royal palace. Here the problem of sources becomes crucial, for there is an obvious distortion between the way in which classical writers portray the exercise of Achaemenid power in Babylonia and the reality provided for us by local sources. But, at the same time, the latter become far less plentiful. For some as yet unexplained reason, the archives of the great temples cease at the end of Darius I's reign and the beginning of that of Xerxes, and the same goes for most of the private archives of the region of Babylon. Nevertheless, rather than seeking catastrophic explanations, it is probably more likely to be the outcome of a reorganisation of local authorities and the country's economic production, which was beginning to have some effects in Xerxes' reign.

Babylonia's position in the empire

At this time, too, the definitive separation took place between the Transeuphratene province and that of Babylonia, which also included Assyria. The link between the Achaemenid sovereign and Babylonia slackened as well, as is shown by the royal titulary in the cuneiform texts: up to the end of the reign of Darius I, the king bears the title 'king of Babylon and the Lands'. During the first years of Xerxes' reign an expanded version appeared: 'king of Babylon and the Lands, of the Persians and the land of the Medes'. Then it was reduced to a short formula: 'king of the Lands', in which mention of Babylon no longer appears, and which would be the norm until the end of the dynasty. From the mid-fifth to the mid-fourth century, Babylonia was not the scene of military operations, except on two occasions, connected with problems of succession: at the time of Darius II's accession in 423, he used the country as a base for recruitment and operations. Similarly, the confrontation between Artaxerxes II and his brother Cyrus the Younger took place in the northern region of Babylonia, and Xenophon has left an account of it in his *Anabasis*. But none of these episodes had any lasting effect on the region. Although military call-ups or levies of troops are attested in Babylonia under Darius II and Artaxerxes II, that does not mean that the province was the theatre of military operations themselves. In fact, we should have to wait for Alexander the Great to see Babylonia participate in the political destiny of the Achaemenid empire, when it gave a favourable welcome to the conqueror.

Names of the reigning Achaemenid sovereigns, from Artaxerxes I to Darius III, according to Babylonian astronomical texts

Artaxerxes I	*Aršu*, otherwise known as *Artakšatsu*
Darius II	*Umasu*, otherwise known as *Darawušu*
Artaxerxes II	*Aršu*, otherwise known as *Artakšatsu*
Artaxerxes III	*Umasu*, otherwise known as *Artakšatsu*
Arses	*Aršu*, son of Umasu, otherwise known as *Artakšatsu*
Darius III	*Artašata*, otherwise known as *Dariyawuš*

Evolution of government

The central administration of the province

During the fifth and fourth centuries, the governor of the province of Babylonia was Persian, often selected from the highest nobility of the empire, who bore the Babylonian title of *pahat* or *bêl pahati* and not that of satrap. Although this word is attested in Babylonia, in the form *ahšadrapannu*, it appears to have designated merely a simple royal functionary.

The Persian governors of Babylonia

Under Cyrus
   Gobryas (I) [= Ugbaru] governor after the viceroyship of Cambyses over the country
Under Darius I
   Uštânu
Under Xerxes
   Zopyros, killed by the Babylonians in a rebellion shortly before 482
   Megapanos [Bagapana], satrap after the second Median war
   Tritantachmes [Cithran-tauxma], son of Artabaros
Under Artaxerxes I (464–424)
   Artarios [Artareme], brother of the king. His son

Menostanes [= Manuštânu] supported Sekyndianos against
Darius II and the family was ousted from government.
Under Darius II (423–404)
Gobryas (II) [Gubaru] is attested from 421 to 417, but may
have remained in office until the reign of Artaxerxes II.
No governor's name is known until the end of Darius III's reign.

As early as the reign of Darius I one may note the first mentions in substantial numbers of Persian administrative titles.
Some refer to dignitaries of the court who owned landed
estates in Babylonia but resided there only when the king was
present in Babylon. But others were local administrators,
superimposed upon or substituted for the administrative
structures of the neo-Babylonian era, such as treasurers (*ganzabara*), those in charge of towns (*umarzanapâta* or *uppadêtu*)
and, chiefly, judges (*databara*), who often bore Iranian names
themselves; this last category of officials went far beyond the
framework of the simple judicial institution and embraced
all those whose task was to have royal law applied: we thus
find judges in charge of overseeing canals or functioning in
special districts: the 'Sealand', the domain of Parysatis. In
Babylonia, finance, the army and royal law were under the
direct control of Persian administrators, and Babylonian officials were basically represented at the local level, which
underwent no major upheaval before the middle of the fifth
century.

Princely estates

The Nippur texts document the existence of a certain
number of princely estates in Babylonia, or those of nobles
such as the treasurers (*ganzabara*): Mithridata under Cyrus,
Bagasaru under Darius I, Šibbu under Darius II. There is
also mention of the estate of the crown prince (*bît mâr šarri,
bît umasupitrû*), a heritage from the neo-Babylonian era that
can be traced from Cyrus to Darius I. In the reign of Xerxes,
we possess the archives of the estate of Mardonios, known

also as one of the major participants in the second Median war. The Nippur texts similarly document the existence of some princely or nobles' estates in Babylonia in the reigns of Artaxerxes I and Darius II: the estate of the crown prince, of Queen Parysatis, or of Arsames, satrap of Egypt. Some dozen other princes (*mâr bîti*) are cited as owning lands in central Babylonia; other estates similarly refer to Persian owners, whose titles are not always supplied, but who belonged to the empire's nobility. The majority of these lands are described as royal gifts (*nidinti šarri*) and were taken from crown domains, most of which were formed from royal estates of the neo-Babylonian period.

New local authorities

Beginning in the fifth century, a profound reform of local authorities in Babylonia took place; the former centres of power embodied by towns and sanctuaries, but also by rural communities, were succeeded by a unified system composed of districts designated by the term *haṭru*. This title applied simultaneously to a territorial, administrative and fiscal unity, but chiefly to the population living there, and possibly the socio-professional community they formed. In a region like Babylonia, where the main factor of wealth was still the labour force, the principal point of reference was the population available to make the most of a territory. Although the system appears to have been extended to the whole of Babylonia, it is at present documented mostly in the centre of the country, around the town of Nippur. It is not always easy to perceive exactly how it worked, as it is intermingled with the system of military colonies and foreign communities established in the Nippur region by the Achaemenids. The names of *haṭru* to be found there, in the reigns of Artaxerxes I and Darius II, refer to professional, military or ethnic designations. The institution of the *haṭru* allowed the various categories of dependants who were not only previously in the service of the crown to be placed under the direct authority of the royal administration, but also sanctuaries or nobles' estates, as well as the families of military colonists settled on royal lands.

Babylonia internationalised

Foreign presence prior to the Persians

The presence of non-indigenous communities in Babylonia in fact dates back to the mass deportations of the neo-Assyrian era: deportees from Kummuh (the classical Commagene) had been settled in the Bît-Yakîn in order to repopulate it. The neo-Babylonian kings continued the practice, the most famous of their deportations being that of the people of Judah, who had been installed in the northern and central parts of Babylonia. But other communities from North Syria experienced the same fate. Some rebaptised the place where they stayed with the name of their home town, and we find a 'town of Judah' (*âl Yahûdu*) in north Babylonia, as well as an Ascalon, a Gaza, a 'town of the Neirabeans', a Qadeš, a Qedar and a Tyre in central Babylonia.

The situation under the Achaemenids

The Persians' arrival was marked at first by a return of Jewish exiles to their own country; Cyrus also authorised the rebuilding of the temple of Jerusalem. Similarly, exiles from the town of Neirab, in north Syria, returned to their home-land early in the reign of Darius I, taking with them the archives of the time of their exile, written in cuneiform. But not everyone went home, and a significant number of exiles stayed put. The Jewish community in north Babylonia would thus found a line there, forming one of the most important outside their country of origin. Furthermore, the empire's administrative requirements brought new immigrants to Babylonia, some of whom received estates on the spot. The Nippur texts indicate the presence of communities with a military purpose, who were installed there in the fifth century as colonists: people from Tyre, Phrygia, Caria, Melitene, Urartu, Cimmerians, Arabs, Indians. Although some of these non-Babylonians appear in cuneiform texts, they rarely used that form of writing for their own archives, and resorted rather to Aramaic, which at that time was the spoken and written language most used in the western part of the empire. It therefore became general practice to add to certain contracts in cuneiform writing on a clay tablet an Aramaic note, scratched or written in ink, which complemented them. Alas, virtually all Babylonia's purely Aramaic documentation, on papyrus or parchment, has vanished, thereby creating a great void in the sources available.

Babylonia, mirror of the East?

The rare pieces of description of Achaemenid Babylonia that we find in Greek sources pose a problem, because they emerge more from the ideological vision of the East that was coming into being in that period in the context of the confrontation between Greeks and Persians than from an objective description. The most famous instance is obviously that of Herodotus: it is difficult to reconcile the few pages he devotes to describing the country, its capital and customs with the reality revealed to us by local sources, to the extent that doubt may legitimately be cast on the very truth of a journey by the historian of Halicarnassus to that region at the end of the fifth century. A certain number of recurrent themes appear, such as the vastness of the open spaces and of the natural elements of the landscape, but also that of the edifices built by people, the enormous amount of resources in produce and labour at the disposal of the king, the social and political organisation based on the sovereign's unbridled despotism, and lastly the absence of any personal worth of individuals on the political plane, which has a deleterious effect on their moral worth. All this leads to a Greek view of an East that is both menacing and fascinating, of which

Babylonia seems to be the archetype, with 'exotic' features which are specific to it but which were probably gathered by Herodotus in indirect fashion in the western parts of the Near East rather than directly verified on the spot.

At the same time a process was being put in place that would extend over several centuries: henceforward Babylonia would no longer assimilate the powers that installed themselves there, whose ideological references lay outside Mesopotamia. This phenomenon began with the Achaemenids and would become more pronounced after Alexander's conquest.

A RESERVE OF SOLDIERS

The system of military estates

The archives of Nippur have enabled us to have a fairly exact idea of the system of maintaining military reserves in central Babylonia. The crown provided land for farmers in exchange for having a fully equipped soldier available: the farmer and family lived on the income from their holding and had to supply a certain number of returns, in precious metal, in kind and in service rendered.

The status of the lands

The size of the farms was proportionate to the type of fighting unit they were expected to provide: thus we see mention of 'bow fiefs' (*bît qašti*) to supply archers, 'horse fiefs' (*bît sîsi*) to supply the equipment and service of mounted warriors, and 'chariot fiefs' (*bît narkabti*) entailing the obligation to do military service in the chariotry. In practice, the bow fiefs appear most often and seem to have formed the bulk of the troops. Supplying a fully equipped cavalryman or chariot in fact represented several people and equipment that was far more costly than that of a simple archer, and relied on estates of greater size; we therefore find chariot fiefs attached to sanctuaries. This system of maintaining a permanent army by allocating land to military colonists was not an Achaemenid invention, and in Mesopotamia harked back to at least the end of the third millennium. There is abundant evidence of it in land termed *ilku*. The bow fiefs similarly preceded the arrival of the Persians, and they are mentioned several times under Nebuchadnezzar II and Nabonidus. Nor did the system always have a military purpose; in the late sixth century we find estates known as *bît ritti*, a type of landholding conferred in return for service, allocated to administrators for their material upkeep. It was not a speciality of the Nippur region, as examples may be found throughout Babylonia; but what seems characteristic of the Achaemenid period is the direct relationship between the bow fiefs, the improved use of crown estates and the system of the *hatru*.

Obligations

The returns provided by the holders of a bow fief were covered in the term 'service' (*ilku*). They corresponded simultaneously to the dues which the occupant of crown land had to pay, and which were used for the upkeep of the royal house, and to the military service to be performed because of the status of the allocated land.

Annual dues levied on a bow fief

'One mina [around 500 g] of silver, representing the whole of his *ilku*-service: the service of king's soldier, the king's flour, the *bâra*-tax and all taxes owed to the king's house, from month 1 of year 3 to the end of month 12 of year 3 of king Darius [II], owing by the bow fief [...]'

The question arises as to whether these obligations were entirely fulfilled by the payment of the sum of money, in which case military service would be recompensed, or whether the latter was actually performed over and above the payment of the money. The general wording indicates that money levied for the *ilku* covered all the obligations; but that by no means implies that the occupant of a bow fief was free to choose to carry out military service or compensate for it by paying a lump sum. That would apply only when the king had no need to mobilise his troops. If the requisition order arrived, the occupant of the estate was duty bound to turn up at his mobilisation site, together with his equipment, as several texts from the Murašû archives prove.

Loan to enable attendance with their equipment at the mobilisation point underwritten by the tenant farmers of the bow fief

'80 *kurru* of dates belonging to Rîmût-Ninurta descendant of Murašû are to be payable by Hannani' and Gubbaia, the sons of Ninurta-êṭir, and Nadin and Arad-Enlil, sons of Sa'ga', of the *haṭru* community of the Šušânu-mâr-hisanni. In month 7 of year 3 of king Darius [II], they will deliver the 80 *kurru* of dates to the town of Hambari. The field of trees and stubble which constitutes their bow fief in the town of Hambari serves as surety for the 80 *kurru* of dates of Rîmût-Ninurta. No other creditor will have priority until Rîmût-Ninurta has paid his debt. They are together guarantors that the nearest [to the place for settlement] will pay for the others. These dates are the equivalent of the money that has been lent to them for military clothing and equipment so that they can go to Uruk. Witnessed. Made at Nippur, the 18th of X of year 2 of Darius [II] king of the Lands.'

How the system worked and developed

The example of Nippur

The interest of the example of Nippur is that it demonstrates the 'classical' working of the system. We note that the bow fiefs are grouped in the *haṭru* communities, which serve as the administrative and fiscal framework, under the authority of an appointed official (*šaknu*) belonging to the royal administration. In the simplest instance, the *haṭru* were installed on royal lands, but some were dependent on estates granted by the king to members of his family or the highest Persian nobility. Enjoyment of these granted estates allowed the beneficiary to avail himself of the income from the land by means of the rent paid by the owners of the bow fiefs; but they continued to be royal property. They were managed by royal administrators, and military service was normally due to the king. In fact, the danger of the system lay, by constituting these noble domains, in allowing the use of military forces in the service of the Achaemenid prince or dignitary for personal ends. The recurrent problem of royal succession among the Achaemenids had the result that at regular intervals several claimants to the throne were in opposition, and the Achaemenid rulers were aware of the fact that, through these gifts, they were providing possible competitors with the military means to uphold their claims if they left them complete autonomy in managing the estates they had been granted and the *ḫaṭru* communities settled there.

Towards land privatisation

At first, the bow fiefs had been allocated, on an individual basis, to a farmer and his family; but not all bow fiefs had the same status: some were fully operational, others served to produce reserve troops (*kutallu*) and bore fewer outgoings. There were also subdivisions, certain of which were described as 'a quarter of a bow fief'. Moreover, as in the old system of the Babylonian *ilku*, enjoyment of a bow fief could be passed on to the holder's descendants or collaterals, on condition that the service continued to be performed. The granting of estates and keeping an inventory of them were placed under the authority of the man in charge of the *ḫaṭru* community to whom the *bît qašti* belonged, who bore the title of appointed official (*šaknu*). He levied the taxes and allocated vacant fiefs. As the system evolved, there appears to have been a trend in some places towards total privatisation: a group of contracts from a township called Šâṭir, between

Uruk and Nippur, shows that by means of inheritance transfers some bow fiefs became multi-ownerships, and that some co-owners could sell the part of the fief that belonged to them. While remaining nominally Crown property, these bow fiefs thus became private family properties. In the same way, those which had been formed on temples' domains gradually regressed to being 'service' lands, linked with the tenure of an office in the sanctuary, and under the Seleucids, at Uruk, we find lands described as bow fiefs belonging to prebendaries.

Tribute and intermediaries

Economic development

As an internal province of the empire, well protected from the exterior, Babylonia was used by the Achaemenids as a granary; it was the part of the Fertile Crescent nearest to the centre of government, and there are several indications that a consistent policy of agricultural development was put into operation there.

Land development

New land was brought under cultivation, the network of canals was maintained on a regular basis, and the Persians initiated some regulation of the Babylonian stretch of the Tigris. The picture drawn by Xenophon of his crossing of the northern part of the country after the battle of Cunaxa portrays a prosperous region. The Persian generals even pointed out to their king, Artaxerxes II, that it would be enough for the Greek troops to retreat into the maze of canals to be able to survive for a very long time. This phase of expansion took place during the continuation of the renewal of Babylonia's agricultural development, which had begun in the seventh century, and went on well beyond the history of the Achaemenid era, right up to the Sassanid period. A new distribution of the population similarly seems to have occurred, resulting from both the development of rural regions and the gradual effacement of the traditional urban authorities; with the exception of Babylon, the large towns began to witness a steady dwindling of their population, to the advantage of a denser network of secondary centres. The establishment of a whole range of nobles' estates which looked after their own management contributed to a more diffuse distribution of administrative activities than previously, and probably explains why several archives of the traditional urban notables ceased. That in no way meant the abrupt disappearance of cuneiform culture, but its practice tended to become concentrated in the traditional circles of the well-read and of religious personnel.

Prices and trade

Thanks to some fairly consistent series of texts of astronomical observations which at the same time record certain economic data, additional information is available on the evolution in the prices of basic produce. Overall interpretation of these data does not fail to pose a few problems of detail, but the general development they map out is enlightening; whereas a classic schema postulated a continuous and major rise in prices throughout the two centuries of Achaemenid rule in Babylonia, ascribed to a maximum exploitation of its resources which would have been siphoned off to Persia, it appears that after an initial period of increases, extending in fact over the fifth century, a period occurred during the fourth century when prices for this basic produce (barley, dates, wool) actually came down. The fifth-century rise in prices may in any case be interpreted not as a sign of a diminution in what was available because of royal levying, but as a result of Babylonia's agricultural development, the expansion of its population and an intensification of trade. The inequality in the distribution of the results of this expansion, however, remains the same as in the preceding periods, and a general enrichment of the population cannot be inferred: the majority of dependent workers and the rural population were little affected by it. The Nippur archives clearly show that small farmers saw no fundamental change in their situation. Similarly, like the greater part of the continental East, Babylonia avoided monetarisation, and trade continued to be conducted in weighed bullion, not in coin. Lastly, the development of the region did not protect it from regular crises in food supplies, the result of seasonal climatic variations.

Tribute, taxes and dependants

Among the levies carried out by the royal administration, beginning in the reign of Darius I a tax was initiated on the sale of slaves, operated by a royal office of records (*karamarru ša šarri*). The same office updated the register of farmlands and developed sites. Among the royal domains, some had the specific function of providing for the king's material upkeep. We thus find the existence of a tax known as *bâra* and an obligation described as 'service of *urašu*', consisting of supplying agricultural produce or a workforce, either *in situ* or to be conveyed to the place where the king was currently in residence. Several deliveries are listed in the reign of Darius I, and until Artaxerxes II. The question that arises is whether all landed properties in Babylonia were taxed by the royal administration, or whether the latter contented itself with the revenues produced by royal land, either managed directly or granted to tenant farmers, who might be military colonists, independent farmers or urban notables.

Undertaking by a subcontractor to transport a royal tax

'Kidin-Nabû, son of Šumaia, will travel to transport the *bâra*-tax due for the king's entry to Susa in year 6 of the king Artaxerxes [II] and carry out the service of agent for the taxes of the oblates, and will effect this transport on behalf of

Kuṣurêa, son of Sîn-ahhê-bulliṭ. Kidin-Nabû, son of Šumaia, has received from the hands of Kuṣurêa, son of Sîn-ahhê-bulliṭ, payment of his wage and his complete equipment matching that of the agents for the oblates' taxes. Zakitu, his mother, daughter of Anu-uballiṭ, stands surety that Kidin-Nabû, son of šumaia, will effectively travel and transport the *bâra*-tax due for the king's entry to Susa in year 6 of the king Artaxerxes on behalf of Kuṭurêa, son of Sîn-ahhê-bulliṭ. If Kidin-Nabû, son of Šumaia, does not set out and does not transport the *bâra*-tax due for the king's entry to Susa in year 6 of the king Artaxerxes, on behalf of Kuṣurêa, son of Sîn-ahhê-bulliṭ, Kidin-Nabû son of Šumaia and Zakitu his mother must pay one-third of a mina [about 166 g] of refined silver to Kuṭurêa, son of Sîn-ahhê-bulliṭ. They are joint guarantors for this payment. Kuṣurêa will be paid at whatever place he chooses. [Witnesses]. Made at Ur, the 4-[…] of year 6 of Artaxerxes [II], king of the country.'

The king had at his disposal on his lands a labour force of dependent workers who were attached to these estates. Their Aramaic (*grd*) and Babylonian (*gardu*) title is the equivalent of what is found in the Persepolis texts in the form *kurtaš*, and they were under the authority of their own specific administration, comprising among others a head of the *gardu* (*gardupâtu*) and an official in charge of their food rations (*pit-ipabaga*).

The system of 'intermediaries'

The example of the Murašû family

The 800 tablets forming the archives of the Murašû family were discovered at the time of the late nineteenth-century excavations at Nippur. They are remarkable not only for the quality of their preservation but also for the writing of the texts, which bears witness to the maintenance to a high level of cuneiform writing, to be found two centuries later among the scribes of the Uruk texts in the Seleucid period. These tablets frequently bear Aramaic epigraphs, showing that the practice of writing had become a mixture in the daily life of Achaemenid Babylonia. The chronological range of these archives is equally interesting, since it covers the end of Artaxerxes I's reign and the beginning of Darius II's, which are sparsely documented by Babylonian texts. Their owners, who hark back to an ancestor named Murašû, are spread over two generations, and may be defined as businessmen playing the role of intermediary between farmers on the crown estates and the royal administration.

Relations with landholders

The activities of the Murašû stemmed from the economic situation peculiar to Babylonia: although the price of land tended to decrease because of the Achaemenid policy of bringing new land under cultivation, that of the workforce, farming equipment, and taxes to be paid for the use of canals for purposes of irrigation and transporting crops remained high. Possibilities for personal investment by the holders of the bow fiefs were fairly limited, and the charges that weighed on this kind of land were heavy. Under normal circumstances, the revenue produced by a bow fief was sufficient to support the holder and family; but some preferred to have a more remunerative supplementary activity, or to concentrate on farming other land which they themselves owned. They then resorted to the Murašû, to whom they leased out all or part of their military estate. The Murašû would install their 'firm's' employees and pay the holder a regular income. They took care of making the necessary payments to the administration and ensured that these were regularly maintained. The Murašû 'firm' in fact owned livestock, equipment and a labour force in large enough quantities to optimise a farm on a large scale, and certain contracts drawn up with the royal administration show that it also leased the use of waterways, thus ensuring its control over the irrigation of the estates situated on their course. The Murašû family's hold over the farming of the bow fiefs was equally strengthened when, in 423, King Darius II called upon their holders to carry out their military service. The resources of the latter at that time were heavily burdened by the cost of equipment and participation in the military campaign being waged by Darius II against Sekyndianos in Babylonia, and some simply could not meet their obligations – on which their right to farm their bow fief depended – except by borrowing the necessary funds from the Murašû. In return, the latter took their land as 'antichretic' security, that is to say, they ensured its working during the period of the loan and paid themselves from the revenue. This isolated crisis therefore had the result of placing a large number of bow fiefs directly at the disposal of the Murašû family.

Relations with the royal administration

The firm's activities included another aspect, which would put it in direct relations with the administration of the *ḥaṭru*; acting on their behalf, the Murašû took care of the regular levying of taxes and rents, and their collection, as well as bringing under cultivation any estates left vacant. By seeing to the marketing of farm produce supplied by the bow fiefs, they were similarly in a position to pay the revenue from these lands directly in precious metal to the royal administration. But it would appear that the Murašû were victims of their own success: their position as intermediaries, and the opportunity they had to build upon the income from the estates they controlled, meant that the profits extracted from this rationalisation of farming benefited neither the holders, who received a reduced income, nor the royal administration, which levied fixed taxes and rents, but remained in the hands of the firm's agents. When their economic power thus extended over increasingly vast domains, and on certain occasions encroached on estates that were nothing to do with them, official complaints reached as far as the royal court. Members of the family were summoned to Susa to appear before the king, and their economic power ended by being dismantled, some time around 421–420. Indeed, the last texts of the archives reveal that, around 410, their activities were restricted to management, by a single agent of the firm, of the livestock belonging to prince Arsames, satrap of Egypt, who is known to have owned several estates in Babylonia. The abrupt cessation of these archives therefore poses a problem of interpretation, according to whether one considers it to be the expression of the end of the firm's activities in Nippur's farming countryside, thus more or less its ruin, or a matter of dead archives having lost their usefulness, though the Murašû continued to pursue this kind of activity without the slightest archivistic trace of it ever being discovered.

Other instances

Other archives show that the Murašû family was not the only one to have profited from the position of intermediary between farming producers and the official administration: a complex group of archives identified as coming from the quarter of the royal palace at Babylon (archives of the Kasr), and dated in the reigns of Darius II and Artaxerxes II, centres on a person named Bêlšunu. It has been possible to follow his career, which led him from the post of governor of the town of Babylon to that of governor of the Transeuphratene province and then of Cilicia, and this has enabled us to identify him with the Belesys of Greek sources. The Babylon texts document his official activities, in a limited fashion, and show mainly that he had at his disposal a group of agents who simultaneously managed his own interests and those of members of the Persian nobility who owned estates in the neighbourhood of Babylon, Borsippa and Dilbat. It is possible that Bêlšunu made the transition from Babylonian businessman to a career in the heart of the Achaemenid provincial administration.

DOCUMENT

Financial activities in the Achaemenid era: leasing a royal tax

'With regard to the collection, at the bridge and river port [of Babylon], of taxes in kind on the boats ascending and descending [the Euphrates], payable at the *bît qîptu*, which is the property of Guzânu, governor of Babylon, and is at the disposal of Širku, son of Iddinaia, descendant of Egibi and Murânu, son of Nabû-mukîn-apli, descendant of the keeper of the sacred boat, have given a lease for a monthly sum of 15 shekels of bright silver at one-eighth [impurity] per shekel, of *nuhhutu*-quality, for a half share – property of Guzânu, governor of Babylon – on the revenues from the bridge which are held in co-ownership by Murânu, son of Nabû-mukîn-apli, and Nabû-bullissu, son of Guzânu, and Hariṣânu, Iqupu [and] Nergal-ibni, the keepers of the bridge, to Bêl-asûa, son of Nergal-uballiṭ, descendant of Mudammiq-Adad and Ubar son of Bêl-ahhê-erîba, descendant of the keeper of the sacred boat.

Bêl-asûa and Ubar will collect the taxes in kind from the boats that put in at the bridge. Silver, revenue [of the taxes] from the bridge each month, will go directly to Širku and Murânu, the co-owners. Bêl-asûa and Ubar will give it to no one else without Širku's authorisation. Bêl-asûa and Ubar are to present any written instruction regarding the bridge tax to Širku and the keepers of the bridge.

Witnesses: Nabû-ittanu, son of Ardiya, descendant of Sîn-ili; Ardi-Marduk, son of Mušêzib-Bêl, descendant of Sippê; Murânu, son of Bêl-iddina, descendant of Šanaši-šu; Nabû-rê'û-šunu, son of Nabû-šum-uṣur, descendant of the *Kânik bâbi*; Nidintu, son of Kalbaia, descendant of Sûhaia. Mušêzib-Marduk, scribe, son of Šum-ukîn, descendant of Bâbûtu. Babylon, the 1st Tašrîtu of year 26 of Darius [I], king of Babylon, king of the Lands. Each has taken a copy.'

The deed was drawn up early in the fifth century (496) at Babylon, and relates to this town where, at least since the reign of Nabonidus, there had been a wooden bridge on stone piers. The river port, literally 'the wharf' (*karû*), was situated on the eastern bank of the Euphrates, south of the vast sacred area of the Esagil, on the edge of the Šuanna district.

As the management and maintenance of the waterways were the affair of the royal administration, it levied taxes for the use of water for irrigation, but also on the installations enabling boats to be hauled along the Euphrates and the large canals, as well as those allowing the loading and unloading of various goods and produce. In the latter instance, the term 'wharf right' was used. Babylon's bridge allowed the same operations to take place, and its use as a landing platform was taxed. Strictly speaking, this was not a river toll levied on the passage of a boat, but a tax on the use of port installations and the supervision that was carried out by the keepers. The tax was paid in an official building known as the *bît qiptu*.

A complicated group of owners of rights

The contract shows that not all of this combination of taxes actually went into the administration's coffers. Half was used to pay the three keepers of the bridge, Harişânu, Iqupu and Nergal-ibni. This system effectively spared the authorities having to pay them a wage, or supplemented their subsistence rations. The other half was the 'property' of two people, Murânu, son of Nabû-mukîn-apli, and Nabû-bullissu, son of Guzânu. It is impossible to determine the origin of the first man's right of ownership, but that of the second is connected to the office of his father, governor of Babylon and first 'owner' of this half of the sums levied. It may be inferred from this that the office of governor of the town – at least in Guzânu's case – included this 'perk', acting as a bonus, in the same way as those allotted to the keepers of the bridge. The interesting point here is that this benefit seems to have passed from the office to the person, since Guzânu had been able to transmit it to his son.

The role of the businessman

The man playing the most important role in the contract is Širku, son of Iddinaia, descendant of Egibi. At all events, it was in his archives that the text was included, in duplicate. Here he is mentioned under one of his two names, his customary civil status presenting him as Marduk-naşir-apli, son of Itti-Marduk-balâțu, descendant of Egibi. Without our knowing the precise reason, this practice of double-naming is attested several times in the private archives of the neo-Babylonian and Achaemenid periods. At least one text in the Egibi family archives specifies that 'Marduk-naşir-apli has Širku as his second name'. The position he occupies here has been his family's own for two generations: he is the businessman of the governor of Babylon, and his duty is to manage the governor's affairs, which means that he plays a part in public as well as private activities. In the same way, his grandfather was in the service of Nergal-šar-uşur before he became king of Babylon, then of Belshazzar, son of Nabonidus; *his* father had for a time managed the interests of Cambyses when he was crown prince.

All in all, we therefore have a document concerning the profits to be obtained by levying a mooring tax on boats arriving at Babylon from the north (descending) or from the south (ascending), by the Euphrates. This tax is not passed on to the state, but is used half to remunerate employees whose duty is to look after the bridge of Babylon, and half to pay the governor of the town, Guzânu, and his son Nabû-bullissu, represented by their business agent, Širku, together with another person, Murânu, whose status remains unknown.

The nature of the contract

The prime aim of the contract is the leasing by the two known as Bêl-asûa and Ubar of the operation of collecting taxes on the bridge and the wharf, against the monthly lump sum of 15 shekels of silver. The term used to designate their payment (*sûtu*) clearly indicates that it is a matter of leasing, not renting; in other words, that it represents part of the total profit actually collected, in the same way as the rent of the tenant farmer is only part of the crop. The guiding principle of this contract is fairly simple, in that it deals with the leasing of the collection of a tax.

The nature of the payments

However, the situation appears more complicated when, in the subsidiary clauses, we read that 'the income in silver from the taxes levied at the bridge will go directly to Širku and Murânu', in other words, payments collected in money are the property of the lessors (Širku and Murânu), and must be paid directly to Širku. This seems to contradict the principle of a flat payment: if the two tax farmers must pay a lump sum of 15 shekels of silver *and* hand over all the silver they collect to Širku and Murânu, what is in it for *them*? To understand, we must dissociate the two payments and take into account that, in Babylonia, taxes of this kind, levied on the cargoes of boats or caravans, were percentages of the freight transported. The collection made was therefore mainly composed of goods in kind: farm produce, animals, craft wares. But what interested the principal beneficiaries, such as the governor of Babylon and his business agent Širku, was to rake in the silver.

The search for metal money

The task assigned to the two lessees, Bêl-asûa and Ubar, was to proceed with the taxation operations, then to market by their own means the goods in kind thus collected, in order to amass the monthly payment of 15 shekels of silver. Their profit in this operation lay in the share that remained to them once the goods they had collected had been sold and the sum of 15 shekels deducted. But if the tax was paid in silver by some boatmen, it was not to enter the trading circuit and was to go directly to the two lessors, Širku and Murânu. From that we may deduce that the greater part of the tax levied was in kind, and that it was probably the two lessees, Bêl-asûa and Ubar, who suggested the fee to be paid, in response to a kind of 'invitation to tender'.

Administrators and entrepreneurs

We may equally conclude that here we are in a well-attested system, on the part of large institutional organisations like the royal palace or the big sanctuaries, of resorting to private entrepreneurs for the marketing of goods in kind. The royal administration paid the governor of Babylon by allocating to him part of the tax levied (for the most part in kind) at the town bridge and wharf. The governor entrusted the management of this revenue to his businessman, Širku, of the Egibi family; he in turn approached entrepreneurs who took on the actual job of collecting the tax and marketing the products collected. They paid him a lump sum in silver, which he himself passed on to his principal, the governor. Širku had it stipulated in the contract, however, that any tax payments made in silver must be passed to him directly, and that he reserved the right to examine 'any written instruction which might arise concerning the bridge tax'. This last clause referred to tax exemptions which might be granted by various civil or religious authorities, and the validity of which it was his business, and that of the bridge-keepers, to judge.

All in all, we can therefore see how, in a non-monetary economic system where metal money circulated fairly rarely, a tax in kind could be transformed into precious metal: thanks to businesspeople from the urban notability, who controlled marketing circuits, the administration had at its disposal, at the end of the circuit, a regular income in silver, without having to take a direct part in either the levying or the marketing of the products of taxation.

Chapter 9

From the Seleucids to the Parthians (331 BC to AD 75)

Mesopotamia, the centre of Alexander's empire in 323, subsequently argued over by the Diadochi, became one of the major provinces of the Seleucid kingdom, starting in 310. Greek settlement there was less important than in the western part of the Near East, despite the founding of Seleuceia on the Tigris. The region therefore kept its own particular features; it did not escape the centrifugal forces that affected the Seleucid kingdom beginning in the second century, and even regained its ancestral divisions between Assyria, which followed its own path, and Babylonia. In the latter there was a gradual emancipation of the south. From the years 140–130, attachment to the Arsacid Parthian empire cut Mesopotamia off from the West for a period of several centuries.

Although the Seleucids introduced some of their administrative practices in their Babylonian satrapy, they did not challenge the traditional organisation, and the sanctuaries continued to play a major role in local economy and society. Private archives reveal a strong polarisation of the urban notables around the temples, up to the first century BC.

Babylonian culture continued to be passed down in the heart of educated circles for nearly three centuries, but the rarity of cuneiform sources does not allow us to follow all the stages of its evolution, except in the case of astronomy. Berossus' attempt to present the fundamental elements of Mesopotamian civilisation to Hellenism does not appear to have met with a wide response, but 'Graeco-Babylonian' tablets (p. 252) prove that the transmission of Babylonian culture was able to proceed by hitherto unprecedented paths. This civilisation died out around the first century AD, in the heart of a country which henceforward obeyed other influences.

THE EVOLUTION OF THE SATRAPY OF BABYLONIA

The Greek conquest (331–305)

Alexander the Great had gained access to Mesopotamia at the battle of Gaugamela (1 October 331), on the territory of the old Assyria. After Darius III's withdrawal to northern Iran, the conqueror had been able to take possession of the entire region without a fight, and entered Babylon on 21 October.

Alexander and Babylon

All the available sources agree in thinking that the transition of power took place peaceably, and the end of Achaemenid domination was well received by the people of Babylon, the more so because their town remained a major centre of the new empire that was under construction, and their traditional practices, especially in religious matters, were unchanged. On his first passage, Alexander stayed only a short time in Babylon, but he set in motion a number of projects for the embellishment of the town and restorations, including that of the Esagil temple. In the Babylonians' perception, their new sovereign seemed to follow on almost naturally from the Achaemenid emperors, as is shown by the title 'king of the Lands' (*šar matâti*) which was given to him. On his return from India (324), Alexander really got to know Babylonia, ascending the Tigris as far as Opis, then visiting northern Babylonia. In extending the development begun by the Achaemenids, Alexander planned some improvement projects for the network of canals. The town itself was for a few months the capital of his immense empire; he installed himself in the royal palace and organised his future conquests.

The restoration of the Esagil temple in Alexander's reign

'A mina of silver, the tithe of Baruqaia, servant of Nabarzanu, has been paid for clearing the land of the Esagil, for the [good] fulfilment of his life, to Bêl [and] Bêltiya. The 6th Šabâtu of year 9 of Alexander, king.

Aramaic note: [document] of the removal of the soil of the Esagil.'

But illness carried off the conqueror on 10 June 323 in the royal palace. The fate of the empire was determined in Babylon, by the agreement reached in the summer of 323 by Alexander's generals, who conferred kingship on Philip Arrhidaeus, Alexander's brother, and his posthumous son, Alexander IV. The kings, whose guardianship had been entrusted to the regent Antipater, fairly soon set off for Macedonia. The major role acquired by Babylon at this time explains why its possession was disputed when conflicts broke out between the Diadochi, who were in charge of the various parts of the empire.

Seleucus and Antigonus

Business texts and Babylonian chronicles serve to illustrate the lively series of events in the country following the death of Alexander the Great. In the autumn of 321, the division of Triparadeisos in Syria allocated the satrapy of Babylonia to Seleucus. He made his entry into Babylon in November 321 and there began to organise his government, levying troops and taxes and having Borsippa's defence wall rebuilt. During 320, Antigonus the One-eyed, leader of the empire's armies, led an expedition against Eumenes of Cardia, which brought him into the neighbourhood of Babylonia. Beginning in late 318, Antigonus secured his grip on the region, gradually stripping Seleucus of his prerogatives. The methods of dating the cuneiform documents enable us to grasp the rivalry then, setting Antigonus against Seleucus: the first had them dated in his name, once the death of Philip III was known (he was assassinated in Macedonia in 317, though texts continued to be dated by his reign for a further year), whereas the second maintained dating by the other king, Alexander IV. In 316, Seleucus finally had to give way, and took refuge in Egypt; there he had to wait more than three years before fortune smiled on him anew. In the spring of 312, Antigonus and his son Demetrius suffered a decisive reverse at Gaza, in Palestine, and Seleucus set off to reconquer his former satrapy. After wintering in Upper Mesopotamia, with a troop of a thousand men, he entered Babylon at the end of spring 311.

The founding of the Seleucid kingdom

Seleucus stormed Babylon's citadel, in which the Antigonian garrison had taken refuge, then had himself acknowledged as royal satrap and general-in-chief throughout the country. The murder of Alexander IV in Macedonia in 310 did not prevent the preservation of his fictitious reign; Seleucus and the loyalist circles dated documents by his reign until 306.

The Seleucid era

Beginning from the reign of Seleucus I, a new system of dating was used in Babylonia, known as the Seleucid period. From a starting point that was fixed retrospectively in the Babylonian year which witnessed the disappearance of the last king of Alexander the Great's dynasty, his son Alexander IV (311–310), the years were counted consecutively, and no longer by successive reigns, as had been the practice for several centuries. Although Seleucus did not assume the royal title until 305, the years 311 to 305 were counted as the first of the Seleucid period. When the Parthians took Babylonia in July 141, a dual system was set up: while maintaining the Seleucid era, an Arsacid period was inaugurated, going back to 171, the start of the reign of the true founder of the dynasty, Mithridates I, known as Arsaces [V] the Great.

When some of Antigonus' generals marched from Media towards Babylon, accompanied by Iranian troops, Seleucus crossed the Tigris, inflicted total defeat on them and incorporated their soldiers into his own army. He then continued his eastward route to take possession of the Iranian satrapies. At the news of these successes, Antigonus sent Demetrius with an army of 19,000 men to Babylon. When he reached it, in September 310, Seleucus was still in Iran, and the strategos Patrocles, whom he had left in Babylon, had the town evacuated. Demetrius seized one of the two citadels Then he left Babylon to the strategos Archelaus and returned towards the Mediterranean. Between 309 and 307, Archelaus increased exactions in Babylonia, without managing to eliminate the resistance of troops who had remained loyal to Seleucus. In the end, it was Seleucus' return from Iran that settled the problem; in 306 he had completely recovered Babylonia and he assumed the royal title for the new year, in the spring of 305.

Seleucid Babylonia (305–141)

Transferring the capital

On his return from the expedition he had led as far as the eastern boundaries of his empire, Seleucus founded a new capital, Seleuceia on the Tigris, near the present-day site of Baghdad. Babylon became a simple regional capital, without in any way being neglected by the sovereign; in 294, he appointed his son Antiochus as co-regent, in charge of all the territories east of the Euphrates. But it was in the coastal regions of the Mediterranean that the fate of the kingdoms that had emerged from Alexander's empire was played out: after the assassination of Seleucus, Antiochus I (281–261) spent the first part of his reign in settling affairs in western Syria and Anatolia, and Mesopotamia remained apart from the conflicts, except between 274 and 271, during the first Syrian war between Antiochus I and the king of Egypt, Ptolemy II. From 271, Antiochus I organised his empire; he came to Babylon in 268, and the restoration of the Ezida of Borsippa probably dates to that time, celebrated by a Babylonian inscription in the name of Antiochus, which is the last known royal inscription in cuneiform. Twenty years later, in 245, following the death of Antiochus II, the third Syrian war brought king Ptolemy III to the edges of Mesopotamia; but disturbances in Egypt rapidly recalled him to his country, carrying away very large amounts of booty.

Regional divisions

While the distribution of power was taking shape in the north of the province, Babylon becoming simply a religious town whereas Seleuceia was the political capital, the southern part pursued a process that had already been under way since the Achaemenids. Indeed, a development of the cult of the god Anu has been noted, taking place during the Persian period, but more obvious attestations put it in the Seleucid era. Whereas in the neo-Babylonian period the goddess Ishtar, and her temple the Eanna, were the town's points of reference, the situation subsequently changed: the god Anu, chief of the Sumerian pantheon, who had been the town's predominant male deity in the third millennium, regained his key status. His sanctuary, the Bît Rêš, was restored on two occasions by Uruk's local authorities, and a ziggurat – the biggest in Mesopotamia – was added. The Eanna survived, but in a limited fashion, and the main worship of Ishtar and her associate Nanaia was performed in the Irigal, a temple close to the Bît Rêš. This development may be ascribed to efforts on the part of the educated circles of Uruk to return to sources, seeking to draw the town back to its Sumerian roots. It is also noteworthy that this emergence of the cult of Anu went hand in hand with the contemporary decline of Babylon, and that Anu seems to have acquired the status in Uruk that Marduk had enjoyed in Babylon. At this time Uruk had the role of capital of the south, and it all seemed as if, after a gap of two millennia, the old dichotomy between the countries of Sumer and Akkad was resurfacing. In parallel, the development of maritime trade by way of the Persian Gulf made the fortune of Antioch of Characene, which replaced an earlier Alexandria, and its connection with the land trade route which reached Palmyra, then the Mediterranean, enabled the former Land of the Sea to acquire the foundations of an autonomy which is evident on the political plane at the end of the Seleucid period.

From the centre to the periphery

The end of the third century saw centrifugal forces at work on the eastern part of the Seleucid empire. Beginning in 239, Scytho-Parnian nomads, led by their king Arsaces, started to settle near the satrapy of Parthia-Hyrcania, east of the Caspian Sea. The gradual occupation of the territory gave them their name (Parthians), but they were still contained until the beginning of the second century, and would not definitively occupy Parthia until the reign of Mithridates I (171–139).

An initial effort to restore order in the Iranian territories was made by Seleucus II between 230 and 227, but it was short-lived, and Mesopotamia was even part of the attempt at usurpation and secession by the satrap Molon, who was in charge of the higher satrapies in 220. It was Antiochus III who, between 210 and 206, re-established Seleucid sovereignty over the east of the kingdom. On his return, he took part in the New Year festival in Babylon (205), then made sure of control over access to the trade routes to India by means of a maritime expedition in the Gulf in 204, which resulted in a treaty with the trading town of Gerrha, in Arabia. His defeat at the hands of the Romans at Magnesia ad Sipylum in 190, however, followed by the peace of Apamea, had grave consequences for the Seleucid kingdom; it lost its western territories and had to pay Rome 15,000 talents of silver. Of course, with south-east Anatolia, Syria-Palestine, Mesopotamia and the whole of Iran, it still represented a considerable power, but Antiochus III was short of resources and sought to obtain them from all the territories under his authority. In 187, he took part in ceremonies at Borsippa and Babylon, where he was presented with the mantle of Nebuchadnezzar II; but he was killed a few months later, while seizing the wealth of a temple of Zeus/Bêl in Elymais.

The arrival of the Arsacids (166–141)

The conquest of Mesopotamia

From 166, the spread of the Parthians to the south of the Caspian Sea cut across the route of the eastern satrapies. Antiochus IV, who was planning an eastern expedition, died after trying to remove the treasure of the temple of Nanaia at Susa, leaving a successor who was a minor. In the west, the Romans arbitrated over the changes of king and played on the dynastic conflict between the sons of Seleucus IV and Antiochus IV. Demetrius I Soter (162–151), son of Seleucus IV, who had been sent to Rome as a hostage in 175, managed to escape, had Antiochus V, son of Antiochus IV, assassinated and then mounted the throne, curried favour with the Romans by means of sumptuous gifts. He put down the rebellion of the Maccabees in Judaea, and rid Babylonia of the tyranny exerted there by the strategos Timarchus. But in 160, the satrap of Characene seceded and formed an independent kingdom of Mesene/Characene, in south Babylonia, a resurgence of the Sealand of the mid-first millennium, with its capital Spasinou Charax, a new name for Antioch of Characene, while Susa and the region surrounding Elymais were similarly detached from the empire and the Parthian king, Mithridates I, began the conquest of Iran. In early July 141, the Parthian army entered Seleuceia. Then a period of several years of disturbances and wars in Babylonia commenced. The region was the theatre for many confrontations: twice the Seleucids tried to regain possession of their territories east of the Euphrates, under Demetrius II in 140, then Antiochus VII in 130, but restored their power for no more than a few months, and finally lost Babylonia completely after the defeat and death of Antiochus VII in 129.

For their part, the Parthians' western expansion was held back by the need to intervene at the same time in the eastern region of their empire against the nomadic tribes who were attacking them. Late in 141, Mithridates I withdrew his forces from Babylonia to send them to the east. He recovered the country between 139 and 130, but his young successor Phraates II was killed in an encounter with Scythian tribes in 129. Parthian rule in Babylonia was in fact delegated to local officials, bearing various titles: general, governor (*pahat*), satrap (*muma'iru*). The outstanding figure was Himerus, a Hyrcanian installed by Phraates II in 129, and one who abused his power. South Babylonia was prey to looting expeditions from Elymais, which had re-formed itself into an independent kingdom, and from Arab tribes, who launched raids as far as Babylon itself. The dynast of Mesene/Characene, Hyspaosines, profited from this to extend his area of influence from the Sealand as far as Babylonia. In 128, he eliminated Himerus, and seems to have exerted his authority over the whole of ancient Babylonia. The sovereignty of the new Parthian king, Artaban I (127–124), therefore remained nominal until his general Timarchus was able to reoccupy Babylon and its region at the end of 127. It was not until 125, however, that the Parthian ruler regained possession of Lower Mesopotamia: he inflicted a heavy defeat on Elam. The death of Hyspaosines in 124 enabled him to resettle himself definitively in Babylonia, and Mesene/Characene itself had to submit in 122. The new Parthian king, Mithridates II (123–88), was henceforward in a position to develop the

Arsacid empire in spectacular fashion: he went up the Euphrates and seized Dura Europus in 113. All the territories east of the Euphrates were now under his rule. But in 91, Gotarzes set up a virtually autonomous kingdom in Babylonia.

Arsacid Babylonia

The chronological data furnished by the astronomical texts enable us near enough to follow the course of Parthian history during the first half of the first century BC, in the reigns of Gotarzes I (91–81), then Orodes I (80–78), up to Phraates III (70–58). From Mithridates II on, Parthian sovereigns took the title 'king of kings'; dating formulae give them the dynastic name of Arsaces (*Aršakâ*), sometimes followed by their personal name (*Guṭarza, Urudâ*) and that of their wife. Starting in the reign of Phraates III, only the dynastic name survives. The documentation available in cuneiform becomes much more rare and almost exclusively of an astronomical nature. Subsequently, only the years 58–57 and the beginning of the last decade of the century, in 12–11 and 7–6, are attested. From 58 BC, indeed, the Parthian empire entered a turbulent period, marked by royal instability that was dramatically accentuated at the end of the century. At the same time, the Parthians carried on a series of offensive or defensive wars, in which they were generally victorious, against the Romans, who in this period eliminated the remains of the Seleucid kingdom in Syria (63) and imposed their protectorate on Armenia. In 66–65, Pompey had challenged the tacit agreement which made the Euphrates the frontier between zones of Roman and Parthian influence, and upheld the claims to independence of the dynasts of Elymais and Media. The forceful reaction of Phraates III (70–58) put an end to this initial encroachment, and the earlier status quo was re-established in 64. Crassus' ill-fated expedition in 53 ended in total defeat at Harrân (Carrhae). When civil war set the Roman territories ablaze,

the Parthians served as a withdrawal base for Pompey's sup-
porters and the other opponents of Caesar. From 40 to 38,
the armies of Orodes II (58–39) invaded Syria-Palestine,
under the leadership of his son Pacorus, getting as far as
Jerusalem. But Pacorus was killed in a minor confrontation,
and the Parthian troops, repulsed by Mark Antony, evacuated the region: the Romano-Parthian frontier was once
again set at the Euphrates.

The crisis of the first century AD

The whole early part of the first century AD was similarly
marked by political instability in the Parthian empire, which
resulted in a veritable civil war, beginning with a member of
a junior branch of the Arsacid dynasty seizing power; he was
Artaban II (12–*c*.38), from Media Atropatene. The Parthian
empire's western territories lived in quasi-autonomy at that
time, with an independent dynasty in Adiabene, the new
name for Assyria, and local governments in revolt, including
the one set up by Asileus and Asineus, two members of the
Jewish community in Babylonia, around 20–35. From 36 to
43, the town of Seleuceia also broke free from Parthian
control, and not until the middle of the first century AD would
that control be gradually re-established in Mesopotamia, in
particular in the reign of Vologeses I (51–76). Throughout
this time the frontier with the Roman empire remained fixed
along the course of the Euphrates. It may be considered,
however, that the process of the disappearance of Babylonian
civilisation properly speaking accelerated during the second
half of the first century; the last datable (astronomical) cuneiform tablet belongs to 75 AD. Henceforward, the country's
history would clearly fall under other influences.

The resurrection of Assyria

Assyria had never fully recovered from the destruction of
614–612 BC. The urban centres of the Tigris valley, with the

exception of Ashur, had been abandoned, and the majority of the population resettled in the hills of the right bank, mainly around Arbela. In the Achaemenid period, Xenophon's *Anabasis* clearly reveals the general paucity of resources along the Tigris when the Greek mercenaries went up it, when Persian troops kept them out of the hilly areas in the east. The Achaemenids had carved out great princely or noble domains in this region, of which Arbela had become the capital, and the 'royal road' also passed through it from Anatolia to the empire's capitals. This area, which had again become essentially rural, remained so after Alexander's conquest, and no important Seleucid settlement is listed there, unless the refounding of Nineveh as a Greek city should be placed at that time. The arrival of the Parthians brought changes: part of the site of Nineveh was reoccupied, and the former temple of Nabû was even restored. In the first century BC, the town had become an administrative centre again, with a mint at its disposal and a governmental structure with an epistates-strategos, Apollonius, mentioned on two inscriptions, around 32–31 BC. Similarly, Kalhu, Ashur (under the name Libana) in the Tigris valley and Arbela on the eastern foothills had become real towns once more; Assyrian religious practices flourished anew, with the same deities (Ashur and Šeru'a), which proves the fairly astonishing survival of a tradition that was sufficiently hardy to have endured through several centuries. In the Parthian empire, Assyria formed a special province, Adiabene, within boundaries that were fairly close to those of the Assyria of the early first millennium. The dynasty who ruled it converted to Judaism in the first century AD. Trajan incorporated Adiabene into the Roman empire in 115, under the name of the province of Assyria, but it became autonomous again in the following year. Recovered by the Romans in 166, then at the end of the second century, it remained under their thumb for some fifty years. A good part of Upper Mesopotamia was transformed into a fortified frontier (*limes*) by the Romans, Assyria forming its eastern tip, with a bridgehead on the Tigris. Nineveh became a rich trading place on the caravan route linking the Far East with the Mediterranean, as evidenced, for example, by the discovery of a particularly elaborate statue of Hercules dating to the first or second century AD, in an era when he was assimilated to the Babylonian god Nergal at Hatra.

SOCIO-ECONOMIC REALITIES

Organisation of the territory

The administration

As Babylonia constituted a satrapy, it was placed under the rule of a satrap (*muma'iru*) installed in Babylon but, like many regions in the Seleucid empire, it included towns and territories of varying status. Some towns, first and foremost Seleuceia on the Tigris, had the status of a city, with their own municipal institutions. The traditional large towns do not seem to have enjoyed the same status, but retained certain privileges, often connected with their religious importance. Such was the case of Babylon, at least until Antiochus IV. In astronomical notes beginning at that date we find mention of 'citizens', *puliṭê/puliṭânu* (cf. Greek *politēs*), of Babylon, which would appear to indicate that the town had acquired the rank of city and supports the reference, in a Greek inscription from Babylon of 166, to Antiochus IV as 'founder of the city' (*ktistē tēs poleōs*). Aside from the territories that were dependent on the towns, the greater part of the rest of Babylonia must have been royal land (*chōra*), but there are very few clues. It would seem that the lands allocated in 253 by Antiochus II to his repudiated wife, Laodicea, and his two sons were taken from this royal domain.

Taxes

Nothing is known about the tribute and the method by which it was levied in Babylonia, but the Seleucid presence is clearly revealed there by the institution of new taxes, or ones taken over from the Achaemenids, on trading operations (*eponiōn*). For the sale of slaves, a tax specific to this type of transaction had to be paid (*andrapodikōn* or *andrapodōn*).

The role of the *chreophylax*

The payment of this tax was recorded by a royal official, the *chreophylax*, and the contract placed in the archives. Because of this, the requirement to write these contracts on parchment or papyrus, accompanied by a small lump of clay bearing the personal seal of the parties to the deed and the *chreophylax*, and deposit them in an official building, resulted in the disappearance of cuneiform contracts on clay tablets concerning the sale of slaves and farmlands. Beginning in the years 37–38 of the Seleucid era (275–273 BC), only the sales of houses and prebends, which were not subject to the *eponiōn* tax, continued to be drawn up in the traditional manner. In the reign of Antiochus III, in year 92 of the Seleucid era (220 BC), the clay tags that accompanied contracts on papyrus or parchment (which had naturally disappeared) were replaced by a more elaborate system of balls or strips of clay in which the contract on papyrus was inserted, and which bore the stamp of the official seals used by the royal functionaries whose job was to collect taxes, and no longer only the personal seal of the *chreophylax*.

Each of these stages – institution by Antiochus I, reinforcement of the system under Antiochus III – corresponds historically to moments when the Seleucid government had to devote considerable sums to its military efforts. They reveal the application of a system of taxation and official recording of sales in Babylonia that was current throughout the empire, and is equally attested in Ptolemaic Egypt. In contrast, the system is no longer attested when Babylonia was conquered by the Parthians.

The use of coinage

Another event connected with the Greek presence was the partial introduction of currency in trade. While coinage spread throughout the Mediterranean basin, beginning in the sixth century, the interior Near East continued to operate with precious metal weighed according to the traditional units of the mina and shekel. Babylonian texts of the Seleucid, then Arsacid, era show that the system remained basically the same, but that silver was fairly frequently used in the form of coins, even to the point of cutting them to obtain the exact weight needed for a transaction. It was therefore not a matter of a conversion to the system of currency, but acknowledgement that, at least at the beginning of the period, these coins were of excellent quality and made of virtually pure silver. A Babylonian chronicle even mentions the circulation of bronze money, in certain circumstances, but that was in times of crisis, linked with the temporary disappearance of silver as the current standard. But that traditional practice affected only the Babylonian population: in Hellenised circles, coinage played its normal role, and Babylon, then Seleuceia, were home to mints striking the coinage of Alexander the Great and then of the Seleucid dynasty.

Temple management

Restoration and administration

Seleucid religious policy did not neglect the Babylonian sanctuaries. It is known that Antiochus I was credited with the restoration of the Ezida at Borsippa. Some sites, such as Nippur, Larsa and Uruk, also had restorations carried out, but others, such as Sippar, did not receive the benefit of the same attention, and the temple of Shamash, apparently in ruins since the Achaemenid era, was not rebuilt. The temples continued to be administered collegially by the assembly of the religious staff and the main prebendaries, under the authority of the *šatammu*. A text from Nippur supplies the hierarchy of the administrative officers of the temple of Enlil in 154 BC: the *šatammu* was assisted by an *episkupusu* (a Greek title that seems to have replaced the former *ša rêš šarri bêl piqitti*), and by an *ammarakalu* (a Persian title equivalent to the former chief scribe of the temple). The members of the temple college (*kiništu*) deliberated in particular over certain appointments, for example examining the technical abilities of new astrologers attached to the temple and determining how they should be paid. For staff holding titular office, it was often a matter of income procured from land in the temple's domain. At Uruk, we find bow fiefs belonging to prebendaries, which have therefore been returned to sacred status and freed from the military obligations that were attached to them in the Achaemenid era.

Appointment of a new astrologer to the Esagil, in 110 BC

'The [...] of year 130 [of the Arsacid era], Bêl-lumur, *šatammu* of the Esagil, and the Babylonians constituting the Assembly of the Esagil have deliberated among themselves and have declared: "The 15-x of year 129 [of the Arsacid era] we have jointly drawn up a memorandum by which we would institute in favour of Nabu-apla-uṣur, singer and astrologer, son of Nabû-mušêtiq-ṣêti, a payment of one mina of silver according to the standard of Babylon [about 500 g] and a piece of arable land, previously belonging to Bêl-apla-uṣur, astrologer, son of Bêl-rîmanni, astrologer, who was appointed to the celestial observation of astrological phenomena [...]."'

Continuing worship

Among the numerous religious texts retrieved at Uruk, several are concerned with rituals. They are often copies, made in the Seleucid period, of canonical texts whose content varied little down through the centuries, such as the series of the lamenter's ritual, which is almost identical to the version discovered in the neo-Assyrian library of Nineveh. But the rituals relating to the worship of Anu are of more immediate topicality since they correspond to the re-emergence of this god, starting in the Achaemenid era; they indicate the updating of far more ancient rituals or the adaptation to this cult of liturgies of the first millennium. These texts enable us to have a fairly precise idea of the gestures performed, the prayers recited and the quantities of foodstuffs forming the daily offerings. The ritual for purifying the temple thus specifies that a torch must be lit on the ziggurat in the presence of the nocturnal stars and afterwards solemnly carried to the various parts of the temple. Similarly, the tablets of Uruk devoted to the ritual of the festival of the *Akîtu* in Babylon describe in great detail the programme for the various days, and indicate the personnel involved, as well as the manipulations they must carry out. One may wonder, however, if in the latter instance the ritual was not first and foremost a text of historical reference, but whose practical aspect had become somewhat blurred. The king's participation in this ceremony had no longer been a reality since the Achaemenid period, and if certain Seleucid kings took part it was only on isolated occasions.

Economic means

Following the reorganisation of local authorities undertaken by the Achaemenid rulers, the temples' domains were probably restricted and the sanctuaries of the final years of the first millennium do not appear to have had such a large workforce as formerly. Religious personnel remained numerous, however, and some texts from Babylon at the beginning of the Greek period show that the temple of Marduk numbered several dozen lamentation priests. But a fusion had taken place between the religious and administrative staff; it is not rare to find people who combine managerial activities with a religious office, and the lists of distribution of food rations are concerned not only with members of the temple staff, but also with their families (wives and children). To ensure the service of the cult and the upkeep of the staff, the temples had their own resources available – less plentiful than formerly, but still considerable by comparison with individual estates – and public and private donations, collected in offertory boxes placed at the temple's entrance. Until the time of the Arsacids, they thus functioned as economic organisations, but increasingly merged. The staff of Babylon's Esagil, for instance, had the task of maintaining other temples in the town; similarly, the management of the temple of Shamash, in the neighbouring town of Larsa, was centralised at Uruk.

Accounts of the Esagil in 94 BC

'1 mina 7 shekels ¹⁄₁₂ of silver [around 526 g], deposited in the *ṣuraru*-purse inside the *hallat*-basket and entrusted on deposit to Rahimêsu. The [...] of year 154 [of the Arsacid era], that is, year 128 [of the Seleucid era]; 18 shekels ⁵⁄₁₂ of silver [around 153 g], deposited in the *ṣuraru*-purse inside the *hallat*-basket and entrusted on deposit to Rahimêsu, the 30-X of year 154, that is, year 128. Taken away. General total: 1 mina 26 shekels ³⁄₁₂ [around 719 g]. Withdrawals on this sum:

[...] 5 shekels ½ [around 48 g] for the charcoal for the burners of the Great Gate of the Esagil, the entrance door of the chapel of Bêltiya, the entrance door of the chapel of Madânu, of the Eturkalamma, of the orchard of juniper trees surrounding the temple, of the temple of Gula Ehursagsikilla, of the temple of Gula Ehursagkuga, for supplying bread for the daily offerings of this temple of Gula, and for the needs of the maintenance staff of the Gates of the Esagil, were paid from the 1-XI of year 218 up to the 11-XII of the same year, from the hands of Rahimêsu.'

Private archives

New data

The distribution of private archives is concentrated on a few sites from the end of the fourth century BC. Setting aside Ur, where the batch of archives of the family of the Barber (*Gallabu*) covers the end of the Achaemenid period and the very beginning of the Greek presence, but subsequently ceases, only two sites have consistently provided archives of this type: Babylon and Uruk. Uruk's archives clearly emanate from the clergy associated with the temple of Anu; those of Babylon are more diffuse, but equally document traditional private activities: money-lending, contracts for developing agricultural land, leasing a house. One of the new features is the presence in the contracts, in far from negligible numbers, of Greek names rendered in cuneiform transcription; but these new names, early in the period, do not correspond to a population of Hellenic origin. First of all, it was an occurrence already attested in the Persian era whereby certain members of the Babylonian population 'borrowed' names from the region's political leaders. A Hellenisation of Babylonian towns must not be inferred from this; on the contrary, it seems as if the Greek population established themselves in structures that were specific to them, especially in the empire's new capital, Seleuceia on the Tigris. Another Greek settlement appears to be attested in an Antioch of the canal of Ishtar, near Uruk, which might explain that true Greeks of Greek origin had a hand in certain private transactions in the town, but not until the middle of the second century BC.

The case of Uruk

The bulk of the documentation found at Uruk for the Seleucid and Parthian periods (chiefly the former) certainly reveals the already mentioned occurrence of a virtually autonomous development of the south of Lower Mesopotamia, probably connected with the vigorous trading activity going on at that time in the Persian Gulf, which was reflected in the great metropolis of southern Babylonia. Even the ancestral site of Girsu, which apparently had not been occupied since early in the second millennium, experienced some sort of activity, as it became the centre of a small principality whose leader, Adad-nâdin-ahi, had a palace built for him during the second century BC on the site of the former temple of the god Ningirsu. The town of Uruk may possibly have enjoyed a special status, like the religious principalities known in the rest of the Seleucid empire, particularly in Anatolia; at its head was a governor appointed by the king, bearing the title *šaknu*. This representative of royal authority was flanked by another local leader, coming from the temple of Anu and having the title *rab ša rêš âli*, 'chief of the officers of the town', or *paqdu ša bît ilâni*, 'appointed in charge of temple affairs'. It is significant that the two leading offices were in the hands of the descendants of Ah'ûtu, one of the great families of Urukian notables since the neo-Babylonian era. Several holders of one or other post had both a Babylonian and a Greek name simultaneously, the most obvious instance being Anu-uballiṭ, son of Anu-balâssu-iqbi, who also had the name Kephalōn, and several of whose direct relatives had a Greek name. Anu-uballiṭ/Kephalōn organised the restoration of the temple and ziggurat of the god Anu, having bricks inserted in the walls inscribed in Babylonian cuneiform and alphabetic Aramaic, in his name, following the example of the former Babylonian sovereigns.

The last Babylonian notables

It has been possible to identify and analyse a certain number of private archives at Uruk which show the persistence of the system of urban notables divided into large family groups: the archives of the descendants of Luštammar-Adad are spread across seven generations and a total of nearly eighty individuals, counting allied families. A particular onomastic phenomenon of paponymy characterises these families. The name of the grandfather is given quasi-systematically to one of the members of the children's generation, and this system seems to have been extended to women, the grandmother's name recurring in that of one of her granddaughters.

Examples of Babylonian transcriptions of Greek names in the Uruk texts

Babylonian form	Corresponding Greek name
Andarniqûsu	Andronikos
Aristukratê	Aristokratēs
Dimgiratê, Di'imukratê	Demokratēs
Di'upanṭe'ussu, Di'ipattûsu, Dippatusu	Diophantos
Kiplûnu	Kephalōn
Nik'arqurasu, Nikarqûsu	Nikarkos
Niqalamûsu	Nikolaos
Panaia	Phanaia

The economic activities of these families are revealed through their contracts, and sometimes show specialised areas; for instance, certain descendants of Ekur-zâkir made efforts, across several generations, to build up groups of prebends by buying shares of blocks of service and combining them. For their part, descendants of Arad-Rêš favoured real-estate investment, buying up tracts of developed land in Uruk which were also grouped together in larger holdings. The most numerous and powerful families, like those of the descendants of Hunzû, diversified their activities into almost every field and went into buying or selling. The absence of contracts concerning slaves and farmlands does not enable us to judge the total value of the patrimony of these families, but the socio-economic circuit into which it falls follows nearly the same rules as in the neo-Babylonian era and reflects identical phases of dispersal and reconstitution. The assets sold were generally very small; prebends in particular related to blocks of service that might be no more than fractions of an hour. Some of the urban plots sold are quoted as the property of the Treasury of Anu, and confirm the close involvement between the temple management and the circle of notables.

Northern Babylonia

The activities of Babylon's notables come within the same context, the more so because the archives appear to emanate particularly from the Esagil complex. Two examples, at opposite ends of the period of Seleucid rule, illustrate the same kind of involvement. The first documents the activities between 277 and 253 BC of Murânu, son of Bêl-bullissu, then of his son Ea-tabtan-bulliṭ, both shipwrights of the sacred boat of the god Bêl (lú nagar giš-má-u₅). The twenty-eight documents mentioning them are divided between promissory notes issued by the temple's administrative authorities and IOUs. Murânu and his son seem to have had the task of distributing the money from the revenue of the *bît abistatu* (perhaps to be understood as the domain of the *epistates*, or chairman) and the revenue of the *taggamânu* (meaning unknown) in subsistence allowances for the artisans (jewellers, weavers) or religious staff (exorcists) of the Esagil. At the same time, we find them lending to private individuals brewing equipment or money which either belong to the temple or come from their own resources. They are therefore not simply officials of the temple of Bêl/Marduk, but rather of a type we have already encountered – businessmen incorporated into a traditional structure, at the heart of which they perform a craft function but also manage its trading and financial activities.

Promissory note for the payment of a ration, in 262 BC

'Letter from Bêl-ibni, the *šatammu* of the Esagil, representative of Nikanor and Babylonians forming the college of the Esagil, to Murânu, son of Bêl-bullissu, shipwright of the sacred vessel: "Pay out of the money at your disposal for the subsistence rations of the [...], 31 shekels of silver, money from the domain of the epistates [provided] by Kiramanne and Tibulisu, the sons of Iddinaia, in the months VI and XII of year 50, to Ea-iddin, son of Marduk-šum-iddin, the [...]" [Made] on 5-VII of year 50 of Antiochus [I] the great king, and of his son Antiochus. A copy [of this note] has been made on parchment.'

The second example is dated at the end of the Seleucid era; eighteen texts illustrate the activities of Râhimêsu over the years 94 and 93 BC. He bears the title 'keeper of the council building' (*nâṣir ša bît milki*), but in reality acts as the Esagil's accountant. In fact, he collects the offerings deposited by private persons at the gates of the temple's chapels, keeps them under his responsibility in a casket called *naštuq* (the Babylonian form of the Greek *narthex*), then has the duty of dividing them among the temple's disbursements, often connected with the purchase of products or payment of wages. It is therefore basically a matter of balance sheets, and Râhimêsu does not seem to have carried on a purely private activity in this context. But at the same time, it should be noted that this kind of management could be leased out; a contract of 89 BC indeed records the leasing by a *kurgâru* of the Esagil of the income produced by these offerings. Right up to the last period of their existence, Babylonian temples involved in their system of internal management people who, while members of their staff, had the relationship with the temple of a private commercial representative.

THE SLOW END OF A CIVILISATION

The transmission of Babylonian culture from within

Families of scribes and training

Among the corpus of learned texts datable to this last period of Babylonian civilisation, some bear often detailed colophons that provide information not only on the structure of the great canonical series on astrology, extispicy and liturgical lamentations, but also on scribal practice. The families of Egibi and Nanna'ûtu in Babylon, Ekur-zâkir and Sîn-leqe-unninni at Uruk, produced men of letters who followed an apprenticeship in their science that was closely linked with the practice of writing. First of all they were apprentices (*šamallû*) before acquiring the title of their speciality: astrologer, conjurer, lamenter, singer/cantor. In the final phase of their training, the *šamallû* copied the great texts of learned tradition, either for the use of their teacher or for the sanctuary that housed them. At that point a tendency to esotericism surfaced, certain colophons specifying that the tablet must not be communicated except to the initiated, others perversely using a numerical cuneiform type of writing, which has not always been decipherable. Most of these tablets are remarkable for the quality of their writing, whereas contemporary business documents use a cursive form that is fairly difficult to read. Although the essence of the learned tradition was handed down on the spot, within the families of the educated or under the aegis of the temples, some scribes continued to seek out texts in libraries other than those of their workplace.

A colophon from Uruk

'Copy by the hand of Šamaš-êṭir, son of Ina-qibît-Anu, grandson of Šipqat-Anu: record-tablet of the rites of the cult of the great gods, of the sacred liturgies, of the royal ritual and divine liturgy of the Bît Rêš, the Irigal, the Eanna and temples of the Sacred Quarter of Uruk, of the liturgical activities of the exorcists, lamenters and singers as well as the experts in their entirety [...] not to mention everything concerning the apprentices, according to the content of the tablets which Nabû-apla-uṣur, king of the Sealand, had carried off from within Uruk. In the time when Kidin-Anu, the Urukean, the exorcist of Anu and Antu, the descendant of Ekur-zâkir, the high priest of the Bît Reš, was able to examine these tablets in the land of Elam, in the reigns of the kings Seleucus [I] and Antiochus, he copied them and brought them back to Uruk.'

Libraries of the literati

It has been possible to identify two private libraries on the site of Uruk, and their contents reflect both the activities of their owners and a concern to supplement their knowledge by the addition of commentaries on certain texts of the series on omens and religion. For instance, in the house of Iqîšaia, an exorcist, descendant of Ekur-zâkir and his son, Ištar-šum-êreš, over 200 tablets or fragments were found, forming a learned library, for the most part dated 318–316. One of those tablets was in neo-Assyrian writing, and bears a colophon of Ashurbanipal; it would therefore come from the library of Nineveh. In the collection are several extracts from the great series on astrological and teratalogical omens, accompanied by texts of commentaries, including one on prices in the astronomical texts, as well as several magical texts, but also some representatives of great Babylonian literature, including extracts from the *Epic of Gilgamesh* and the *Exaltation of Ishtar*. The temple of Anu itself kept a library of scholarly tablets.

The external transmission of Babylonian culture

Berossus

Berossus is known as a priest of Bêl/Marduk of Babylon, at the end of the fourth and beginning of the third century BC, thus a contemporary of the first Seleucids. He wrote a work in Greek, traditionally quoted as *Babyloniaca*, or sometimes as *Chaldaica*, which he must have composed around 281 for the information of Antiochus I, with the aim of presenting a survey of all that was known about Babylonian civilisation. At the end of his life, Berossus left Mesopotamia to settle in the island of Cos, under Ptolemaic rule, where he taught 'Chaldaean' astronomy and astrology, apparently with great success. Berossus has acquired partly legendary aspects, and Hellenistic tradition turned him into the prototype of the Chaldaean astrologer, attributing the invention of a certain model of sundial to him. Pliny the Elder reports that, to honour his knowledge of astronomical predictions, the Athenians had erected a statue of him in one of their gymnasia and, according to Pausanias, his wife Erymanthe gave him a daughter named Sabbe who would become the famous Babylonian Sibyl. Berossus' work has not come down to us directly and probably did not have very wide circulation, since all the writers of antiquity who quote it rely on a summary of the *Babyloniaca* drawn up by the Milesian Alexander Polyhistor in the first century BC. There was a copy of the *Babyloniaca*, however, in the Library of Alexandria.

The *Babyloniaca*

Notwithstanding its chronological type of presentation, Berossus' work does not claim to be historical in the Greek sense of the term. His aim was to present Greek readers with 'the history of the sky and the sea, the first birth, kings and their deeds', but according to the traditional Babylonian conception of the past. The chronological improbabilities, the outstanding position attributed to Babylon, regarded as the birthplace of humanity, the account of the reigns nearest to Berossus' own period, especially those of Sennacherib and Nebuchadnezzar II, emphasising their respective actions as destroyer and rebuilder of Babylon, reveal this outlook. So Berossus did not assemble the documents he uses for his personal benefit, but rather to give a glimpse of what was traditionally taught to the educated in Seleucid Babylonia. At no time is it an 'inquiry' into Mesopotamian history, but more the presentation of the Babylonian concept of human history, as it was passed on in the scholarly circles of his time. The astronomical parts of Berossus' work include information about the moon, which is portrayed as a sphere, one half of which is luminous and the other dark, revolving round the sun. It has been noted that the level of astronomical knowledge matching this description of the moon is that of the fifth tablet of the Babylonian *Epic of the Creation*. It obviously does not match the level attained in the Seleucid period, and that casts doubt on the eminent position ascribed to Berossus as the one who introduced Babylonian astronomy into the Greek world.

The Graeco-Babylonian texts

Among the learned tablets of Uruk there is a text in cuneiform but which is a transcription from an original in Aramaic. Its existence reveals a kind of exchange of knowledge between the traditional culture of educated Babylonians and that which predominated at the time in the Near East. But henceforward this exchange is best attested in Greek writings from Babylon, in Babylonian or Sumerian, inscribed in both cuneiform and the Greek alphabet; the latter had the advantage, among alphabetic scripts, of noting vowels as well as consonants, thus allowing a faithful transcription from a Babylonian or Sumerian original. The use of Greek as the language of culture under the Seleucids, and also under the Arsacids, means that here it is not necessarily a matter of the transmission of Babylonian knowledge to well-read Greeks. The practice of bilingual Graeco-Babylonian texts provides an indication of how a process was able to develop locally for passing on information by means of a common language/writing (*koinē*) that was more widespread than Sumero-Akkadian cuneiform. A fair number of these little texts are in fact extracts from lexical lists which we know formed part of the initial training of educated Babylonians. Once they had mastered the vocabulary and the ability to read the originals in cuneiform, it is probable that the well-read in that terminal phase of Babylonian culture transcribed them onto a material better adapted to cursive Greek script, such as parchment or papyrus. It is therefore assumed that, although the effective practice of cuneiform writing must have disappeared in the second half of the first century AD, knowledge of the language and Sumero-Akkadian texts could have survived for a few more decades in learned circles of the western part of the Parthian empire. The death blow would have been inflicted by the Roman armies that ravaged Babylonia and destroyed Seleuceia in the reign of Marcus Aurelius, in AD 165.

The last traces

Babylonia after the first century AD

According to the present state of documentation, the end of official worship in the Esagil occurred at the end of the Arsacid Parthian era. Part of the sacred area of the Esagil, cluttered with the debris which had piled up to a height of several metres, had already been occupied by individual buildings as early as the end of the first century BC. While being used for residential purposes, some of them also had an official function, especially a large dwelling complete with a peristyle, built to the south-east of the Esagil, in which a kind of sacred treasure was found. This edifice had been in use until the beginning of the Sassanid period, which leads one to suppose the continuance of religious practices perhaps up to that time. Under Šahpur II (310–79), mention is still found of a 'priest of the king Bêl', and a Greek inscription from Borsippa even seems to indicate the practice of a Babylonian cult up to the fourth century. Nevertheless, it is clear that the old Assyro-Babylonian civilisation no longer awoke any echo in the country. The Sassanid empire drew its political ideology from Iranian traditions, even though its capital was at Ctesiphon, on the Tigris. Babylonia's population was in the process of Arabisation, and the languages of its vernacular and culture were Syriac Aramaic and Greek; the outstanding religious communities were Jewish, Christian, Nestorian, Mazdean or Manichean. There was no longer any support to perpetuate the Assyro-Babylonian civilisation, so it gradually died out at the time when the Sassanid empire was establishing itself.

Magi and astrologers

It was certainly not due to chance that cuneiform writing lasted longest in the fields of astronomy and astrology; the remarkable conformity between the method of notation of astronomical data and the cuneiform system made the use of another form of writing pointless. Moreover, this scientific field was truly specific to Babylonia. Once the mathematical bases of their astronomy were established, knowledge of a centuries-old corpus of observations and interpretations of omens enabled Babylonian astrologers to spread their speciality through neighbouring regions and to Rome itself. This process was accompanied, however, by a loss of the primary meaning of their science, which became reduced to the not always lawful practice of horoscopes and astrology, which ensured the celebrity of the 'Chaldaean' astrologers, and then the magi.

DOCUMENT

Religious activities in the Seleucid period: renting out a prebend

'Kidin-Anu, son of Anu-ahhê-iddin, [grand]son of Nanaia-iddin, descendant of Hunzû, has spoken of his own accord in these terms to Anu-mâr-ittanu, son of Anu-ušallim, descendant of Luštamar-Adad:

"Give me for ten years 1/6 plus 1/15 plus 1/6 of 1/60 of a day, on the 11th and 12th days of the month, that is, in total, 402 litres 1/2, [forming] your prebend of sacrificial butcher before Anu, Antu, Ishtar, Nanaia, the lady of the Bît Rêš and all the other gods and their sanctuaries, for all the months of the year, [with] the income of the *guqqû*-offerings and that of the *eššeššû*-ceremonies.

"I will perform your office and will give you two sacrificial-butcher portions, two heads [of sheep], as well as two portions of meat [...], each month, and what is due [to you] as a share of the *eššeššû*-ceremonies, all that forms the benefice of this prebend, as well as four sacrificial butcher half-portions for a year on all the sheep offerings and a half-portion of the *ṣudû*-meat: that is what I will give you for this daily prebend."

Anu-ušallim has heard him and has given him 1/6 plus 1/15 plus 1/6 of 1/60 of a day, on the 11th and 12th days of the month, [forming] his prebend of sacrificial butcher, for him to fulfil the office for a duration of ten years. He will carry out his duties effectively. Kidin-Anu, son of Anu-ah-ušabši, pledges himself to carry out the sacred service, fulfil the office and make the payments corresponding to this prebend of sacrificial butcher.

Anu-mâr-ittanu will not challenge the contract until the ten years have completely elapsed and will not withdraw this prebend from the hands of Kidin-Anu to give it to anyone else. Kidin-Anu will not challenge the contract until the ten years have completely elapsed and will not abandon this prebend. Anyone who might alter the terms of this written contract will pay the other party 1/3 of a silver mina without further ado. Each has taken a copy of the contract.

Witnesses: Balâṭu, son of Anu-ah-ittannu, descendant of Luštammar-Adad; Nidinti-Anu [I] and Anu-bêlšunu [I], the sons of Tanittu-Anu, descendant of Luštammar-Adad; Anu-mukîn-apli, son of Lišir, descendant of Kidin-Anu; Anu-uballiṭ [I], son of Rihat-Anu, descendant of Luštammar-Adad; Nidinti-Anu [II], son of Kidin-Anu, [grand]son of Anu-zêr-lîšir, descendant of

Hunzû; Anu-ah-ittannu, son of Anu-balâssu-iqbi, descendant of Luštammar-Adad; Anu bêlšunu [II], son of Ina-qibit-Anu, descendant of Ah'ûtu; Anu-uballiṭ [II], son of Rihat-Ishtar, descendant of Ekur-zâkir; Ina-qibit-Anu, son of Anu-uballiṭ, descendant of Kur'î.

Ishtar-šum-ereš, scribe, son of Anu-erîba, descendant of Kur'i. Uruk, the 4th Du'ûzu of year 97 of the king Antiochus [III].

Seals of Anu-bêlšunu [I], Anu-mukîn-apli, Anu-ah-ittannu, Nidinti-Anu[I], Nidinti-Anu [II], Anu-bêlšunu [II], Anu-uballiṭ [I], Ina-qibît-Anu, Anu-mâr-ittannu, Anu-uballiṭ [II], Balaṭu.'

This work contract was made between two religious notables of Uruk in the reign of Antiochus III (222–187): the owner of a butcher's prebend entrusts its effective performance to one of his colleagues. The text carefully specifies all the elements that make up the prebend, the benefices and incomes related to it and the way in which they are to be shared out.

The practice of worship at Uruk in the Seleucid era

In year 97 of the Seleucid era (216–215 BC), the sanctuaries of Uruk in south Babylonia continued to function following a centuries-old tradition: each day, food offerings were brought before the gods' statues and 'consumed' during a divine repast. Uruk's main temple in that period was that of the god Anu, the former supreme deity in the Sumerian pantheon, who had regained all his erstwhile lustre in what, two thousand years earlier, had been the land of Sumer. Anu was associated with his divine wife Antu; a number of other female deities remind us that Uruk had been the town of Ishtar, above all in the neo-Babylonian and Achaemenid periods. Under the Seleucids, her temple, the Eanna, had fallen dormant, and henceforward the cult was managed in a centralised manner by the clergy of Anu; hence the allusion at the opening of the contract to the principal deities of Uruk and 'all the gods in their sanctuaries', who had the right to secondary chapels within the sacred complex. Texts of rituals bear witness to the provision of meat for the divine statues in very large quantities: three cattle, fifty-eight sheep and eighty poultry were prepared each day to be served before the statues of Anu, Antu, Ishtar, Nanaia and the other gods in their sanctuaries.

The role of the prebendaries

To look after the preparation of the food offerings, the temple administration divided the tasks among several specialists, title-holders to 'service sectors' measured in time. The prebend involved here is that of the sacrificial butcher, a task that consisted in slaughtering the sheep to be offered, butchering the meat and seeing to its preparation. The service connected with the prebend comprises a technical element, but also involves participation in a certain number of weekly or monthly 'feasts', like the *guqqu*, and rituals, like the *eššeššu*. These ceremonies were originally linked to the monthly cycle of the moon, but had increased in number at Uruk, as in the Seleucid period there were as many as eight in certain months.

Measuring the 'service sector'

The holder of the prebend, Anu-mâr-ittannu, is the owner of a service block or sector that is effective on the 11th and 12th of each month, but which covers only part of the day of worship. The share he possesses for each of these days is '1/6 + 1/15 + 1/360 of a day'. In Babylonia, as for the majority of scientific applications, computation of daily time relied on a sexagesimal system. In the astronomical texts, for instance, the 'day' (the time between two sunsets) was divided into 12 'double hours' (*bêru*), themselves containing 30 equal subdivisions (that is, in total 360 basic units), which were measured by the flow of a water clock. Here, a system of association of fractions of a day on a similarly sexagesimal basis is used, resulting in a total of 85/360 of a day. But it is difficult to convert the system into contemporary standard units, since it is based on the moment of sunset as the starting point for measuring the length of the day. Furthermore, the recapitulation of the total that is made in the request presented by Kidin-Anu remains incomprehensible, since it is expressed in a measure of capacity and refers to a system that is unknown to us. It is certainly not that of the water clock, because it is usually the 'weight' of the water that has flowed, measured in minae and shekels, that serves as reference, and not its capacity.

Remuneration

The pay of a sacrificial butcher comprises a fixed base, made up of subsistence rations that may be paid in kind or sometimes in silver, its total proportionate to the length of the service sector. In his capacity as a member of one of the most important categories of prebendaries, together with the bakers and brewers, he has an equal right to a part of whatever of the offerings is redistributed after their 'consumption' by the divine statues, or to a part of the meat that was not used for their repast. Neo-Babylonian regulatory texts in fact show that when a sheep was slaughtered for the gods' meal, the entire animal, including the fleece, the head and the cheap cuts, was divided among a certain number of those who were entitled. Of these, the most important were the king and the summit of the temple's religious hierarchy, especially the high priest. But certain prebendaries also figured in this list and received pieces that were allotted beforehand: thus the sacrificial butcher traditionally received the sheep's head. Lastly, participation in the ceremonies and rituals entailed the collection of special bonuses which also came from the offering meals.

The basis of the contract

Kidin-Anu, the lessee, puts the proposition to Anu-mâr-ittannu that he should carry out his service as butcher in his place on the 11th and 12th days of the month. Out of the benefices attaching to this prebend, he will keep a part and return the rest to him. The principle of the work contract was commonplace among the prebendaries. For those whose monthly service sector did not exceed a few hours, it was not really a matter of true professional activity; they could therefore grant its effective performance to a colleague in the form of a work contract or transferable lease. The advantages attached to the prebend were thus shared between the owner and the executant. By this contract, Kidin-Anu pledges himself to carry out regularly the service connected with the prebend, with its obligations of attendance and the regularity of the meat deliveries that go with it. On his side, the lessor, Anu-mâr-ittannu, pledges that he will not resort to the services of anyone else. And both agree on a period of ten years for this contract, which cannot be broken without payment of a compensatory indemnity of twenty shekels of silver.

The form

Constructed in the form of a verbal contract, this agreement follows a lay-out that was already in force in the neo-Babylonian era, but which had become the norm in Seleucid times: request/agreement/guarantee-clauses/witnesses/date. The list of witnesses, several of whom belong to the same family group as the owner of the prebend, Anu-mâr-ittannu, that of the descendants of Luštammar-Adad, illustrates the specific features of Seleucid onomastics in Uruk. There are several instances of homonymy due to the decrease in the 'stock' of personal names. In order to avoid any confusion, careful note was made of the names of father and ancestor, sometimes also of the grandfather. The localisation of Uruk also explains the strong predominance of personal names formed with that of the god Anu. Equally noteworthy is the system of dating, also peculiar to the Seleucid period, as it functions by a unified computation of the years since the official start of the Seleucid era (3 April 311). The witnesses and the lessor of the prebend have put their seals on the clay of the contract, and their names are carefully recorded alongside each imprint.

The milieu of the Urukian prebendaries

The prebend of sacrificial butcher is a movable asset, quantifiable by its duration and the total profits it earns. But it also carries an element of prestige, since it enables its holders to enter the close-knit circle of the religious personnel attached to the temple of Anu, who take part in the ceremonies and rituals. The two parties to this contract, Kidin-Anu and Anu-mâr-ittannu, as well as the witnesses present, all belonged to that environment; they were fairly few in number, but left abundant private archives which give evidence of the maintenance of the traditional situation of the Babylonian clergy in the Seleucid era. They were grouped in a few vast families, defined by the name of their eponymous ancestor (Luštammar-Adad, Hunzû, Ekur-zâkir, Kurî), and kept up the use of cuneiform in their private dealings (contracts) and official affairs (by recopying the great works of the scholarly and cultural tradition).

The splitting up of these prebends has often been noted; originally, they had been formed of service blocks or sectors counted in fractions of a month, but in the Seleucid era they frequently appear simply as hours or even fractions of an hour. The principle of the division of prebends through the device of shares of an inheritance does much to explain this splitting into smaller units. But it has also been observed that, overall, the number of prebendaries did not increase very much; the division of certain prebends was matched by the reconstitution of others through purchases or, as in this instance, by leasing. In total, the rights of ownership may appear to be split up, but the reality of the service continued to be unified, the more so because the temple administration and the college formed by the prebendaries exercised the right to inspect any changes.

A complicated remuneration

In the agreement made between Kidin-Anu and Anu-mâr-ittannu, the latter grants the former the share of income constituted by the upkeep allowance. But he reserves the bonuses for himself: part are monthly, composed of two butchered 'portions', two heads, two allocations of meat (not identified), and allocations connected with the *eššeššu* ceremonies; another is annual, made up of four 'half-portions' of butchered meat and a 'half-portion' of *ṣudû*-meat. Unfortunately, the exact composition of these bonuses eludes us, because for the Seleucid period there has been no trace of the administrative and accounts sections of the archives in the form of records in which the prebendaries' names were inscribed, together with the duration of their service sector and the amount of their remuneration.

The economic power of the temples of Uruk was therefore still considerable at the end of the third century BC, with large flocks and staff who made a handsome profit out of the system of redistributing offerings. It is very likely that the whole of the resources redistributed in this way extended beyond the strict circle of the prebendaries and went towards the food upkeep of a good many of Uruk's religious notables.

Conclusion

Two major facts characterise Mesopotamian history in the first millennium: one in the institutional field, royal power and its evolution, the other in the socio-economic field, the coexistence of what are known as the 'great organisations' (palace and temples) with the private economy.

The monarchic institution is typical of Mesopotamian states. It had been established in this region for centuries, and rested on a strong ideological foundation, perpetuated by the circles of the educated and the clergy. According to the traditional view, royalty had 'descended from the skies' in antediluvian times. The Babylonian pantheon itself was based on that principle, from the time when Babylon's political and cultural primacy had been definitively established by the founding text of the *Epic of the Creation*, around the thirteenth century BC. The divine delegation of royalty and its autocratic development are best documented in Assyria; there, at the king's coronation, the god Ashur assigned to him the task of ensuring that his (Ashur's) pre-eminence over all countries was recognised, by means of either diplomacy or war.

Although the propaganda texts continued to celebrate the king as dispenser of justice, protector of the weak and pastor of his flock of subjects, his main field of action was military. He derived a major part of his legitimate right to the throne from his victories and conquests, his ability to enlarge the scope of the civilised world in the course of his campaigns and to triumph over natural and human obstacles. At the time of the crisis experienced by Assyria during the eighth century, it was symptomatic that the weakening of royal power was counterbalanced by the increase in power of the head of the army, the *turtânu*. Similarly, the majority of neo-Babylonian kings in the sixth century saw themselves as conquerors, even though the essential part of their field of action was confined to the western area of the former neo-Assyrian empire. The dynastic changes accepted by the Babylonians were subsequently directly connected with military victories: of Cyrus in 539, Darius in 521 and Alexander the Great in 331.

In Upper Mesopotamia (Assyria), as in Lower (Babylonia), the basis of the local economy was agriculture; dry in the north, irrigated in the south, with livestock breeding throughout the territory that was not given over to crops. In the absence of any notable technical development, the major element of economic evolution was the labour force available: Assyrians, Babylonians, then Achaemenids and Greeks paid great attention to ensuring that Mesopotamia had at its disposal a workforce of farm workers in sufficient numbers, either by expanding the system of rural dependency or by bringing new populations into the region, willingly (by favouring immigration and a form of rural colonisation) or forcibly (by deportations). The second key to agricultural development was control of working capital (animals and equipment). The establishment of vast production structures in the great organisations – palaces and sanctuaries – enabled resources to be assembled that were in general sufficient to ensure farm production proportionate to their needs. The private capitalisation achieved by the families of urban notables (especially in Babylonia) was added to palace and temple resources, which were further fuelled by the tributes imposed on territories that had been conquered or subdued by the kings of Assyria and then Babylonia.

After a marked phase of economic decline during the second part of the second millennium, revealed by the abandonment of certain sites and the restriction of the urban perimeter of the large Mesopotamian cities, the first millennium was rather a period of expansion, but over a very long timespan and with numerous accidents. For example, Assyria's agricultural economy was chiefly developed between the ninth and early seventh centuries, then disintegrated at the end of the neo-Assyrian empire. Assyria did not regain any economic dynamism until the third century. In Babylonia, the beginning of the first millennium was marked by a converse happening: the lasting settlement of Aramaean and Chaldaean populations took place in competition with the traditional methods of working the land. Babylonia's reluctance to enter the Assyrian sphere of influence and, later, the empire was reflected in the ravages due to an almost permanent state of war between the ninth and seventh centuries, with particularly destructive episodes such as the treatment meted out by Sennacherib to the city of Babylon in 687. The neo-Babylonian political period (610–539) was therefore chiefly a phase of rebuilding the economic structures. During the Achaemenid period the development of Babylonia continued (contrary to the traditional picture of an over-exploited province), and accelerated to culminate during the first centuries AD.

Political chronology

The dates of reigns indicated are those of the effective rule of the kings over Mesopotamia. Names in italics are those of usurping sovereigns. The names of the Arsacid kings in square brackets are not attested by cuneiform documents.

Kings of Assyria	Kings of Babylonia
Ashur-dan II (934–912)	
900 Adad-nêrârî II (911–891)	Shamash-mudammiq (?–900)
Tukulti-Ninurta II (890–884)	Nabu-shum-ukîn I (899–888)
Ashurnasirpal II (883–859)	Nabû-apla-iddin (888–855)
850 Shalmaneser III (858–824)	Marduk-zâkir-shumi I (854–819)
Shamshi-Adad V (823–811)	Marduk-balâssu-iqbi (818–813)
800 Adad-nêrârî III (810–783)	Baba-ah-iddin (812)
Shalmaneser IV (782–773)	5 unknown kings (?)
	Ninurta-apla-[...] (?)
	Marduk-bêl-zêri (?)
	Marduk-apla-uṣur (?)
Ashur-dan III (772–755)	Erîba-Marduk (769–761)
750 Ashur-nêrârî V (754–745)	Nabû-shum-ishkun (760–748)
Tiglath-pileser III (744–727)	Nabû-nâṣir (747–734)
	Nabû-nâdin-zêri (733–732)
	Nabû-shum-ukîn II (732)
	Nabû-mukîn-zêri (731–729)
	Tiglath-pileser III-Pûlu (728–727)
Shalmaneser V (726–722)	Shalmaneser V-Ulûlaiu (726–722)
Sargon II (721–705)	Merodachbaladan II (721–710)
	Sargon II (709–705)
Sennacherib (704–681)	Sennacherib (704–703)
	Marduk-zakir-shumi II (703)

		Merodachbaladan II (703)
700		Bêl-ibni (702–700)
		Ashur-nâdin-shumi (699–694)
		Nergal-ušêzib (693)
		Mušêzib-Marduk (692–689)
		Sennacherib (688–681)
	Esarhaddon (680–669)	Esarhaddon (680–669)
650	Ashurbanipal (668–627)	Shamash-shum-ukîn (667–648)
		Kandalânu (647–627)
	Ashur-etel-ilâni (630–626)	
	Sin-šum-lišir (626)	Sin-šum-lišir (626)
	Sin-šar-iškun (626–612)	Sin-šar-iškun (626)
		Nabopolassar (626–605)
	Ashur-uballiṭ II (612–610)	
610	*Fall of Harrân, end of the Assyrian empire*	
600		Nebuchadnezzar II (604–562)
		Amêl-Marduk (561–560)
		Neriglissar (559–556)
		Lâbâši-Marduk (556)
550		Nabonidus (555–539)
539	*Cyrus' entry into Babylon*	

Achaemenid Kings
Cyrus (539–530)
Cambyses (530–523)
Bardiya (522)

Nebuchadnezzar III (522)
Nebuchadnezzar IV (521)

500 Darius I (522–486)
Xerxes I (485–465)
450 Artaxerxes I (464–424)
Darius II (423–405)
400 Artaxerxes II (404–359)
350 Artaxerxes III (358–338)
Artaxerxes IV–Arses (337–336)
Darius III (335–330)
331 *Conquest of Mesopotamia by Alexander*

Macedonian Kings

Alexander the Great (330–323)

Philip Arrhidaeus (323–316)

Antigonus Monophthalmos
(315–311)

Alexander IV (323–306)

311 *Beginning of the Seleucid era (3 April)*

Seleucid Kings

300 Seleucus I (305–281)

Antiochus I (280–261)

250 Antiochus II (260–246)

Seleucus II (245–226)

Seleucus III (225–223)

200 Antiochus III (222–187)

Seleucus IV (186–175)

Antiochus IV (174–164)

Antiochus V (162)

Demetrius I (162–151)

150 Alexander I Balas (150–146)

Demetrius II (145–141)

141 *First entry of the Parthians into Seleuceia on the Tigris (between 2 and 8 July)*

Arsacid Kings

Phraates II (141–130)

Antiochus VII (130–129)

128 *Definitive loss of Mesopotamia by the Seleucids*

Arsaces (128)

Hyspaosines of Characene (127–126)

100   Artaban I (127–124)

Mithridates II (123–88)

Gotarzes I (91–81)

Orodes I (80–78)

Sinatrukes (77–71)

Phraates III (70–58)

50   Orodes II (58–39)

Phraates IV (40–3)

Beginning of the Christian era

[Phraates V (AD 3–4)]
[Orodes III (4–6)]
[Vonones (7–11)]
[Artaban II (12–38)]
[Vardanes (39–45)]

50   [Gotarzes II (43–51)]

[Vologeses I (51–76)]

75   *The last datable cuneiform astronomical tablet*

[Pacorus II (78–109)]   [Vologeses II (77–8, 89–90)]
[Artaban III (79–80)]
[Osroës (89–90)]

Glossary

adê A sworn covenant binding his subjects or vassals to the king by an oath of absolute loyalty. Used chiefly in the Assyrian empire, the term was current until the beginning of the Persian period in Babylonia.

ahšadrapannu Babylonian form of the Persian word meaning 'satrap'. In Babylonia it did not necessarily designate only the governor of the province, but also minor administrators.

ahu rabû The 'great brother' was the title borne by the high priest in the temples of Babylonia.

andûrâru A royal edict abolishing debts and cancelling forced sales, taken by some neo-Assyrian kings, most often on their accession. It reveals a state of latent economic crisis.

âšipu Exorcist, specialist in the magic arts who, with the help of the god Ea, combats the spiritual attacks of evil in the form of possession or illness. Some had the special task of protecting the royal personage, but all were closely connected with the temples and the circles of experts. The term *mašmašu*, 'exorcist', was used as a synonym.

atû Doorkeeper, attested chiefly in Babylonian temples, where he had to keep surveillance on access to the sacred areas and comings and goings, in order to avoid possible sacrilege and, above all, the theft of precious objects, foodstuffs or raw materials deposited in large quantities in the storehouse buildings.

bâbanu The part of the royal palace served by the principal gate and given over to official, administrative and economic activities.

barû A diviner, especially with the task of hepatoscopy and the techniques of extispicy (interpreting the liver and entrails, respectively).

bêl pahâti/pihâti, pahat Chief of a provincial district. A term generally translated as 'governor'.

bêl piqitti Head of the administration in Babylonian temples, coming from the royal administration, hence the title *ša rêš šarri* often attached to him. The term also signifies, rather vaguely, anyone holding office in the administration.

bîtânu The part of the royal palace occupied by the royal apartments and the women's house, access to which was under strict control.

bît mâr šarri The whole of the estate and apartments granted to the crown prince in the neo-Babylonian and Achaemenid eras.

bît redûti Under the Sargonids, in Assyria, this building was occupied by the heir to the throne, who learned his 'trade' there. Administrative and diplomatic correspondence was handled, analysed and then passed on to the sovereign.

ekal mašarti Acting as a sort of arsenal in the neo-Assyrian era, this architectural complex could also be used for government functions.

erib bîti A term in Babylonia designating those who had the right of entry into the sacred part of the temple where the deity dwelt.

errêšu A farmer autonomously working temple or royal land taken on a lease, and paying part of the crop as rent.

ešrû A tithe levied by sanctuaries on the farming revenues from royal and private lands.

gardu A word designating dependent workers attached to land on crown estates in Achaemenid Babylonia. Found in Iran under the Elamite word *kurtaš*.

ginû Daily offerings, mostly of food, made to the gods for their upkeep. The term *sattukku* was also used.

gugallu The official responsible for the allocation of water for irrigation and, often, for the agricultural district pertaining to it. The *gugallu* belonged to the administration of the temples or royal lands.

guqqû Ceremonies occurring on certain feast days of the month, marked by more plentiful offerings than the usual daily diet of the *ginû* or *sattukku*. The term *sellu* was also used.

harrânu Describing a route or expedition (military or commercial), this word was applied to contracts setting up limited trading partnerships.

haṭru A local district set up in the Persian era in Babylonia, simultaneously designating the territory, the administrative body and the community who lived there.

idû A form of remuneration for work similar to a wage, but working on the principle of a worker's hiring his labour, for the most part farming.

ikkaru A labourer, responsible for farming a plot granted by a large institutional owner, or working in a team on an estate directly farmed by the temple or the crown. Most of the *ikkaru* were dependants paid subsistence rations.

ilku Military or civilian service owed to the king by those of the population who did not enjoy any special exemption.

imittu An overall estimate of the anticipated production made by the owner of leased land, shortly before the harvest of dates or cereals, to determine the share to be paid by the tenant farmer.

iškaru The system used in Assyria by the royal administration, consisting of supplying artisans with their raw materials and determining the quantity of finished products they should deliver.

išparu The weaver in charge of preparing material. Generally, spinning and weaving were women's activities. Fulling and laundering were seen to by the *ašlakku*. The *išparu* was mainly concerned with the shaping and dyeing of garments and their decoration with various embroideries and adornments. The *išparu* of Babylonian temples attended to the garments of the staff, but chiefly those of the gods.

iššiakku A word of Sumerian origin, originally designating the head of a principality or small kingdom, subordinate to the orders of a more important king. By virtue of this, the king of Assyria was therefore the delegate of the god Ashur, the only true king of the country, and he made this position clear in his title by describing himself as *iššiak Aššur*, 'vicar of the god Ashur'.

kalû A special category of religious officiants whose duty was to recite lamentations as a group in order to move the gods to compassion or call for their aid, accompanying themselves on percussion instruments. The language of the lamentations was a particular form of Sumerian, called Emesal, knowledge of which lasted in Babylonia until the beginning of the first century BC.

kidinnûtu An exemption granted by the king from certain taxes and service due for the army or by way of free labour. The big towns of Assyria and Babylonia benefited from this, especially if they were the seat of a major sanctuary. The king could abolish this privilege should there be a rebellion.

kiništu The college of the temple, assembling the heads of the administration, the principal religious dignitaries and those in charge of the artisans in the temple service. This college gave rulings on the internal organisation of the sanctuary and certain allocations of responsibilities.

kudurru An inscribed stele, often adorned with divine symbols, duplicating a real-estate deed, the result of a purchase or royal gift. Most of the *kudurru* took the form of a boundary marker of property and were placed in temples under the protection of the local deity.

kurgâru A sacred actor, often in female attire, who took part in ritual representations: some myths were 'acted out' in the temple in honour of the principal deity.

kurru A measure of capacity and surface area used in Babylonia in the first millennium. The *kurru* was the equivalent of 180 litres or one and a half hectares.

kurtaš See *gardu*.

kurummâtu Subsistence ration in cereals, wool and oil, given to slaves and dependent workers by temples and the royal administration. The term also designates the minimum upkeep to which each family member has a right in private households.

limmu Eponym used to date the year in Assyria. At first reserved for high-ranking dignitaries of the court, following a fixed order, the use of eponymous dating became solely linked to royal favour under the Sargonids.

maddattu, mandattu A word designating the tribute due to the king of Assyria by those who, willingly or forcibly, acknowledged his sovereignty. In Babylonia, the term was used in private contracts to describe the yield in money or craftwork of a slave or person held as surety.

mahâzu Holy town. A term designating, in Babylonia, most of the urban large towns which were the seat of a major sanctuary, and which often had the benefit of exemptions.

malâhu Boatman. In the temples, he would be the prebendary responsible for maintaining the sacred vessel that enabled the divine statue to be moved from place to place.

manzaltu Service 'block' measured in months, days or fractions thereof, during which a prebendary performed his function.

manzaz pâni The term is translated as 'courtier', but implies chiefly access to the king's person, a privilege reserved in Assyria for a small minority who enjoyed the king's favour.

mâr bâni A term meaning 'a well-to-do man of substance', typifying *a priori* any person of free status, but in actual fact essentially the notables of Babylonian towns.

mašmašu See *âšipu*.

maṣṣartu Military watch carried out in the service of the king. It serves also to designate, in a general way, all tasks performed for the king, including the observation of the night sky by the astronomers.

maššartu An overall allocation in kind supplied to the prebendaries for them to prepare the meals served as offerings to the gods. The unused part (*pappasu*) was their perquisite.

mina A unit of weight (*manû*), the name of which is formed from a root meaning 'to count'. The mina corresponded more or less to 500 g in Assyria and Babylonia. It was subdivided into 60 shekels (*šiqlu*) and 60 minae made the weight of a talent (*biltu*). The weight value of the mina varied, however, according to the regions of the Near East. In the neo-Assyrian era in particular, for trade in the west of the empire, the 'Carchemish mina' was used, which had a heavier weight than that of Mesopotamia.

muma'iru The office of one who carried out the instructions of a superior. In the Seleucid period, this term was used for the satrap of the province of Babylonia.

nagâru An artisan who specialised in woodwork, from furniture to chariots and boats. In Babylonian temples, it was a prebendary office when the furniture or vehicles to be made were for the gods.

nâgiru A herald whose duty was to proclaim and orally transmit the king's instructions. In Assyria, the *nâgir ekalli*, 'palace herald', was one of the great personages of the court, and by virtue of this title was responsible for a frontier province.

nâmurtu See *tâmartu*.

naptânu A meal. The word was used especially for the ceremonial of the meals served as offerings to the gods four times a day and consumed by them, the remains of which were shared among the principal dignitaries of the temple.

narû Singers and musicians, the *narû* recited or chanted hymns to the gods to celebrate their glory during most religious ceremonies.

nuhatimmu A term designating the 'bakers' who prepared bread, groats and semolina for the meals of the gods or king. The title 'chief baker' (*rab nuhatimmi*) was actually that of one of the high-ranking dignitaries of the Assyrian court. In Babylonian temples, the one in charge of the bakers (*šâpir nuhatimmi*) was the representative of the category of prebendaries whose duty was this type of food preparation. He centralised their allocations and redistributed them.

nukurribu An arboriculturist who specialised in looking after palm-trees and the artificial fertilising of date-palms or in the planting and maintenance of other fruit trees. The *nukurribu* were also in charge of the vegetable gardens spread around the foot of the trees.

papâhu The equivalent of the *cella* of Graeco-Roman temples; the room in which the representation of the principal deity of the temple was enthroned in majesty.

pappasu See *maššartu*.

paqdu An administrative term describing one appointed to a particular office.

parakku A pedestal, which might have several steps, on which a statue or symbol of a deity was placed in majesty.

qîpu A term designating a high-ranking administrative official. In Babylonian temples, he came second or third in the hierarchy of the sanctuary's top administration.

rab bânî A special category of prebendaries. They were the owners of plots of the garden adjoining the rural temple of the Akîtu, whose task was to keep the temple supplied with market garden produce and dates.

rab bîti A steward.

rab bît kîli Head of the 'prison'. In Babylonian temples, he had the necessary flour milled for the temple's requirements by people who were in irons or in custody.

rab šaqê Grand cupbearer to the Assyrian court, responsible for the drinks served to the king. This post was held by someone close to the sovereign, as it called for complete loyalty. Its holder was thereby one of the highest dignitaries of the court, and played a part in government decisions and actions. He was at the same time responsible for a frontier province.

rê'î alpê The official in charge of the cattle for the gods' meals, he saw to fattening them on barley. This profession, like the following two, was governed by the system of prebends.

rê'î sattukki In Babylonian temples, the one in charge of the sheep for offerings; he collected them from the shepherds of the steppe and fattened them in the sanctuary sheds.

rê'û ša šizbi An office similar to the one above, but to do with unweaned animals, especially lambs. He probably also looked after the preparation and supply of milk products served as offerings.

ša ina muhhi quppi ša šarri The official in charge of managing the royal funds in neo-Babylonian temples, supplying the sovereign's offerings and recouping the share due to him.

šaknu A very general term to designate an administrative official charged with issuing commands. In Babylonia, the *šakin ṭêmi* carried out the function of governor of a large town.

šalšu The third man in the basic structure of Assyrian administration, made up of the holder of the office, his assistant (*šânû*) and this co-assistant.

šamallû An apprentice who begins to master a skilled or intellectual technique under the guidance of a teacher. The term was often used of scribes in training, who perfected their knowledge of cuneiform writing by copying the great scientific, literary or religious texts.

ša muhhi sûti The one in charge of cultivating and levying farm rents on land placed at his disposal by a temple, he performed the functions of a kind of lease farmer at the end of the neo-Babylonian period.

šangû Originally an administrative official of a temple, the *šangû*, in first-millennium Babylonia, was the one responsible for the worship of a god, and sometimes for the entire temple, as at Sippar or Larsa.

šanû See *šalšû*.

ša rêšilša reš šarri The one who is close to the king, ensures his protection, transmits his instructions or carries out his order. In Assyria, a good number of the *ša rêši* were eunuchs. Under the Sargonids, the head of the *ša rêši* became virtually responsible for the Assyrian army.

šar puhi A surrogate king who was set up when bad influences, often determined by astronomy, threatened the true sovereign. At the end of the ill-omened period, the substitute king was put to death.

šatammu Head of the administration of the temple in

Babylonia. Coming from the clerical hierarchy, he ran the sanctuary together with the *bêl piqitti* and the *qîpu*. In certain towns his office was devolved to the *šangû*.

sattukku See *ginû*.

sellu See *guqqu*.

sêpiru A scribe writing in alphabetic Aramaic on a flexible medium (papyrus or parchment).

shekel Unit of weight, basic subdivision of the mina, the shekel (*šiqlu*, from the root meaning 'to weigh') equalled about 8.33 g. Most of the sums of money used for payments were expressed in shekels. A *kurru* of barley or dates was usually worth a shekel of silver, according to a traditional, but theoretical, equivalent.

šibšu See *sûtu*.

simmagir The title of a high-ranking dignitary in Babylonia, responsible for the province of the same name and part of the royal army. Before mounting the throne, Neriglissar had held this office in the reign of Nebuchadnezzar II.

sirâšu The brewer whose job was to prepare the fermented drink based on malt and barley or dates, described as 'beer', which was the most widespread alcoholic drink in Mesopotamia. Next to the *nuhatimmu*, the *sirâšu* were the other great category of prebendaries in charge of preparing the meals served as offerings to the gods, and like them were provided with their own administrative official, the *šâpir sirâše*.

širku Translated as 'oblate', this word designated the slaves of a Mesopotamian temple, dedicated by a private person to the deity, taken in by the temple among the deprived, or having voluntarily entered its service.

sissinnu A form of special remuneration for arboriculturists who looked after the upkeep of the palm-groves, corresponding to a wage in money or a quantity of dates agreed on in advance.

sukkallu Put in charge of a mission, the *sukkallu* fulfilled the functions of minister and ambassador at the same time. The *sukkallu dannu* in the Assyrian court was thus a kind of prime minister or grand vizier.

šušânu A category of dependent workers, most often in the service of the crown. They had the same obligations as the *gardu*, and similar status.

sûtu A measure of capacity equal to 6 litres. The term was also used for a farm rent, especially the one that the tenant of a palm-grove had to pay. The rent for a cereal farm was termed *šibšu*.

ṭâbihu The butcher whose task was to slaughter the sheep served as a meal to the gods, butchering them and preparing the meat. The term was also used to describe those charged with personally guarding the king. In the neo-Babylonian era, the head of the *ṭâbihu* was one of the chief military officials.

tâkultu A sacred meal consumed by Assyrian kings with the gods in their temples, and governed by a detailed ceremonial.

tâmartu or *nâmurtu* A welcoming present made by his vassals to the king of Assyria, its value and size proportionate to the respect they wished to show him. It was actually a form of tribute.

tamirtu Land irrigated by a waterway which also served to mark out a rural district for the officials (especially the *gugallu*) who managed the farming estates, private or official, which might be found on it.

ṭupšar enûma Anu Enlil An expression designating specialists in astrology and astronomy, capable of interpreting the great divinatory series of astral phenomena and proceeding with the corresponding astronomical calculations.

ṭupšarru A scribe who specialised in Sumero-Akkadian cuneiform writing on clay tablets.

turtânu The head of the army in the first part of the neo-Assyrian period and responsible for the frontier provinces of the west, he became one of the most powerful men in the state, sometimes taking on part of the royal function, as illustrated by the careers of Dayyân-Ashur or Shamshi-ilu. To lessen this power, Assyrian kings duplicated the office, then, under the Sargonids, entrusted responsibility for the army preferably to the head of the *ša rêši*.

ubšukkinakku The place in the temple (generally a court-yard) in which the gods, in the form of their statues, met in assembly to decide and pronounce the fate of the country.

u'iltu Format of cuneiform tablet commonly used for money-lending contracts. The term eventually came to be used for IOUs in general.

ummânu Specialists in the most varied arts and techniques. The word applied as much to specialised craftsmen as to experts in cultural or divinatory tradition. Supported by their mastery of the various aspects of knowledge, at the end of the first millennium in Babylonia, the *ummânu* claimed the status of sages, the only possessors and transmitters of traditional wisdom.

urâšu Service due to the king or his government in Achaemenid Babylonia by certain holders of lands, in the form of offers of service (hauling boats) or deliveries of farm produce.

Bibliography

Amiet, Pierre, *Art of the Ancient Near East*, New York: Abrams, 1980.

Boardman, J., et al. eds, *The Cambridge Ancient History*, III.1. *The Prehistory of the Balkans, The Middle East and the Aegean World, Tenth to Eighth Centuries BC*, 2nd edn, Cambridge: Cambridge University Press, 1982.

Boardman, J., et al. eds, *The Cambridge Ancient History*, III.2. *The Assyrian and Babylonian Empires and Other States of the Near East, from the Eighth to the Sixth Centuries BC*, 2nd edn, Cambridge: Cambridge University Press, 1991.

Bottéro Jean, *Mesopotamia: Writing, Reasoning and the Gods*, trans. Z. Bagrani and M. van der Mieroop, Chicago: University of Chicago Press, 1992.

Briant, Pierre, *From Cyrus to Alexander: A History of the Persian Empire*, trans. P. T. Daniels, Winona Lake, IN: Eisenbrauns, 2002.

The Cambridge History of Iran, II. *The Median and Achaemenian Periods*, Cambridge: Cambridge University Press, 1985.

Dandamaev, M. A., *Political History of the Achaemenids*, Leiden: Brill, 1990.

Frye, R. N., *The Heritage of Persia*, London: Weidenfield and Nicolson, 1962.

Grayson, A. Kirk, *Assyrian and Babylonian Chronicles, Texts from Cuneiform Sources 5*, New York: Augustin, 1975.

Oppenheim, A. Leo, *Ancient Mesopotamia: Portrait of a Dead Civilization*, revised edn, Chicago: Chicago University Press, 1974.

Parrot, André, *Nineveh and Babylon*, London: Thames and Hudson, 1961.

Roaf, Michael, *Cultural Atlas of Mesopotamia and the Ancient Near East*, Oxford and New York: Facts on File, 1990.

Roux, Georges, *Ancient Iraq*, 3rd edn, London: Penguin, 1993.

Sources of the texts quoted

Page 15: Description of the ruins of Nineveh in 1644
J.-B. Tavernier, *Les Six Voyages en Turquie et en Perse*, Maspero, La Découverte, 1981.

Page 24: The forces of economic life in Mesopotamia
L. Oppenheim, *La Mésopotamie, portrait d'une civilisation*, Gallimard, 1970, p. 98.

Page 33: The contingents of the Qarqar coalition
K. Grayson, *Assyrian Rulers of the Early First Millennium BC II (858–745 BC)*, Toronto, 1996, p. 23.

Page 47: One of Ashurnasirpal II's campaigns in the east of Anatolia in 865
K. Grayson, *Assyrian Rulers of the Early First Millennium BC I (1154–859 BC)*, Toronto, 1991, pp. 219–20.

Page 73: The *Census of Harran*
F. M. Fales and J. N. Postgate, *Imperial Administrative Records*, Part II, *State Archive of Assyria XI*, Helsinki, 1995, no. 201, pp. 122–3.

Page 80: The titles of Ashurnasirpal II
K. Grayson, *Assyrian Rulers of the Early First Millennium BC I (1154–859 BC)*, Toronto, 1991, no. 56, pp. 320–30.

Page 87: Extract from a deed of exemption in the reign of Ashurbanipal
L. Kataja and R. Whiting, *Grants, Decrees and Gifts of the Neo-Assyrian Period, State Archives of Assyria XII*, Helsinki, 1995, no. 25, pp. 24–5.

Page 93: Colophon of a tablet from Nineveh, in the name of Ashurbanipal
H. Hunger, *Babylonische und assyrische Kolophone*, Neukirchener Verlag, 1968, no. 329, p. 103.

Page 101: The king of Assyria and his servants: letter from the exorcist Adad-šum-uṣur

S. Parpola, *Letters from Assyrian Scholars to the Kings Esarhaddon and Assurbanipal*, Neukirchener Verlag, 1970, no. 121, pp. 89–91.

Page 127: Governors of Babylonia's provinces

E. Unger, *Babylon. Die heilige Stadt nach der Beschreibung der Babylonier*, Berlin, reprint 1970, text no. 26, p. 291.

Page 132: Transmission of an order from Nabonidus concerning the cult offerings at Uruk

P.-A. Beaulieu, *The Reign of Nabonidus, King of Babylon 556–539 BC*, New Haven, 1989, p. 119.

Page 138: The dreams of king Nabonidus

L. Messerschmidt, 'Die Inschrift des Stele Nabuna'ids des Königs von Babylon', *Mitteilungen der Vorderasiatischen Gesellschaft* 1/1, 1896, pp. 73–83.

Page 165: The life of Babylonian notables: Lurindu's marriage

F. Joannès, *Archives de Borsippa La famille Ea-ilûta-bâni*, Paris, 1989, p. 3.

Page 170: Land management: leasing contract

F. Joannès, *Textes Babyloniens d'Époque Récente*, Paris, 1982, pp. 137–8.

Page 183: Regulations for the division of a sheep offering

G. Mac Ewan, 'Distribution of meat in Eanna', *Iraq* 45, 1983, pp. 187–98.

Page 196: Example of a commentary

J.-M. Durand, 'Un commentaire à *TDP* I, AO 17761', *Revue d'Assyriologie* 73, 1979, p. 159.

Page 197: Association between portentous elements

E. von Weiher, *Spätbabylonische Texte aus Uruk IV*, Mainz, 1993, pp. 99–100, no. 159.

Page 199: An extract from the *Epic of Erra*

Jean Bottéro, *Mythes et Rites de Babylone*, Paris, 1985, pp. 241–3.

Page 206: Names of the reigning Achaemenid sovereigns

A. Sachs, 'Achaemenid royal names in Babylonian astronomical texts', *American Journal of Ancient History* 2, 1977, pp. 129–46.

Page 212: Annual dues levied on a bow fief

A. Clay, *Business Documents of the Murashû Sons of Nippur Dated in the Reign of Darius II (424–404 BC)*, Philadelphia, 1904, no. 18.

Page 213: Loan underwritten by the tenant farmers

A. Clay, *Business Documents of the Murashû Sons of Nippur Dated in the Reign of Darius II (424–404 BC)*, Philadelphia, 1904, no. 61.

Page 217: Undertaking by a subcontractor to transport a royal tax

H. H. Figulla, *Business Documents of the New-Babylonian Period*, 1949, London, pl. XXVI, no. 48.

Page 222: Financial activities in the Achaemenid era

G. Contenau, *Contrats néo-babyloniens II. Achéménides et Séleucides*, Paris, 1929, no. 196.

Page 228: The restoration of the Esagil temple in Alexander's reign

D. Kennedy, *Late-Babylonian Economic Texts*, 1968, London, no. 6.

Page 241: Appointment of a new astrologer to the Esagil

D. Kennedy, *Late-Babylonian Economic Texts*, 1968, London, no. 144.

Page 243: Accounts of the Esagil in 94 BC

D. Kennedy, *Late-Babylonian Economic Texts*, 1968, London, no. 151.

Page 246: Examples of Babylonian transcriptions of Greek names

D. Weisberg, *The Late Babylonian Texts of the Oriental Institute Collection*, Malibu, 1991, pp. 81–3.

Page 248: Promissory note for the payment of a ration

D. Kennedy, *Late-Babylonian Economic Texts*, 1968, London, no. 118.

Page 249: A colophon from Uruk

F. Thureau-Dangin, *Rituels Accadiens*, Paris, 1921, p. 86.

Page 255: Religious activities in the Seleucid era

G. Mac Ewan, *Texts from Hellenistic Babylonia in the Ashmolean Museum*, Oxford, 1982, no. 36.

Index